GENDER AND LANGUAGE

GENDER AND LANGUAGE: THEORY AND PRACTICE

Lia Litosseliti

Hodder Arnold

A MEMBER OF THE HODDER HEADLINE GROUP

First published in Great Britain in 2006 by
Hodder Education, a member of the Hodder Headline Group,
338 Euston Road, London NW1 3BH

www.hoddereducation.com

Distributed in the United States of America by
Oxford University Press Inc.
198 Madison Avenue, New York, NY10016

British Library Cataloguing in Publication Data
A catalogue record for this book is available from the British Library

Library of Congress Cataloging-in-Publication Data
A catalog record for this book is available from the Library of Congress

ISBN-10: 0 340 809 590
ISBN-13: 978 0 340 809 594

1 2 3 4 5 6 7 8 9 10

Typeset in 10 on 13pt Times by Phoenix Photosetting, Chatham, Kent
Printed and bound in Malta

What do you think about this book? Or any other Hodder
Education title? Please send your comments to the feedback
section on www.hoddereducation.com.

Contents

Acknowledgements

Thanks to

Louise Mullany and Yasemin Bayyurt for their collaboration in producing sections of this book.

Joan Swann, Nigel Edley, Judith Baxter, Margret Grebowicz, Bethan Benwell, Markus Perkmann, Maria Koutsoubou, James Gardener, Lisa Stewart and Eva Martinez for their comments and ideas.

Shields Russell, for his unfailing support and encouragement.

Introduction

Gender and Language is a diverse and rapidly developing field, which has both academic and popular appeal. The 'turn to language' across the humanities and social sciences, and the impact of critical linguistics and discourse analysis, have contributed to a reframing of questions on gender and language. This book provides a broad overview of key issues and questions, and aims to do so in both theoretical and practical ways. It introduces key theoretical concepts and frameworks and illustrates and exemplifies the relationships between gender and language use, by looking at specific texts (spoken and written), situated in specific contexts. In addition, each chapter contains questions and suggestions for further reading, to allow those new to the field to locate the issues discussed in that chapter critically and in context.

In this book, the word *text* is used to refer to both spoken and written language, including dialogue. Contrary to text, which can exist physically – a transcript of a conversation or a newspaper article – *discourse* is a broader term and less easily defined. *Discourse analysis* involves analysis of the text as product, but is ultimately concerned with language in a social context, shaped by discursive and socio-cultural practices. A central theme running through the book is that language *both reflects and creates* how we see the world; and how we see the world includes assumptions about gender and gender inequalities. *Gender* is used in this book not as a grammatical, but as a social category. If *sex* relates to a biological and generally binary distinction between male and female, then gender refers to the social behaviours, expectations and attitudes associated with being male and female. Sex is binary, but 'the traits assigned to a sex by a culture are cultural constructions', socially determined and alterable (Wodak, 1997: 3). In this sense, gender and *gendered identities* are both social and individual, but also variable; they vary from one generation to the next, from one situation to another, and among language users who belong to different groups in terms of age, ethnicity, race, religion, class, sexuality, or education. The concepts mentioned here are initially discussed below, and elaborated and illustrated throughout the book.

First, it is necessary to provide some background on how theories of gender and language have developed. The feminist movement has undoubtedly influenced thinking in the social sciences and humanities, including linguistics, over the past 30 or 40 years. Since the 1960s, the scope of feminist thought has become wider and more diverse and its impact more profound. As a political movement, feminism has tried to render women's experience visible and to both identify and combat the sources of gender inequalities. The earlier wave of feminist intervention tended to see women's involvement in the domestic domain as an expression of their exclusion from the male world, while later work emphasized the special and distinct nature of women's outlook on social life.

Scholarly and popular debates on gender and feminism have centred on shifts: women entering professions such as medicine and law; girls doing better than boys at school; shifts in gender roles, where women are not only mothers and housekeepers, and men are not only workers and providers; shifts towards equal opportunities and increased gender awareness. Gender and language research during the past three decades has run parallel to such debates, and has been similarly preoccupied for a long time with gender *difference*. Gender and language research, as an umbrella term, refers to cross-disciplinary discussions of both the ways in which language is used *by* men and women, and the ways in which language is used to say things *about* men and women. In Part I of the book, we will see that past theorizations of gender and language ('deficit', 'difference', 'dominance') revolved mainly around how language has been used by women and men differently, while more recent approaches are concerned with how women and men are constructed through language.

These more recent and complex approaches, which started gathering pace in the late 1980s and 1990s as a result of the influence of post-structuralism, turn to the role of *discourse*, which is generally seen as *language as social practice*. Past approaches have been characterized by a 'static conception of distinct male and female identities, apparently fixed once and for all in childhood' (Talbot, 1998: 144). But the ways in which language, identity and social context interact have not been taken into account until recently. Johnson also points out that the view of men and women as binary opposites (and thus essentially different) 'needs to be seen within a much broader tradition in linguistic thinking generally, the roots of which are to be found in structuralist approaches to language' (Johnson and Meinhof, 1997: 14). Such approaches see language as a closed system with internal rules, and not as a dynamic entity influenced by external social factors and used variably by real speakers and writers.

As we will see in Part I, the current and new directions in the study of gender and language, in terms of theoretical and analytical frameworks, are the result of a critical rethinking of linguistic analysis, feminist theory and feminist linguistic analysis. This also involves a lack of consensus on how to evaluate the claims of the literature, and to what extent to revisit previous assumptions. Broadly speaking, current thinking is based on different research paradigms *across disciplines*, the importance of meaning which is situated within immediate and socio-cultural *contexts* and within particular *communities of practice*, the centrality of *discourses* and the *discursive construction of a range of gendered identities*. These are explored in detail throughout the book, but it is useful first to briefly introduce them in this section.

Context is important within a view of language as social practice, and it incorporates the social situation, linguistic co-text, genre, and (gender and other) relations between speakers and hearers, writers and readers. As Fairclough (1992) has argued, context includes those *discursive practices* pertaining to a given text, and the relevant *social practices* (see Chapter 3). Generalizations outside a particular conversational context are now seen as inherently problematic, and increasingly gender and language research has focused on particular men and women in particular settings. An acknowledgement that gender is complex also involves looking at the ways in which gender interacts with other identity categories such as ethnicity, age, class, race, education, and sexual orientation. In addition, gender is produced through people's participation in *communities of practice* where groups of people engage in a mutual endeavour, such as a classroom or a workplace (see Part II). Current theories are interested in the ways in which gender identities are formed and reproduced, through participation in multiple communities of practice (Eckert and McConnell-Ginet, 1992).

In terms of analytical frameworks, current thinking has also led to an emphasis on *discourse analysis*, and *critical discourse analysis* (CDA), as valuable frameworks for exploring a range of text types for their contribution to the construction of gender. If past approaches had assumed that people use language in certain ways because of who they are, (critical) discourse analysts suggest that people are who they are (partly) because of the way they use language (Cameron, 1998). And at the same time, people activate power whenever they produce meaning. Here, CDA is particularly useful, in that it aims to understand social issues, inequalities, and ideologies, by exposing the subtle role of discourse in maintaining them (the 'hidden agenda' of discourse). Once we consider that this agenda serves particular interests and acts against others, it becomes clear that a critical (feminist) discourse analysis cannot remain descriptive and neutral (see Chapter 1).

Different definitions of *discourses* are given in Chapter 3, but for our purposes here, we can think of discourses as ways of seeing and experiencing the world (including gender) from a particular perspective. Discourses are manifested in texts and work to represent, maintain, reconstitute and contest gendered identities and social practices.

As mentioned earlier, language does not simply reflect social reality; it is also constitutive of that reality, through an ongoing process of negotiation, modification and restatement in which all speakers, writers, listeners and readers are involved. As we will see in Chapter 3, gender is socially and culturally constructed; our gender identities (our sense of who we are as gendered subjects) are largely constructed through the discourses we inhabit and negotiate. The plural form *identities* is used to emphasize the current thinking of identities as multiple, diverse, fragmented, and shifting. In addition, our gendered identities are not simply about being male or female, but about *doing* or *performing* one's gender at any one time. One example of this can be seen in sex workers' speech on the telephone, where they typically perform the 'powerless' femininity that clients expect (see Chapter 3, for this and other examples). In order to define ourselves as masculine or feminine, we make choices among norms of language which are seen as appropriate and intelligible for performing masculinity or femininity (Butler, 1990). In this sense, identity formation is an ongoing and dialectical process, rather than a set of attributes: who we are is being constantly shaped by the taken-for-granted concepts and assumptions embedded in discourses, and vice versa. Further, identities (and gender identities) are not only multiple and shifting, but sometimes also contradictory.

ABOUT THIS BOOK

The book engages with the above issues and the questions they raise, in theoretical and applied ways. The theoretical frameworks discussed and the examples of language use provided aim to demonstrate the various strands and directions of research in this area, towards a more critical re-evaluation of previous work and the theorization of gender and language in non-essentialist ways.

The book is structured chronologically in Part I. Chapter 1 summarizes early feminist and non-feminist approaches to the study of gender and language. It focuses on key elements of early study in this area, such as sexist language, and language change and intervention. It also traces the emergence of feminist linguistics. Chapter 2 concentrates on past approaches, which have been primarily concerned with the investigation of differences between male and female speech, and with the varying interpretations of such differences – the long-running debates surrounding the 'dominance' and 'difference' paradigms. Chapter 3 examines more recent theorizations of gender and language, which question any straightforward notion of gender differences, and conceptualize gender in more productive ways. Instead of a reliance on binary and generalized distinctions between male and female language use, the focus is on gendered discourses and identities (femininities and masculinities) and on gender as a contextualized and shifting practice, rather than a relatively fixed social category. The move away from seeing gender as a set of behaviours imposed upon the individual by society, and towards gender as enacted or accomplished, is discussed through examples.

Part II is based on the assumption that it is both difficult and counter-productive to make global statements about women's and men's language: 'if gender identities are not fixed, then it is difficult to imagine how the linguistic resources used in their construction can be the same from one situation to the next' (Johnson and Meinhof, 1997: 23). The chapters in this part look at how gender is discursively constructed – and to what effect – in education (Chapter 4), in the media (Chapter 5), and in the workplace (Chapter 6). The issues and theories discussed in Part I are further exemplified in Part II. For example, the theories of 'difference' and 'dominance' are demonstrated through analysis of interaction in the classroom and in the workplace. Also, sexist language and gendered discourses are identified in media texts and in workplace interaction. The discussion extends to the power relations and ideologies pertaining to these texts, for example, those contributing to gender inequalities in the workplace.

Finally, Part III provides a broad introduction to some of the principles, approaches and decisions involved in conducting research on gender and language. It can be used as a starting point for researchers in the area and a resource for those who are teaching and studying gender and language. This part introduces key principles of feminist linguistic research and provides samples of activities, study questions, and resources.

The questions and extracts used in each chapter are suitable for either self-study or classroom use. I have used the majority of them effectively in my teaching of Gender and Language courses at universities, and in the process of supervising dissertations and research projects in this area. Their aim is not to offer clear-cut or correct answers, but rather to encourage readers to reflect on the issues raised, clarify their understanding, and engage with 'real' texts critically. The questions are guided, in the sense that the content of the chapter in which they are embedded provides the ideas, suggestions and directions necessary for addressing them. In most cases, this is done explicitly in the parts immediately following each question or extract; in some cases, it will be necessary to read the whole chapter, or other parts of the book, before going back to address some of the questions. There is sign-posting for the reader, when it is necessary to do this, and generally, for moving from one section of the book to the next. Each chapter is provided with a summary.

Further readings at the end of each chapter are selected with one criterion in mind: they consist of key sources where many of the issues discussed in that chapter are overviewed and explored comprehensively and in much more detail than is the case in this book. They include a mixture of 'classic' key texts and recently published ones. In most cases, the lists of further readings are short, because the key texts suggested are more than adequate in initiating those new to the subject, and in providing access to a whole range of other discussions and sources. Where specific chapters in suggested readings are particularly relevant, and where readings relate to a specific area covered in the book, this has been indicated.

This book is the product of fascination and engagement with what is a constantly developing field. As with any project, there are necessarily omissions in it. Some of these are the result of spatial constraints and the scope of the book (for example, discussions on gender, language and sexuality); others are the result of an 'Anglo-centric' bias in the research we are conducting, reporting and disseminating, for which we are all responsible (hence the relatively fewer examples from different languages and cultures). However, I hope that the book will be useful in offering the new reader an informed account of past, current, diverse, and controversial voices in the field; an understanding of the complexity of this area of study; and a thought-provoking examination of some of the ways in which theory permeates practice.

It is an exciting time for gender and language work. Collaborative research is being produced across several academic disciplines. The literature in the field is expanding (at the time of writing) to include more pedagogically-oriented texts, and the number of students studying and researching gender and language as part of their degrees is rising. I hope this book will contribute to this excitement and will make critical questions about gender and language accessible to more readers.

THEORIZATIONS OF GENDER AND LANGUAGE

Putting gender and language on the map

> There is no neutral discourse: whenever we speak
> we have to choose between different systems of
> meaning, different sets of values.
>
> (Coates, 1998: 302)

This chapter introduces some key assumptions about language and about gender. It describes early (feminist and non-feminist) approaches to gender and language, and moves on to discuss sexist language. This includes examples of sexist usage, lexical gaps and asymmetries, connotative differences, and the use of generic expressions. It also examines different ways of describing and classifying women, which can result in their invisibility and stereotyping. This is followed by looking at language change and linguistic intervention (e.g. using sex-neutral vocabulary, reclaiming words, creating new terms and guidelines for non-sexist language use). The chapter concludes with a summary of concerns for feminist linguistics.

A VIEW OF LANGUAGE

In the Introduction, a shift in assumptions about language is mentioned, which is also relevant for our understanding of gender and language: the shift from the view that we use language in certain ways because of who we are, to the view that who we are is partly because of the way we use language. This perspective assumes that language does not simply *reflect* social reality, but is also *constitutive* of such reality, in other words, it shapes how we see ourselves and the world. If language use is constitutive rather than indexical, then it has the potential to help establish and maintain social and power relations, values and identities, as well as to challenge routine practice and contribute towards social change.

Question 1
In what ways can language shape how we see ourselves and the world?

To address this question, one can consider, for example, why one person's 'terrorist' is another person's 'freedom fighter'; the contexts in which one would use the terms 'liberal', 'collateral damage' or 'axis of evil'; what people mean by 'woman of colour', 'hooded youths', 'male nurse', or 'spinster'; and how much information is conveyed (or not) by the term 'domestic violence'. In addition, violent, shocking, or high impact events, for example, war, provide vivid and highly charged contexts where language is paramount. During the Second World War, the Japanese were constructed as the dehumanized enemy, described as 'specimens' to be 'bagged'. In Rwanda, during the 1994 genocide, the Tutsis were described as 'cockroaches', the target of 'bush-clearing' by the Hutus, who were ordered to 'remove tall weeds' (adults) and 'shoots' (children). The killing of people in wars has typically been reconceptualized as 'action', 'severe measures', 'evacuating', or 'rendering harmless'. In many cases, 'war' has become 'conflict', 'killing fields' have become 'free fire zones', and 'killing civilians' has become 'collateral damage' (Bourke, 1999, 2001). These re-conceptualizations help constitute particular versions of events, such as a bombing, and particular social and power relations, such as those between 'us' and the 'other' (whoever the doer(s) and the receiver(s) of an action may be). Similarly, in terms of gender, the use of phrasing such as 'male nurse' or 'female doctor' or 'lady doctor' effectively constitutes particular versions of the social world, where it is necessary or important for speakers to index gender in that way.

The view of language not as a fixed or closed system, but as dynamic, complex and subject to change, assumes that every time we use language, we make meaningful selections from the linguistic resources available to us (Antaki, 1994). This is hardly a straightforward process, not least because these selections are embedded in a local/immediate, as well as broader/institutional and socio-cultural context (Antaki, 1988, 1994; Fairclough, 1992). Consider, for example, a public debate on the topic of abortion. The language that may be used to write or talk about this topic must be viewed in the context of the particular social occasion (e.g. at school, in parliament, in the media); of the medium (e.g. spoken, written); of who argues (e.g. a doctor, a legislator, a campaigner); for what purpose(s) (e.g. to convince, to change a situation) and from what perspective. The range of perspectives on abortion may vary according to the participants' age, sex, education, race, class, or religion, but also their expectations, experiences, knowledge, expertise, and involvement. Different perspectives will also reflect and promote different assumptions (or discourses, as we will see in Chapter 3) around gender, for example, about women's position in a society, their relative power in terms of decision-making, the role of parenting, a society's views about sex, and so on. It then becomes obvious that in order to understand the role that language plays in establishing and maintaining any social relations, including gender relations, we have to look outside of language itself, at the wider social processes in which language plays a part (Graddol and Swann, 1989).

SEX AND GENDER

The terms *sex* and *gender* are sometimes used interchangeably as synonyms. Language and gender theorists have generally made a distinction between sex as physiological, and gender as a cultural or social construct. According to this distinction, *sex* refers to biological maleness and femaleness, or the physiological, functional, anatomical differences that distinguish men and women, whereas *gender* refers to the traits assigned to a sex – what maleness and femaleness stand for – within different societies and cultures.

Gender can then be seen as a broader, a more encompassing and complex term. As Graddol and Swann (1989) state, the many different life experiences of women and men cannot be simply explained by biological differences between the sexes. Biological differences cannot account for the fact that a person may be more or less 'feminine' and more or less 'masculine'. Further, the many variations of maleness and femaleness over time/from one generation to the next, across cultures, and across contexts, show that the traits assigned to a sex by a culture are socially determined and learned, and therefore alterable (Wodak, 1997; Talbot, 1998). Current theories of gender recognize not only that behaving as men or women within a society will vary from one situation to the next, from one social grouping or community to another, and according to different goals, aims, and interests, but also that people are active agents involved in their own 'gendering' or 'doing gender' (see Chapter 3).

The distinction between sex and gender is important and political. Biological explanations of socially constructed differences between men and women are often used to justify male privileges or reassert traditional family and gender roles, for example, women's so-called 'natural' role as mothers and nurturers (see Talbot, 1998, for other examples). Unsurprisingly, feminists have strongly criticized biological explanations of 'natural' differences between the sexes for perpetuating gender myths, stereotypes, and imbalances that are ultimately damaging for both women and men.

Question 2

Identify other examples of biological explanations of gender differences. What are their possible effects and implications?

In addition to assumptions about women as carers/nurturers and men as providers, other examples relating to Question 2 may include 'men as active' vs 'women as passive', 'male rationality' vs 'female emotionality', men as more suitable for certain jobs than women and vice versa, and the pay gap between male and female employees (see also Chapter 2, Beyond difference, p. 40).

Theorizations of the distinction between sex and gender have developed in recent years. As we will also see in Chapter 3, rather than simply talking about a biological sex and a social gender, we have come to ask more complex questions about the processes of gendering, questions of agency in these processes, and questions around gender ideologies. In addition to discussions of gender as context-dependent femininities and masculinities and not as a set of traits characterizing women and men, recently there has also been discussion of sex as a less clear-cut dichotomy. The latter can be seen in cases of inter-sexed infants – born as both male and female, or as neither, or as indeterminate – who tend to develop the gender identity of the sex assigned to them at birth (Giddens, 1989; Lorber and Farrell, 1991; Bem, 1993; Bing and

Bergvall, 1996; Cameron, 1997). For a discussion of how some societies (often in industrialized parts of the world) are less likely to assign binary biological categories than others, see Epstein (1990), Jacobs and Cromwell (1992), and Hall and O'Donovan (1996). Some theorists go even further, to suggest that the concept of two sexes is 'unreal' and purely a cultural construction or perception in discourse (Butler, 1990). The result of such debates is that assumptions about dichotomies in relation to both sex and gender are being challenged.

Question 3

Consider the following topics being debated in some European countries at the time of writing:

- the preaching, by some Christian groups, of sexual abstinence to teenagers;
- boys' academic under-achievement;
- the ban on wearing Islamic head-scarves in French schools;
- single-sex schools;
- the pay gap between women and men in paid employment;
- the availability of contraception to girls and boys under 16;
- the provision of maternity and paternity leave for employees.

First, would it be possible in each case to talk about the sexes (men, women, boys, girls) without saying something about gender?

Second, would it be possible to talk about gender without saying something about race, ethnicity, religion, class, sexuality, education levels, and the geographical/historical/political/social context pertinent to each of these issues?

PRE-FEMINIST LINGUISTICS

Early pre-feminist linguistic research moved between the view that women's and men's language signals biological differences, and the view that it symbolizes social gender roles, whereas feminist linguists have argued for the latter (Cameron, 1997).

The former approach can be found as early as 1922, in the work of Danish linguist, Otto Jespersen. Jespersen made claims about certain gender differences (discussed in Cameron, 1990): women using more adverbs of intensity (e.g. 'awfully pretty', 'terribly nice') due to a tendency to hyperbole; women not finishing their sentences, due to not having thought out what they are going to say; men being linguistic innovators (e.g. coining new words) and women having a less extensive vocabulary than men. While there are various reasons for criticizing such claims – especially their reliance on 'folk linguistics' (widely held beliefs about language) and stereotypes rather than rigorous systematic research – it should be noted that not much else was written on the subject at the time.

This is in contrast to the enormous amounts of gender and language research that we have seen since the early 1970s, up to today, and with it, a wealth of different approaches, assumptions and methodologies (see Chapters 2 and 3). It is worth pointing out here that different methodological and analytical assumptions about sex and gender, about language and its different aspects, and about notions of 'truth' and 'reality', will produce different research in terms of both results and claims. This is important for understanding that, generally speaking, early research on gender and language focused on gender from the perspective of the speakers' biological sex. For example, language variation studies focused on sex-preferential linguistic usage, that is, men and women's tendencies to speak in their own and different ways. These ways sometimes involved phonological gender differences and sometimes gendered conversational styles (see Trudgill's (1974) work on sociolinguistic variation in Norwich; Cheshire's (1978) research on dialects; Labov (1990) for a discussion). Trudgill found that in many styles (e.g. both casual and formal speech) women used fewer non-standard forms than men, and that the use of non-standard forms, such as multiple negation, was associated with working-class speakers and with male speakers. Trudgill claimed that women are more status-conscious than men. However, such a biological explanation ignores women's and men's social roles and positions, for example, the fact that many women's jobs require them to be more 'well spoken', or that many women 'perform' well-spokenness in conforming to the types of social behaviour most expected of them. It also ignores the fact that gender differences involve differences in orientation to other social categories, and therefore effects of gender in variation cannot be reduced to notions of male/female speech as 'more or less conservative' (Eckert, 1989).

As gender and language study became more sophisticated and more complex, the questions asked moved from the micro-level of sociolinguistic investigation to a broader consideration of language as social practice. But most research studies in the 1970s and the 1980s focused either on gender and language use, and specifically gender differences, or gender (bias) in language as an abstract system, with the focus on the lexicon/individual words (Sunderland and Litosseliti, 2002). We will look at the discussions on gender and language use, and gender differences, in Chapter 2. The emphasis on gender bias in language is particularly evident in arguments over the notion of sexist language, which is discussed next.

SEXIST LANGUAGE

The term 'sexism' was coined in the 1960s, probably by analogy with the term racism, to describe 'discrimination within a social system on the basis of sexual membership' (Wodak, 1997: 7). Sexism makes sense within a historically hierarchical relationship between men and women, where one is the norm, and the other marked as 'other' or inferior, and in relation to a wide range of social practices where women (and in some cases men) are exploited, manipulated or constrained because of their sex.

If language is a powerful medium through which the world is both reflected and constructed, then it is important that sexist language should be both critically examined and questioned (a discussion of the difficulties with defining what counts as 'sexist' follows below). From the 1960s until today, such questioning has involved a shift from looking at gender bias in language as an abstract system, to looking at bias in language use and at potentially sexist discourses, which may be obvious, or subtle, or even unarticulated. We will deal with the latter in Chapter 3, and in the rest of this book. There are a number of areas that have been highlighted regarding the former, i.e. gender bias in language as an abstract system. One of them is the problematic use of pronouns, particularly the (arguably) generic use of 'he', 'him', 'his' to refer to both men and women. Feminists such as Spender (1990) believe that language is man-made, with male forms being seen as the norm and female ones seen as deviant. Some have claimed that the use of *generics* 'he'/'him'/'his', as well as 'man'/'mankind' and expressions like 'the man in the street', to refer to both men and women, reinforces this binary understanding of norm and deviance, promotes male imagery, and makes women invisible. These claims exemplify the 'dominance approach' (see Chapter 2), in that the use of generic expressions is seen to be preventing women from expressing and raising consciousness about their own experience, and perpetuating men's dominance and exploitative behaviour.

In addition to the male being treated as the norm or unmarked term and to women being hidden behind such terminology, feminists have objected to the use of generic expressions such as 'man', saying that they are not true generics (Graddol and Swann, 1989). Spender illustrated this with an example that is acceptable in English: 'Man is the only primate that commits rape'; and an example that is not: 'man being a mammal that breastfeeds his young'. Another example where it becomes obvious that 'man' is not a true generic is the sentence 'Man has difficulty in childbirth' (Hekman, 1990). In addition to criticisms regarding the restriction and exclusion of women, the use of generics can be misleading and confusing. For a detailed discussion and a number of examples in this area, which has been the subject of much controversy, see Graddol and Swann (1989). For a thorough investigation into gender-variable pronouns and gender marking in languages other than English, see Hellinger and Hadumod (2001).

Other areas of bias in the English language as an abstract system include the following:

- *sex specification* in the language (e.g. the now outdated 'authoress', or the use of 'she' to refer to countries, boats, motor cars);
- *gratuitous modifiers* (Miller and Swift, 1981) that diminish a person's prestige, drawing attention to their sex (e.g. 'woman doctor'/'lady doctor') – and while historically the focus for those opposing sexism has been on discrimination against women rather than men, another example of a modifier would be the phrase 'male nurse';
- *lexical gaps or under-lexicalization*, for example having many more terms for promiscuous women than for men (Stanley, 1977) and no female equivalents of terms such as 'henpeck', 'virility', 'penetration';

- *semantic derogation* (Schulz, 1975), where a term describing a woman initially has neutral connotations, but gradually acquires negative connotations, and becomes abusive or ends up as a sexual slur (e.g. 'lady', 'madam', 'mistress', 'queen'); relatedly, there are many more negative terms for women than for men, particularly pertaining to sexual behaviour and denoting women as sexual prey (Cowie and Lees, 1987; Cameron, 1992);

- *asymmetrically gendered language items*, i.e. single words used to describe women, for which there is no equivalent for men, and vice versa. For example, the use of 'fireman'/'policeman'/'chairman' (prior to linguistic intervention, see next section); the use of 'Mrs' to label only women, thus arguably reinforcing a patriarchal order; and the difference in status between lexical items such as 'master', 'bachelor', 'governor', 'god', 'wizard', and their female equivalents;

- *connotations of language items*, such as 'girl' (which may sometimes indicate immaturity, dependence, triviality, e.g. compare 'weatherman' to 'weathergirl'); 'lady' and 'woman', both of which are often used euphemistically for decorum or to obscure 'negative' associations with sexuality and reproduction; and the nurturing connotations of 'mothering', compared to those of the term 'fathering'.

As will become evident later, bias in the language does not necessarily entail bias in language use, and as we will also see in Chapter 3, sexist discourses may or may not draw on sexist language items. Words have more than one meaning, and language users' intentions are obscure and unpredictable. Couched within words are presuppositions about gender, that is, many taken-for-granted assumptions about women/men, girls/boys, gender relations, roles and expectations. The identification of sexist wordings is a good start towards raising awareness about how differences in the meanings of words 'reflect differences in the traditional roles accorded to women and men in our society' (Graddol and Swann, 1989: 113). Newspapers, for example, are full of examples of wordings which are used to portray women in negative or limiting ways, i.e. wordings which:

- depict women as sex objects and on the basis of their appearance rather than their intellect or capabilities (e.g. 'a blonde');
- define women in terms of home, family, and domestic roles (e.g. 'mother of three'), in ways that are seldom used for men;
- trivialize women (e.g. using 'girl' for a much wider age range than 'boy' would be used; also 'weathergirl');
- judge women (e.g. 'ladette', 'career woman').

Consider the following examples from the sports section of the British broadsheet newspaper *The Sunday Times*. The extracts are from two pieces about tennis, which are written by the same writer, and appear on the same page of the paper.

Extract (1A)

From *The Sunday Times*, 23 January 2000 (Sports section)

By Richard Evans

Hewitt keeps home fires burning

The Australian wonder boy's dream lives on as Newcombe amends his Davis Cup script

UNDETERRED by heavy showers, another record-breaking crowd packed Melbourne Park by day, and by night they returned for what is becoming a happy ritual – another victory by Lleyton Hewitt. It was his 13th of the year and his fourth of the Australian open, and all bets are now off as to just how far the Adelaide Express can run before he hits the buffers.

Hewitt is a phenomenon, but even 18-year-old legs have their limits, and with the men's doubles and mixed also on his agenda, this amazing athlete cannot go on running and out-hitting the world's best players.

Or maybe he can. There was little sign yesterday as he outclassed a fairly classy performer in Adrian Voinea, the Perugia-based Romanian, who was suffering from a leg strain as well as his usual inability to concentrate over the distance.

...

Kournikova plays it cute in off-court games

Romantic gossip and garish fashions are creating more of a stir than results in the women's championship

ANNA KOURNIKOVA looked fetching in powder blue as she practised during a brief sunny spell in the afternoon, but Serena Williams, on the late shift in the Rod Laver Stadium, re-appeared in her scarlet number with its low-cut black top and her red shoes. ...

It was one of those days when the tennis never quite managed to divert one's attention from the gossip ricocheting off the walls of the long corridors that link the players' area with the cosmopolitan press room.

Most of it centred on the titillating possibility that Kournikova, the little blond from Moscow, might actually be entering into what is euphemistically called a relationship with the tall and handsome Mark Philippoussis.

At the risk of being called a cynic, I doubt whether Kournikova has discovered what a real relationship means. She has plenty of friends, most of them male, who spend much of the time gawking at her. The fact that they seem to be among the better-looking members of the men's locker room could be sheer chance, or it could be her choice. They are certainly numerous.

...

© *The Sunday Times*

The extracts illustrate well some of the issues discussed in this chapter so far, and raise certain questions:

- In what ways do participants' sex and gender interact in the extracts, and to what effect?
- Is there anything surprising or inappropriate about the descriptions, given the purpose of the texts?
- Is there evidence of asymmetrically-gendered language, or sexism (as discussed earlier) in the extracts?

By way of addressing some of these questions, one can argue that the excessive emphasis on women's appearance is inappropriate or irrelevant in contexts where a woman's profession is the focus. One may further argue that such emphasis is offensive in contexts where a similar emphasis for men is unlikely, and where men are described in terms of other achievements (e.g. prowess, performance in their chosen field). An analyst would pay particular attention to the words used to describe the male characters – 'wonder boy', 'a phenomenon', 'amazing athlete', 'classy performer', 'tall and handsome' – compared to those used to refer to the female characters: 'cute', 'fetching in powder blue', 'in her scarlet number', 'the little blond from Moscow'.

If Extract (1A) above represents a rather obvious and exaggerated example of sexist language as discussed in this chapter, it is also worth reflecting on these questions in relation to more subtle examples. Extract (1B) is from an interview in *The Sunday Times* with Dr Heather Clark, a member of the Royal London hospital's helicopter emergency medical service.

Extract (1B)

From *The Sunday Times*, 9 May 1999
Flying high on the excitement of saving lives
INTERVIEW – Eleanor Mills meets Dr Heather Clark

[A photograph of the interviewee is accompanied by the caption:

Trauma queen: helicopter doctor and dancer Heather Clark admits she is an adrenaline junkie]

Opening sentence by interviewer:

When Dr Heather Clark hacked open a man's chest and performed open-heart surgery on the floor of a busy East End pub, she became a national hero ...

'My heart is in my mouth and my whole body floods with adrenaline when I get that call and head for the helicopter,' admits Clark. 'It's certainly a buzz. When you get in, you never know what you're going to – it could be a major incident with lots of casualties, or a road accident, or anything. ...

'With this job, the day is always varied, you never know what you will be doing. Also, it is the only area of medicine where you really save people on the spot. Where you really know instantly that you have made a difference …

'But although it is exciting, you learn to never be blasé about death and injuries. Sometimes you lie awake at night worrying that if you had done something different they might have survived.'

Sitting opposite Clark, it is hard to believe she is really 35 years old – she looks about 20 – or that someone so tiny could have the strength necessary to cut open bodies and save lives. At 5ft 1in, with size 3 feet and big blue eyes, she looks like a china doll. In her orange boiler suit stuffed with equipment – 'It's terrible, I look like a Teletubby', she says modestly – Heather could be a child dressed up as a doctor.

Yet, it would certainly be wrong to judge this woman by appearances. 'I know I am small, but I am incredibly fit', she insists. 'You have to be in this job as we often have to run quite a way from the helicopter to the patient carrying a pack weighing 15 kilos and all the kit in my suit, which is another 8 kilos or so.' …

She is not married but does have a boyfriend – 'another doctor, so he understands about my crazy hours'. … 'But I suppose I'm used to it, as a junior doctor I regularly did a 100-hour week. … There is no way the government should be increasing the hours junior doctors work as they just suggested, it is dangerous, you just can't function.'

Could she do her present job if she had children?

'Well, the male doctors who work here all have children – but how their wives put up with the hours I will never know. They are never home. As a woman it would be much more difficult. You would have to employ a nanny and you wouldn't be a proper mother. But doctors only join the helicopter team for six months at a time.' …

© *The Sunday Times*

In addition to the questions asked of the previous sports page extracts (Extract 1A), this example is useful for thinking about the less explicit ways of describing, defining, and trivializing women. These can be seen in the choice of lexical items and expressions such as 'trauma queen', 'china doll', and 'child dressed up as a doctor', which would be both inappropriate and confusing if used to describe a male doctor. (For further discussions, see Cameron, 1998; also Pauwels, 1998.) The fact that these terms are used by a woman is a reminder that women themselves often play a role in reproducing and perpetuating sexism. The view of 'language as sexist' is often simplistic, in assuming that the sexes are in binary opposition to one another and that a hierarchical relationship between them is always in place – however, what is needed is a broader understanding of where potential sexism resides (see later).

Extract (1B) also raises broader questions about the importance of establishing meaning beyond single words. As Poynton states (1989), sexist meaning may be constructed in other levels of language, beyond the lexical level: grammatical choices, such as choosing particular pronouns or adjectives over others, as well as discourses (social meanings and practices – see Chapter 3) contain particular ways of seeing and acting in the world. To interpret the expression 'proper mother' in the extract above appropriately, one needs to go beyond words, to navigate through the whole range of possible meanings, values and ideologies implicated in such language use. These issues will be discussed in Chapter 3 in some detail.

Above all, the extract raises questions about the problematic definition of sexism:

■ Is there direct or evident sexism in this example?
■ What are some of the difficulties in describing parts of the extract as sexist?

These difficulties are explored in the following section.

CHANGING LANGUAGE

Language evolves historically and as the needs of its speakers change, not necessarily with politically motivated intervention. Typically, language changes as a result of social, political and economic processes, such as lifestyle changes, new experiences, encounters with technologies and communication media, colonization, or migration (see Beard, 2004, for examples). This is not a predictable process, and it doesn't affect all languages in the same way; for example, Japanese has not changed nearly as much as English has over the years. Change in language may precede or may follow change in social structures. Language changes as a result of a dynamic relationship between opposing forces of conservation and innovation, and with such change come more choices (Cameron, 1995). But choice has 'altered the value' of the terms we use to talk and write about gender, and has 'removed the option of political neutrality' (ibid.: 119).

The argument that language can be sexist has, for a long time, guided efforts to promote gender-inclusive language. These efforts are based on the premise that language is always changing, and that we can, and should, actively influence such shifts. Action for linguistic change can help raise consciousness about the ways in which people and groups are represented, described, defined, and constrained in discourse. Such awareness-raising may eventually lead to fairer representations and the empowerment of those people and groups – not only women, but also men (see August, 1995), as well as those discriminated against on the basis of their race, religion, age, education, disability, or sexual orientation.

Linguistic intervention for change, as regards gender, has taken the form of guidelines and equal opportunities policies (e.g. in industry and in classroom teaching); awareness training seminars in organizations (see Chapter 6); the promotion of gender-neutral terms in job advertisements (e.g. fire fighter); and various codes of practice (for some examples, see Graddol and Swann, 1989). Such intervention has had a number of aims. First, it has aimed to promote a more inclusive language. Notable examples include the use of the words 'persons', 'people', 'Ms', 'they' and 'them' (e.g. 'Each speaker will have one hour for *their* presentation'), and opting for 'chair' rather that 'chairman', 'flight attendant' rather than 'airhostess', 'doctor' rather than 'woman doctor', etc. (See also Pauwels, 1998, for attempts to change gender-inflected languages.) Second, intervention has aimed to increase women's visibility, for example by avoiding the generic pronouns 'he'/'his'/'him', adding the female pronoun ('he or she', 's/he'), opting for reversal ('she or he', 'women and men'), or using the generic 'she'. And, third, change has also focused on establishing, reclaiming or changing the meaning of particular words, such as 'partner', 'queer', 'patriarchy', and 'chauvinism'.

These forms of linguistic intervention however, both face and pose a number of problems. One difficulty has been that attempts at intervention are often faced with ridicule (e.g. the mocking of terms such as 'herstory'); marginalization, as a result of claims that language is a trivial concern (Blaubergs, 1980); or appropriation and denial, for example, claims that change is too difficult or impractical, or that it interferes with our freedom of speech. The introduction of the term 'Ms', as an alternative to 'Miss' and 'Mrs' – which label only women, and arguably reinforce a patriarchal order where women's marital status becomes important – has not necessarily been effective in combating sexism. This is because, for some people, 'Ms' refers to 'older unmarried women, divorcees and strident feminists – in other words to "abnormal" and "unfeminine" women' (Cameron, 1992: 122; Dion, 1987). These reactions have a lot to do with the fact that, in the 1970s and the 1980s, linguistic intervention was advocated strictly as a small part of the wider project of feminist intervention – and both have been resisted and marginalized.

Linguistic intervention is also problematic, when confronted with the non-tenability of language that is neutral: non-sexist, non-racist, and so on. As Coates puts it, 'there is no neutral discourse: whenever we speak we have to choose between different systems of meaning, different sets of values' (1998: 302). In addition to language itself changing, our use of language is constantly changing, in order to accommodate and convey a range of meanings, concepts and values. Different people may ascribe different meanings to a particular word (Graddol and Swann, 1989). As meaning is situated in context, the question becomes one of intentionality and interpretation: how do speakers and writers use language (including 'sexist language') from one time to another, from one context to the next? And how do people interpret others' language differently within different contexts (times, places, events, social/cultural/value systems)?

It is clear that a so-called sexist word may be used in non-sexist ways. It may be used in an ironic way, or in a different way within a particular community, as in the case of the reclamation of 'queer' or 'dyke' as positive terms within gay speech communities. The opposite can also happen. As Sunderland and Litosseliti (2002: 5) illustrate, a gender-neutral word such as 'people' can be used in a sexist, or at least non-gender-inclusive, way: 'The commons were popular with Newburians and other locals. People took picnics, "walked out" with their girls, picked bluebells and primroses in season' (*The Independent*, 5 January 1990). In parts of the world such as Saudi Arabia, where sex segregation in public places is obligatory, one finds signs on restaurant doors marked 'singles' (exclusively for men) and 'families'; yet the former term is not neutral, and the latter not only is not inclusive of all women, it also defines women exclusively in relation to their husbands, children, and relatives. Also, to quote an anecdotal example, the fact that I use the gender-neutral title 'Dr' in front of my name does not stop people (contacting me by phone or email) from asking to speak to 'him'.

Similarly, the removal of many racist terms from our language does not entail the elimination of racist sentiment and behaviour. In fact, efforts to eliminate such sentiment are not necessarily free of racism or sexism themselves, as illustrated in the language used by Malcolm X (seen in Spike Lee's 1992 film) in speeches: 'The Earth belongs to us . . . the black man'; and in written form: 'We must protect our most valuable property . . . our women'. (For an account of different 'frames' or perspectives when talking about race, see Rattansi, 1995, and for a good example of recent work on discourses of racism, see van Dijk, 2005.)

In short, meaning cannot be inferred by words alone, but by inferential work that involves many situational and contextual parameters. What we therefore need to challenge is the 'particular "discursive practices" in which sexist assumptions are embodied by linguistic choices, rather than to keep on asserting that "language" is globally and generally sexist in itself' (Cameron, 1990: 18). We will be looking at discursive practices in Chapter 3, but the key point to make here is that changing sexist language will not *by itself* eliminate sexism in our society. Effective change has to come from both personal and institutional levels. In addition, a focus on language has to be part of a focus on gender inequality in general, and viewed in the context of wider social and institutional change. For example, a change in the language used in rape reporting and in court examination of rape victims (for analyses of such language, see Lees, 1996; Wood and Rennie, 1994; Ehrlich 2004) needs to materialize within the context of legal and social changes. Such changes would involve, most notably, a more realistic co-relation between crime and convictions; at the time of writing, only 5 per cent of defendants whose rape cases come to court are convicted, and the conviction rate has been falling rapidly in the UK in the past 20 years (from 24 to 5 per cent), according to *The Observer* (31 July 2005). Changes would also involve the provision of better support for victims, and the inclusion on the agenda of male rape. Our language regarding how rapists and their victims are perceived and treated can then reflect as well as help consolidate the legal, institutional and social developments in this area.

Undoubtedly, there have been profound changes in recent decades in terms of raised awareness about gender issues, as well as gender and language. Yet, the complexity of our language choices, the pressures of a climate of political correctness, and the success of feminist campaigns over language, may mean that we are now faced with different, more insidious, forms of sexism than in the past, when instances of sexist language were relatively easily identified. Mills (2002) claims that sexist language today is liberally and apolitically used by people, in ways where it is assumed to be ironized; this means that there is an assumption that people 'know it as sexist', thus implying that they could not possibly be using it in earnest, but only in a humorous, knowingly ironic way (Christie, 2000). We can see this in how 'sexist' jokes are produced and received (Sunderland, 2004), in much of the discourse found in men's magazines as well as advertisements (see Chapter 5 for a detailed discussion) and in the contradictory discourse of managers in organizations (see Chapter 6).

If we look again at Extract (1B) above, we see that any claims about sexism in this text would be based on a notion of sexism as indirect or built on presuppositions, for example, about women's appearance, or women's role as mothers. One will have to unpack these presuppositions, and work through their various meanings, before being able to hypothesize about sexism in the text. Even then, resistant and/or feminist readers of the text are often typecast as 'too serious', 'over-reacting' or 'politically correct' when they attempt to articulate their own resistant readings. But 'political correctness' should not be equated with 'anti-sexism'. Mills (2002) points out that 'political correctness' has damaged and de-stabilized anti-sexist practices. Anti-sexist practices are localized, complex, and linked to campaigning over real concerns. In contrast, 'political correctness' is 'an abstracted set of rules extrapolated by the media from these practices and generalized to absurdity' (e.g. 'personhole cover' instead of 'manhole cover') with the alleged aim of protecting the sensibilities of minority groups (ibid.).

To sum up, the debate on sexism is complex and fraught with difficulties. When sexism was overt and outside the context of well-established political debates, it was easier to identify, and possibly to address, through deliberate efforts of intervention. But without the option of political neutrality on issues of (and not only) gender, sexism may take different – much more insidious, and arguably more dangerous – forms. Therefore, while raising awareness about sexism and sexist language remains an important step towards change, any deliberate efforts of intervention in order to raise such awareness *have* to be accompanied by broader changes in our discourse practices and in social and institutional structures. In addition, they have to be based on an understanding that both sexist and anti-sexist practices are localized and will vary widely (in terms of approach, seriousness, interpretation, and effectiveness) from one context to the next.

THE EMERGENCE OF FEMINIST LINGUISTICS

This chapter has started by providing a backdrop to early approaches to gender and language. In the following two chapters, we will look at how our approaches have developed and what new directions have opened up with the emergence of feminist linguistics. To understand the background of these developments, it should be stressed that not all *gender and language research* would align itself with *feminist linguistics*, because its interest in feminism as a political movement or theory may not be evident or made explicit.

Feminist linguistics is interested in identifying, demystifying, and resisting the ways in which language is used, together with other social practices, to reflect, create and sustain gender divisions and inequalities in society (Talbot, 1998). For a long time, an exploration of these ways has concentrated on gender differences (primarily in talk) in terms of intonation, pronunciation, vocabulary, syntax, conversational strategies, and interactional or discursive patterns (see Chapter 2). Gender and language studies in the 1960s, the 1970s, and the 1980s have focused almost exclusively on women's language, rather than men's. This can be seen as an understandable and necessary response to the sustained historical exclusion of women in a patriarchal world order in general, and their exclusion in androcentric research in particular. In contrast to past approaches, the focus of feminist linguistics today is not on 'women's language'. A feminist approach has a critical view of gender, one not just concerned with differences, and it accepts that differences must be theorized too (Cameron, 1997). A critical view of gender also accepts that we need to focus on the relationships between femininity and masculinity, and to extend our preoccupation with women outside the normatively female, i.e. white heterosexual middle-class women.

Mills (2002) identifies three chronological waves in the history of feminism, and although feminist linguistics developed within linguistics rather than within feminism, these can help us place the development of feminist linguistics in context. Pre-modernist or 'first-wave' feminism can be associated with the suffragette movement in the nineteenth and twentieth centuries. Modernist or 'second-wave' feminism in the 1960s can be associated with political resistance against sex discrimination and with the promotion of equal opportunities as well as the emancipation of women. Along the same lines, the development of gender and language research during this second wave has focused on discrimination and sexist vs inclusive language, has emphasized aspects of difference and of dominance in interaction, and has celebrated femaleness (see Chapter 2). Finally, 'third-wave' feminism, with its more critical, constructivist, and post-structuralist theoretical paradigms shares a lot with current thinking within feminist linguistics. According to Mills (2002; also summarized in Baxter, 2003: 5), 'third-wave feminism' is concerned with the diversity, multiplicity, performativity, and co-construction of gender identities within specific contexts and communities of practice, and on the politics of power construction and subject positions (see Chapter 3). Feminist linguistics shares these assumptions and principles. It aims to theorize gender-related linguistic phenomena and language use, and to explicitly link these to gender inequality or discrimination, on the assumption that linguistic change is an important part of overall social change. Feminist linguists assert that people produce their identities in social interaction, in ways that sometimes follow and other times challenge dominant beliefs and ideologies of gender. Further, 'as new social resources become available, language users enact and produce new identities, themselves temporary and historical, that assign new meanings to gender' (Bucholtz, 1999: 20). As we will see in Chapter 3, the scope of feminist linguistic work is broad and multidisciplinary, especially as a result of overlapping with theories of critical linguistics and critical discourse analysis (CDA).

SUMMARY

■ Language reflects and constitutes our social world in a dynamic way; it constructs particular versions of events and particular social and power relations.

■ 'Sex' and 'gender' dichotomies have been challenged, and both are better seen as continua of maleness and femaleness. Biological explanations of socially constructed differences between men and women have also been challenged for justifying male privileges and perpetuating gender imbalances.

■ Early research on language and gender contained biological explanations that ignored women's and men's social roles and positions. Studies in the 1970s and the 1980s focused on gender (bias) in language as an abstract system, with an emphasis on individual words, and on gender and language use, with an emphasis on gender differences.

■ Attention to bias in the language concentrated on generic pronouns and expressions, sex specification, modifiers, lexical gaps, 'semantic derogation', asymmetrically gendered language items, and connotations of words. These have the potential to reinforce binary understandings of norm and deviance, promote male imagery, and make women invisible.

■ Sexist wordings portray women as sex objects and, judging on the basis of their appearance rather than intellect or capabilities, they define women in terms of home, family and domestic roles, and trivialize women.

■ Language changes historically and as a result of social processes, and to a lesser extent through politically motivated intervention (e.g. codes of practice, equal opportunities policies). Such intervention has aimed to promote a more inclusive language, increase women's visibility, and establish, reclaim or change the meaning of particular words. These attempts have often been met with ridicule, marginalization, appropriation and denial.

■ There is no neutral language. The possibilities of intentionality and interpretation mean that a 'sexist' word can be used in non-sexist ways, and vice versa. Meaning resides in inferential work that involves many situational and contextual parameters.

■ Language change can and should happen alongside wider changes in our discourse practices and our legal, institutional and social structures.

■ Sexist and anti-sexist practices have been de-stabilized as a result of more complex language choices, the climate of 'political correctness', and the advances of feminism. The debate on sexism is complex and fraught with difficulties.

■ Feminist linguistics is interested in identifying, demystifying, and resisting the ways in which language is used to create and sustain gender inequalities. On the basis that linguistic change is an important part of social change, it aims to theorize those ways and link them to gender inequality or discrimination in societies.

FURTHER READING

Beard, A. (2004) *Language Change*. London: Routledge.

Bing, J. and Bergvall, V. (1996) The question of questions: beyond binary thinking, in V.L. Bergvall, J.M. Bing and A.F. Freed (eds) *Rethinking Language and Gender Research: Theory and Practice*. Harlow: Longman.

Cameron, D. (1990) *The Feminist Critique of Language*. London: Routledge (especially Chapter 1; also Chapters 7 and 9).

Cameron, D. (1992) *Feminism and Linguistic Theory*, 2nd edn. New York: St Martin's Press (Chapters 1, 2 and 10).

Coates, J. (1993) *Women, Men and Language*, 2nd edn. Harlow: Longman (especially Chapter 1, see also 2003, revised 3rd edn).

Goddard, A. and Patterson, L.M. (2000) *Language and Gender*. London: Routledge (see the activities).

Graddol, D. and Swann, J. (1989) *Gender Voices*. Oxford: Blackwell (especially Chapter 1).

Talbot, M. (1998) *Language and Gender: An Introduction*. Cambridge: Polity Press (Chapters 1, 3 and 11).

Other references

The Sunday Times, 9 May 1999.
The Sunday Times, 23 January 2000.
The Observer, 31 July 2005.

2 The 'language of women':
lacking, powerless, different

> It is [...] not simply that women and men are seen
> to be different, but that this male–female
> difference is superimposed on so many aspects of
> the social world that a cultural connection is
> thereby forged between sex and virtually every
> other aspect of human experience.
>
> (Bem, 1993: 2)

This chapter introduces and problematizes past theoretical approaches to the study of gender and language: 'deficit', 'difference' and 'dominance' approaches. As mentioned in the Introduction, these approaches have tended to focus (each to a different extent) on how women and men use language differently, rather than on how women and men are constructed through language. Similarly to early research in this area (Chapter 1), they also focused on gender from the perspective of the speakers' biological sex. This chapter overviews the theoretical models and discusses key studies within each one. The chapter is not intended as a comprehensive discussion of these theories (for there are books that do this very well; see below and Further Reading), nor as a clear-cut description of them as distinct (for they overlap in time and as theories). Rather, it aims to provide the background for the ways in which the field has developed, and to show how elements of past approaches have influenced current thinking in gender and language. In other words, the focus is on the progression of theoretical and methodological frameworks, which then led to the reframing of the original questions and the shift from words to discourse (Chapter 3).

WOMEN'S LANGUAGE AS DEFICIENT

The gendered language debate has been guided by two main theoretical positions: *theories of dominance* in the late 1970s, and *theories of difference*, predominantly in the 1980s. The former treats differences as indicative of women being dominated in interaction, while the latter explains differences as a result of women and men belonging to distinct sub-cultures. They will be discussed in detail in the following sections of the chapter. Both positions, but especially dominance, can be seen as products of the political climate for women at the time (for instance, efforts to expose bias and avoid sexist language), and as a reaction to existing 'deficit' models of women's language. Jespersen's theories, and to an extent work by Trudgill (1974), both discussed in Chapter 1, represent 'deficit' models, in that they make claims about female language being an inferior version of male language. According to Jespersen's 1922 controversial piece, the deficiency of women's speech can be found in their use of 'hyperbole', their 'incoherent sentences', 'inferior command of syntax', 'less extensive vocabulary', and 'non-innovative' approach to language (Jespersen, 1990). His comments about the greatest orators and literary artists being men – such 'linguistic genius […] rarely found among women' – would be risible for many readers today and, in addition, he has been criticized for making these claims on the basis of intuition rather than empirical research. But this was one of the first articles to address issues of gender difference in language, and was surprisingly influential on the research that followed.

But probably the most influential early feminist work on gender and language (and in many ways a 'deficit' model) has been Robin Lakoff's pioneering, and greatly criticized, 1975 book *Language and Woman's Place*. Although Lakoff's claims approach gender and language from a 'difference', and occasionally from a 'dominance' perspective, they are fundamentally claims about women's language as lacking, weak, trivial, and hesitant – in short, deficient when compared to men's language (though also see Livia, 2004). Lakoff claimed that this weakness can be seen in certain features that are typical of women's speech: their 'empty' vocabulary, for example, the choice of adjectives such as 'lovely' and 'adorable' and colours such as 'beige' and 'lavender'; their weaker expletives, e.g. 'oh dear', as opposed to stronger expletives; their trivial subject matter; and their tendency to be over-polite where men would be direct. She also asserted that women use intonational patterns that indicate uncertainty and seek their interlocutor's approval. An example of this would be:

Man: When will dinner be ready?
Woman: Oh … [*with rising intonation*] around six o'clock?

Other features which are seen to indicate such insecurity on the part of female speakers are tag questions (e.g. 'It is a lovely day, *isn't it?*') and the use of more intensifiers and qualifiers (e.g. 'so', 'really', 'well', 'a bit') than male speakers.

> Women's speech seems in general to contain more instances of 'well', 'you know', 'kind' and so forth: words that convey the sense that the speaker is uncertain about what he (or she) is saying, or cannot vouch for the accuracy of the statement … [These words] appear … as an apology for making an assertion at all.
>
> (Lakoff, 1975: 53–4)

Question 1
What assumptions is Lakoff making in the quote above?

Lakoff is assuming that the women's heavily qualified statements and use of tag questions are signs of their uncertainty and efforts not to force their own, subordinate, view onto their interlocutor. However, such explanations have received a lot of criticism, on the basis that they ignore the context and the possible different communicative functions of tag questions and qualifiers (also known as 'hedges'). As Cameron *et al.* show in their own studies of tag questions (1988), the relation between linguistic form and communicative function is complex, thus making it difficult to state *a priori* what tag questions do. Holmes (1986, 1990) is also critical of any straightforward association of qualifiers (such as 'you know') with hesitancy. Studies by Coates (1996b) and Fishman (1990; discussed later) show, for example, that such techniques can have a different function, namely to include the other speaker and to keep the conversation flowing. In addition, most subsequent research (following Lakoff) agrees that the use of any form depends on many variables, apart from gender, such as the participants' status and relative power, their objectives, their role in interaction, the type of activity and the overall context.

Where Jespersen ignores issues of dominance in society, i.e. that men have been *allowed* to become great orators and writers, Lakoff often highlights these issues to explain women's alleged linguistic inferiority in relation to men. So, for example, the use of tag questions is interpreted as one way of seeking approval through politeness, while rising intonation is seen as diminishing women's contributions and disadvantaging their power positions in more serious contexts. Lakoff also highlights issues of difference, and one of the significant points she makes is that girls are from an early age taught or socialized to speak like 'little ladies', which results in more polite speech and the avoidance of strong statements; this is seen in contrast to boys, who are taught to be more forthright. However, she has been criticized for ignoring the possibility that politeness can also be used strategically by women to affect or change power relations (see, for example, Cameron and Coates, 1989).

In general, Lakoff's work has been criticized for its lack of empirical data, that is, for a reliance on her own intuition and casual observations, and for her use of cultural stereotypes as a way to study gendered language. At times, her claims have been misrepresented as putting forward a view that all women use all the features of women's language, whereas Lakoff intended to focus on the pervasiveness of media stereotypes as models of behaviour that men and women follow. In terms of criticisms about her 'armchair theorizing', it is important to be aware that her work was describing 'a particular ideology of femininity rather than an empirical description of it' (McElhinny, 2004: 130). But a valid criticism is directed at the fact that this work, like most research at the time, is blind to linguistic differentiation, that is, the fact that a linguistic feature may have various functions, and to social differentiation (differences in terms of class, age, race, etc.). Further, social differentiation is culture-dependent: features of women's language that are seen as powerless in the USA, for instance, can be an index of prestige in Japan (Ide, 2004). Criticisms of Lakoff's work, as well as generally of work by 'difference' theorists (see below), raise some important broader questions about the study of gender and language. As Bing and Bergvall (1998) assert, these theorists tend to reinforce the female–male dichotomy by asking questions that assume the existence of a binary. Such questions not only presuppose that women and men *do* speak differently, but also, on the basis that the language of women is found to be deficient, they reinforce the perception of *women* as deficient (ibid.; and Cameron, 1996).

Question 2

Consider each of the features of 'women's language', as described by Lakoff. Think of as many *functions* of the same feature as possible, and of different *situations* where the same feature is used in different ways.

If we accept that features like tag questions, hedges, minimal responses (e.g. 'yeah', 'right'), and so on, can function not as signs of hesitancy, but as conversational facilitation strategies, we still need to ask questions about who is doing the facilitating, in what ways, and in what situations and settings. Is facilitation a 'norm' of female speakers and female groups, a burden shouldered by subordinate speakers, a strategy used to control the interaction, or a combination of these at different times and in different settings (Cameron *et al.*, 1988)? Different situations, for example, casual conversation between friends or unequal encounters in the workplace, make different demands on speakers – demands for indirectness, politeness and attention to the power dynamics. Consider the following extract from a business meeting in a retail company in the UK (Mullany, 2003). The first speaker, who chairs the meeting, is here attempting to convince the others (who are subordinates) to run their own induction day, similar to what the sales department in the company had previously done.

Extract (2A)

Sue:	Do you feel that (-) we need to do perhaps something like (-) the sales department did?
Jasmin:	Set a date to sort it out
Sue:	Cos as Steve's quite rightly pointed out, all it's all been done for us and the things etc why don't we just take advantage of that? (.) Steve's offered his support with perhaps John? (-) Err you know perhaps to run that (.) why don't we just set a date now?
Jane:	Yeah
Sue:	And say right okay let's do it
Steve:	Just get everybody in
Jane:	Yeah

(Mullany, 2003: 136)

As it appears, the extract could be used as an illustration of Lakoff's claims regarding the linguistic forms or strategies associated with women's speech style. Sue is drawing on numerous co-operative mitigation strategies, such as questions and qualifiers (e.g. 'you know', 'just', 'right'). Her style is indirect ('perhaps' is used a number of times) and characterized by collaborative rapport-building (e.g. 'do you feel that', 'why don't we', 'let's'). These features could be treated as signs of hesitance or uncertainty however, in this context, they appear to work as ways to facilitate or control the meeting and influence the decision-making process. It is important to know that, in this case, Sue's status in the organization is higher than that of the other participants. But is it important to know that Sue is female? In fact, the names in this extract have been swapped around. In reality, the female managers indicated above were male, and vice versa. How does this influence our reading of the extract, in the light of Lakoff's comments? These issues are explored in the rest of the chapter. (For details on this extract, and other examples of workplace interaction, see Chapter 6.)

Lakoff's 1975 book has recently been re-released, with the author's annotations and comments on past and current debates, and accompanied by other researchers' new contributions (Bucholtz, 2004). This collection acknowledges the importance of *Language and Woman's Place* in initiating an in-depth discussion of the issues that were to be followed up and critiqued for decades later by researchers in diverse fields (e.g. politeness theory), and in contributing to the expansion of linguistic theory (Bucholtz, 2004). Lakoff's most recent commentary on her original work productively clarifies and expands on some of her previous claims. For example, she talks about how politeness strategies are negotiated by speakers in tandem with managing the power dynamics in interaction. This balancing of attention to politeness and issues of power underlies indirect language, and it can vary by gender as well as other factors; for instance, Lakoff refers to other groups (e.g. gay men, academic men, upperclass males, hippies) that manifest features of women's language as a result of opting out of worlds where stereotypical male bravado as a way to compete is the norm. But she also makes the important point that, as in the 1970s, women still often find themselves in a 'double bind' situation where, if they use direct language they are accused of being unfeminine, and if they 'talk like a lady' they risk being ignored or treated as incoherent and non-serious. In this sense, dominance issues still remain relevant today, and indeed Lakoff suggests that, while attempting to identify the linguistic uses that discriminate against groups of people, we need to change the social positions that make certain groups powerless (Bucholtz, 2004).

The commentaries accompanying the re-release of Lakoff's original work are useful in challenging some of her claims and in expanding her work to areas previously neglected – notably the study of women other than white middle-class women, and the study of men, as well as sexuality. As Morgan (2004) points out, the study of the everyday interaction of 'other' women and men (African-American, Hispanic, Asian) has been ignored, even by feminist researchers. These groups are viewed in opposition to the 'norm' and are marginalized through the study of their most extreme varieties of language use, such as inner city gang talk. Similarly, Lakoff's assumptions about parallels, in terms of powerlessness, between gay speech and women's speech, are today challenged (see Gaudio, 2004; Leap, 2004) for reinforcing limiting stereotypes.

Having said all this, Lakoff's methods are consistent with her disciplinary community at the time, in terms of the centrality of native speaker intuition, and in terms of omissions in researching 'other' groups (Hall and Bucholtz, 1995). Despite presenting a deficit view of women's language, *Language and Woman's Place* is an important work written from a feminist perspective; it explains the 'inadequacies' of women's language in political and cultural terms, rather than seeing them as 'natural' sex differences (Cameron, 1990). It also marks the beginning of studying actual speech behaviour in context, and of asking more critical, social questions about language.

CONVERSATIONAL LABOUR: WHOSE POWER?

In the late 1970s, and into the 1980s, gender and language research was characterized by an interest in interaction and (mis)communication within mixed-sex and (progressively) single-sex groups. It was also guided by an emphasis on the politics of researching women's language, and particularly the need to be more critical about 'deficit' models of analysis that portray women in negative ways. As part of a more political climate, the emphasis on exposing patriarchy – the social structures and ideology contributing to women's oppression – was being extended to language. We thus saw an interest in exposing bias in the language (e.g. generics, lexical items, etc. discussed in Chapter 1) and in language use (e.g. verbal harassment, everyday interaction). Relatedly, during this time there was campaigning for alternative and inclusive language use, and many radical feminists proposed ways of creating women-centred language and meaning. Even non-verbal gestures, such as eye contact, touching, smiling, or intonation, became foci for exploring unequal power relationships (Thorne and Henley, 1975).

In her monumental piece, *Man-made Language* (1980), Dale Spender argued that, as a result of patriarchy, meaning is defined by men (e.g. literally by writing dictionaries) and male language is treated as the norm. As we saw in Chapter 1, generic expressions ('man', 'mankind', 'he'/'him'/'his', etc.) can reinforce a 'male as norm' ideology and render women invisible. Spender criticized Lakoff precisely for treating male language as the norm, and viewing women's language as lacking in comparison. She pointed out that, rather than women's deficiency, what is at stake is the deficiency of social order (Spender, 1980). According to this 'dominance' model, any differences between women's and men's language are indicative of women being dominated in interaction, and the ways in which women and men interact both reflect and perpetuate male exploitative behaviour.

Question 3
In what ways can language be used to dominate and control interaction?

In addition to generic expressions, dominance theorists concentrated on specific aspects of interaction, particularly questions, hedges or qualifiers, back-channelling, interruptions, topic initiation and topic control. These are discussed below.

Pamela Fishman's (1983) linguistic investigation re-visited some of the features discussed by Lakoff, from a more empirical and dominance-oriented perspective. Her study of conversations by three heterosexual couples in their homes found that women tended to use more tag questions (two and a half times as many as the men), more hedges such as 'you know' (twice as often as the men), and half as many statements as men. However, Fishman argued that the function of such strategies was interactional and facilitative, rather than a sign of women's insecurity and hesitancy. Women appeared to be using them in order to include their interlocutor in the conversation, and in order to keep the conversation flowing by getting the attention of the unresponsive male (see Fishman, 1990, for a detailed discussion). Questions and hedges do conversational work by trying to get a response from the other speaker. This was the case with the women in Fishman's study, who used twice as many attention getters (e.g. 'this is interesting') as the men, and made greater effort than the men to be supportive through the use of minimal responses/back-channelling (e.g. 'uhmm', 'yeah', 'very nice').

Fishman's assertion is that, far from being uncertain, women are skilled communicators facilitating interpersonal relationships (see also McMillan *et al.*, 1973); but that, in routine mixed-sex interactions, they are the ones responsible for providing conversational support and keeping the conversation going. That women are forced to be what she called 'conversational shitworkers', reflects women's inferior social position, rather than their inferior social training or inferior inherent ability. This position is further reflected in Fishman's discussion of topic initiation: the strategies speakers use to introduce new topics in conversation, and the listeners' response or lack of response to these topics (Table 2.1).

Table 2.1 Topic initiation: summary of Fishman's findings (1983)

Topic initiation	Success	Failure	Uncertain	Total
Male	28	0	1	29
Female	17	28	2	47
Total	45	28	3	76

Table 2.1 shows that men are more successful than women in initiating new topics, and therefore tend to dominate the conversational agenda by talking about what *they* want to (see also Coates, 1996a, 1997). This, combined with Fishman's claim that men do not provide the necessary attentiveness responses during conversation, supports her argument about unequal power relations between the sexes. Although she has been criticized for the small number of participants in her study, Fishman's research has been useful in acknowledging the impact of social structures and power relations on conversation, and in situating behaviour in interaction. It has also drawn attention to the situational context when exploring gender in talk.

Zimmerman and West's study (1975) is another key contribution to the 'doing power' in interaction paradigm. Using data of informal talk among people in public places (such as coffee shops) in a university community in California, Zimmerman and West found that male speakers assert an asymmetrical right to control and develop topics of conversation, and that they do so without evident repercussions. In the cross-sex conversations analysed, 96 per cent of interruptions were by males to females. Significantly, in the conversations between men, there were very few interruptions. Similarly to other research, where interruptions are found to be a way for the dominant participant to achieve control (e.g. Goffman's work, 1976, on parent–child interactions, where parents were responsible for 86 per cent of the interruptions), Zimmerman and West treat interruptions as a form of dominance. They speculate that male control of macro-institutions in society is similarly exhibited through maintaining control at the micro-level of conversation. One example of this would be the following extract (from Zimmerman and West, 1983), where = indicates an interruption:

> **Female:** I guess I'll do a paper on the economy business he laid out last week
> if I=I can=
> **Male:**   =You're kidding!=
> That'd be a terrible topic.

Zimmerman and West's analysis further shows that, not only did men interrupt women (rather than men), but also men used delayed minimal responses more often, and that these responses were longer delayed when talking to a woman (see Coates, 1993). There are, however, subsequent studies that refute Zimmerman and West's findings. For example, James and Clarke (1993) did not find gender differences in the use of interruptions, and Bilous and Krauss (1988) claim that there are more interruptions in female–female than in male–male pairs. (For a critical overview of the literature on gender and interruptions, see James and Clarke, 1993.)

What follows is an extract from a focus group, where the participants (who are in their late thirties/forties, living in a town in England) discuss the topic of marriage (Litosseliti, 1999). Interruptions are indicated by the symbol = and full transcription conventions are listed on page 36. Extract (2B) can be used as an exercise for considering some of the issues raised by dominance theories: for example, who interrupts who, how are topics initiated and controlled, how minimal responses are used, and who keeps the discussion going.

Extract (2B)

> **Phil:**   [...] it used to be that when you got married you'd got tax breaks / and
>   that was a single major advantage / so the state recognised that you were
>   different over someone who =
> **Irene:**   = you were more likely to get promoted if
>   you were married / *[Nods of agreement]*
> **Phil:**   oh yeah / a career move / it made sure you weren't gay for a start / you
>   were SAFE / *[Nods of agreement]*
> **Anna:**   did you experience any (...)? /

Irene:	I haven't experienced it personally but =
Anna:	= cause I've LOST a job as a result of being married / I was very young and it was a very long time ago and I hadn't quite worked out what was going on / I was invited to apply for a job it was a kind of set up and I sailed through the interview and I thought this is jolly nice . it's a very good thing . and then they said your husband . what does he do? . and I said he's doing so and so . and when will he finish doing it? . in about eighteen months . OH thank you very much and GOODBYE / that was the end! *[She laughs]* / so it took me a LONG time to understand what had happened / and I realised that I could have been any candidate for that job but I was NOT going to get it / I was not going to get it because my husband was likely to complete what he was doing and would be wanting to move and . if he was moving I would be leaving and / you know . *[Ironically]* you CAN'T trust women ! /
George:	*[In the same tone]* and even if you stay you're gonna have BABIES ! /
Anna:	yes HOPELESS ! HOPELESS! (…) / *[Laughs]*
Simon:	it's interesting that . because . if that reverses you'd probably expect =
Anna:	= oh what a surprise ! / *[Laughs]*
Simon:	as a MAN you're always regarded as being . you know the safe option if you were married / you know . if you're a young man unmarried then you will not (…) but if you're married . you have dependants . you have a stable relationship . you're a much safer bet /
Mary:	and you obviously made more money when you came down to promotion / I've known of young girls who have been passed over for promotion and the excuses were (…) he's married and he's got a baby on the way /
George:	Matt Busby the famous Man-United manager always encouraged his players to get married / and he was always trying to find suitable wives for them / for that reason . cause he didn't want his players out all night *[Laughs]*

[Discussion later moves to the topic of wives taking their husband's name]

Phil:	[there are] very practical reasons =
Simon:	= no I think it's more than that actually / I think this taking the same name is sometimes a symbolic thing / certainly in my first marriage I wanted my name to (…) / but my relationship now is very different from my first relationship . it's very much two individuals / I think I'd be quite happy if Mary kept her own name /
Irene:	I think a side of you feels as if you're giving in / I feel as if I was giving up something =
Phil:	= it's pretty bad when you feel that this is your husband's name

Irene:	yes
Phil:	that strikes me as very much a putdown /
Irene:	I still don't think that it's MY name / my name is X / it's how I was born and it will always be / I like X but it's not my name /
Anna:	so it's the name you go by ! /
Irene:	yes that's right / [*Laughs*]
Simon:	I can sympathise with that / I think if the situation reversed I would be very unhappy losing my name /
Irene:	I was . perhaps I was 36 I think when I got married / and so yeah I had my own name for a long time / it was me /
George:	[*referring to him and his wife having different surnames*] whenever . you know like the car needs to be serviced and they ring up and they say is it Mr X . and they use her name . and I suddenly become HER /
Lia:	what is that like? /
George:	well I say I'm NOT Mr X but =
Irene:	= and it's not important / it's unnecessary
George:	but yes you get a glimpse into what it feels like to actually not having . being who you want to be /

(Litosseliti, 1999)

Transcription conventions used in Extract (2B)

.	pause (a stopping fall in tone or break in rhythm)
[pause]	long, noticeable pause
/	utterance boundary indicated by intonation
=	interruption (by the utterance immediately following)
(…)	inaudible, indecipherable speech
[…]	omitted text
?	utterance meant or understood as a question (rising intonation)
!	exclamatory utterance (animated tone)
in CAPS	spoken with emphasis
[*in italics*]	non-linguistic aspects (laughter, gestures, etc.)

It is necessary to address issues of dominance carefully and critically. First, we need to be aware of different ways to define (and analyse) interruptions, e.g. decide whether to include overlapping speech, attempted interruptions, or silent interruptions in analysis. In addition to the content of the interruption, we need to account for the larger context in which it is embedded, the direction and content of the conversation up to that point, the participants' conversational style, their cultural and other background, and the relationships between participants (James and Clarke, 1993). Further, similarly to the discussion of tag questions above, we need to consider the multi-functional nature of interruptions and simultaneous talk – indeed of all talk. Interruptions need not be interpreted solely as dominance signals, as they can be supportive speech acts (e.g. back-channel utterance), and depend on the particular participants' interactional goals (Bilous and Krauss, 1988; Wooffitt, 2005; see also Tanaka, 2004, for co-operative interruptions in Japanese).

This last point concerns the biggest criticism of dominance paradigms of gender and language in general: the correlation of attributes, such as gender, with specific forms of speech behaviour, such as interruptions or minimal responses; and locating the source of domination through such linguistic strategies. Dominance theorists do not really attend to the effects of conversational contexts, topics and genres, objectives, styles and rules for speaking, when examining specific forms (Borker and Maltz, 1989; Tannen, 1993). Also, they fail to recognize the possibility that some men may unintentionally dominate a conversation, or that women may, in certain cases, *choose* not to interrupt. Indeed, dominance theories often over-emphasize the subordination of women, and assume that all men in all cultures are in a position to dominate women. But, at the same time, they are useful – particularly as a reaction to deficit theories – for their greater emphasis on sociocultural factors and for challenging the right of males to control language. Finally, in methodological terms, dominance studies do rely more on data to support their claims than previous studies – even though a bias towards the analysis of language used by white, middle-class, heterosexual couples still exists.

TALKING DIFFERENCE

While any differences in female and male language are seen by dominance theorists as evidence of male privilege, those assuming 'difference' (an approach gathering pace in the early 1980s) attribute such differences to the different socialization of women/girls and men/boys. In contrast to a view of women as weak (deficit) and as victims (dominance), there is an attempt during this time to see women's language not just as different, but as positively valued. Such a re-evaluation of women's language is based on a theorization of differences as a result of participation in different male and female 'sub-cultures' (see Maltz and Borker, 1998).

Based on Gumperz's (1982) 'two cultures' model for inter-ethnic communication, Maltz and Borker developed a cultural difference approach to male–female communication and miscommunication. They claimed that it is the differences in the cultures of boys and girls, rather than in power status or inherent male–female differences, that causes difficulties in male–female communication (Maltz and Borker, 1998). They propose that different conversational patterns originate in childhood (between the ages of 5 and 15), when boys and girls learn to use language differently through interacting primarily in single-sex peer groups. They further acknowledge that gender is only one of many cultural influences on language use.

In the UK, this difference perspective was developed in research by, among others, Coates (1993 and elsewhere), who, by re-addressing the evidence for differences in sociolinguistic research, preferred to talk about women's and men's 'styles', rather than 'women's speech'. In addition to children participating in gender-specific sub-cultures with distinct male–female styles of interaction, Coates discussed the diverse ways in which women and men are socialized into different gender roles. This may happen through adults providing different linguistic models for children, talking to children differently according to their sex, having different preconceptions of boys and girls, and responding differently to a linguistic strategy used similarly by boys and girls. She claimed that the linguistic usage and interaction styles (interruptions, swearing, politeness, silences) of women and men reflect precisely these differences (Coates, 1993).

Question 4
What are some of the ways in which adults talk to boys and girls differently, and some of the ways in which adults respond to them differently?
What are the possible effects of such talk?

Cultural differences, such as the pressure (intentional or not) on girls to 'be nice' and polite and on boys to be strong and competitive, are likely to lead to the learning of different interaction styles and the adoption of different linguistic choices by girls and by boys. Some of these choices, and the related broader gender ideologies, often work to disadvantage girls and women. For example, as we saw earlier, women risk being called unfeminine when they use direct language, and not taken seriously when they 'talk like a lady'. While boys and men can argue in direct and confrontational ways (and be seen as 'assertive' or 'strong'), girls and women do so at the risk of being called 'bossy' or 'difficult' (Sheldon, 1997). This also depends on the situation and there are a number of studies claiming that girls can skilfully negotiate the demands at the same time for competitive and co-operative behaviour (ibid.; Goodwin, 1980, 1998; Eckert, 1990; Sheldon and Johnson, 1998).

The (cultural) difference approach also became influential in the USA, as seen especially in Deborah Tannen's book, *You Just Don't Understand: Women and Men in Conversation* (1990). Tannen, among others, pointed out that dominance may be only one of the factors behind gender differences in speech, and sometimes not a factor at all. Her explanation for differences was also based on the different socialization or acculturation of boys and of girls: the idea that girls and boys grow up being socialized so differently, and with different conversational expectations, that communication between them is like communication between two different cultures. In her book, she urged men and women to understand that this difference is the source of misunderstandings and miscommunication between them, and to stop blaming each other.

A number of popular books aimed at lay audiences, such as John Gray's *Men are from Mars, Women are from Venus* (1992), are loosely based on the same premise. Such books also illustrate that some of the ideas emerging from linguistic research are catchier than others. Tannen's claims are also widely used in gender awareness programmes that have become part of training in organizations (e.g. the distinction between so-called male and female management styles; see Chapter 6). In fact, Tannen's work represents a rare case, where linguistic research findings have reached multiple audiences, such as academic as well as public audiences (for a discussion of relevant issues, see Cameron, 1995).

Tannen's analysis of videotaped conversations between same-sex friends at different ages showed that girls communicated by sitting closely together and supporting each other through eye contact, while boys were fidgeting and only spoke at intervals. This she interpreted as a clash of styles which can lead to miscommunication. In addition, she made a distinction between female 'rapport talk', characterized by an emphasis on listening and involvement, and male 'report talk', where speakers focus on exhibiting knowledge, initiating and dominating the conversation. Her findings have been criticized (see especially Cameron, 1992) for reifying such differences while ignoring issues of power and male dominance, for perpetuating gender stereotypes, and for putting greater responsibility on *women* to understand men's language and behaviour. In response to the first criticism, Tannen has pointed out that one cannot claim that men are dominating women just because they appear to interrupt them in interaction. In this sense, her findings may be seen as trying to redress the balance on behalf of men. Also her findings are useful in highlighting the importance of context, and exploring conversational styles that are situated.

The idea of re-evaluating women's language is an important one for difference theorists, who have put more emphasis than previously on studying all-female groups. It is an important shift, in that it marked the beginning of an interest in analysing women's everyday talk within their own speech communities. This is particularly evident, from the 1980s onwards, in a number of studies that have examined 'gossip talk' and have emphasized its positive function (Jones, 1990; Coates, 1988, 1996a; Holmes, 1995). Far from gossip being a trivial aspect of women's speech, these researchers claim that it is an integral part of their construction of 'self', key to female subculture, and therefore culturally significant. Through discussing and re-evaluating social norms, women are able to construct, negotiate, and maintain their personal identities – something illustrated in analysis of talk among women friends (Coates, 1996a). This claim relates to the idea that groups of women establish identity differently from men: that whereas women may treat gossip as co-operative work that requires a lot of positive feedback and prompting, and avoids indirect disagreement, talk among men tends to contain little feedback and a lot of open disagreement or criticism (Coates, 1996a, 1997; Pilkington, 1998). In other words, women may pursue a conversational style of solidarity and men may opt for one based on competitiveness. However, the question that must be addressed is whether and to what extent it is the latter that is taken more seriously as 'real talk' – an issue not really critically addressed by difference theorists.

Question 5

Re-read Extract (2B). Can you see evidence of the linguistic choices and interaction styles that are associated with women's and men's language, according to difference theorists?

Contrary to those assuming dominance, difference theorists did not blame any group for the miscommunication (Crawford, 1995), and also helped to offset the negative view – maintained by the deficit and dominance models – of women as weak and as victims. However, they still did not account for the similarities between the speech of women and men, nor for the diversity of speech styles that exist between different groups of women and different groups of men. In addition, difference theorists mostly ignored the important power dimension, and sometimes (as with Tannen) seemed to reduce gender to a simplistic and innocent cultural distinction. But, as Uchida (1992) convincingly argues, it is inappropriate to see 'power' and 'culture' as two separate independent concepts, because social interaction is influenced by social hierarchy, and more specifically, occurs in a patriarchal social context. Rather than being 'disinterested quests for the truth', studies of difference in unequal societies 'inevitably have a political dimension' (Coates and Cameron, 1988: 5–6). In addition, theories cannot just make claims about the existence of separate sub-cultures without trying to explain their existence – something that those assuming difference have not achieved. In fact, there are also arguments that boys and girls are socialized together through childhood, rather than separately (Uchida, 1992). Those arguments aside, what is missing from difference models is a critique of the reasons why children are 'socialised into gender roles which place them into a polarised structure of difference and opposition, that is masculine versus feminine as exclusive categories' (Simpson, 1997: 201).

Ultimately, the problem with difference – and indeed with all traditional models in the field – is the *lack of a complex conceptualization of gender* (alongside other variables), and, again, the *assumption of difference*, with the polarization that ensues from it. We turn to these in the section that follows.

BEYOND DIFFERENCE

Dominance and difference models are not mutually exclusive. Both have strengths and have played their part in progressing feminist thinking. They are valuable at a theoretical level, in developing the ideas which led us to eventually ask more complex questions about gender, and at a political level, in foregrounding feminist issues on language use, such as the use of more assertive styles (Cameron, 1990).

However, both models have conceptualized gender in a simplistic way, not only by assuming a straightforward link between form and function (e.g. tag questions as indicators of uncertainty, interruptions as an attempt to dominate), but also by not paying enough attention to how gender interacts with other social and contextual parameters: race, class, age, ethnicity, region, sexual orientation, setting, culture (see, among others, Bergvall *et al.*, 1996; Bing and Bergvall, 1998; and Swann, 2002). Traditional models have neglected the study of men in general, of women other than the normative white, middle-class, heterosexual females, of homosexual speech, and generally of research contexts other than Anglo-American ones. Further, the sociolinguistic methodologies of the 1970s and 1980s, which closely observed speakers' conversational patterns and strategies, have often been blind to the specific social and economic conditions of women's lives (Cameron and Coates, 1989).

The insufficient contextualization of gender and the failure to view gender as part of a complex system of intersecting social variables are the key reasons why these models are not currently influential within feminist linguistics. We now acknowledge that, when they exist, differences between the female and male 'register' can be subtle and variable; that dominance and difference can both be at stake; and that any generalization about gender differences is limited to a specific group or community situated in a social context. It has also become evident

> that when the specifics of how gender is constructed across race, class and culture are studied, males and females within a given cultural group are often found to have more in common than do females across cultural groups, or males across cultural groups.
>
> (Christie, 2000: 14–15)

In their analysis of courtroom language behaviour, for instance, O'Barr and Atkins (1998) showed that the features of 'women's language' are not restricted to women, and that the differences are not between men's and women's language but between powerful and powerless styles of language used by both men and women. In other words, gender turns out to be an issue of social rank or social power. Similarly, the choice of formal or informal features, which has long fuelled arguments about women as more conservative speakers, may be determined less by gender and more by the age of the interlocutors and their relationship, as well as culture (see Tanaka, 2004, for examples in Japanese). We also know, from research in all-black speech communities (Nichols, 1983), that women's language choices primarily reflect those available to them in their own small speech communities and particular social networks. Any language variation must therefore be understood in terms of the norms of these communities and networks – where gender is only one of the many parameters involved.

Question 6

If we conceptualize the interactions of gender, class and race as intersecting circles (West and Fenstermaker, 1995), what are some examples where different members of groups share some, but not all of these characteristics?

In addition to insufficient attention to contexts and overlaps, another key reason why theories of difference and dominance are less influential today is their over-emphasis on gender *difference*. Both frameworks view gender as a binary opposition, ask questions that presuppose a dichotomy, and concentrate on gender differences while mostly ignoring similarities. As Bing and Bergvall (1998) point out, evidence of gender similarities is often overlooked, while findings about the essential difference between men and women are over-reported and reproduced by both scholars and the general public. Barnett and Rivers (2004) suggest that one reason for this is that over-generalized and headline-grabbing findings about gender differences have emerged from a few small, non-representative studies, and subsequently have been picked up by the news media and other researchers. They are also critical of methodologies that are designed to find difference (e.g. some statistics) where differences are slight and the overlaps and similarities are significant.

The problem with *gender polarization*, 'the ubiquitous organization of social life around the distinction between male and female' (Bem, 1993: 2) – from modes of dress to social roles, expectations and experiences – is that it results in 'mutually exclusive scripts for being male and female' (ibid.: 80); and more importantly, that 'underlying androcentric social institutions transform male/female differences into female disadvantage' (ibid.: 192). There are numerous examples of how gender polarization can make it easier – and even legitimate – to limit women's opportunities and access to positions of power in organizations, public office and education. Bing and Bergvall (1998) mention cases where employer discrimination against women (i.e. women not being hired for certain jobs) has been defended in courts on the basis of assumed fundamental and 'natural' gender differences. As mentioned in Chapter 1, such biological explanations of gender differences can help justify male privileges and reinforce gender stereotypes and imbalances. Some of the most prevalent 'explanations' concern women's 'natural' or 'inherent' role as mothers, carers, and nurturers, men's 'inherent' tendency to be active, competitive, assertive and aggressive, and women's 'natural' emotionality (refer back to Question 2 in Chapter 1). It is precisely such traits and such roles, historically associated with women, that have been relegated to inferior status – although men can also be disadvantaged by such stereotyping (e.g. fathers' rights to custody of their children, and men as victims of violence).

Question 7
What are some concrete examples where gender polarization effectively justifies the limiting of options – in terms of educational, vocational, public office or political opportunities – for women? And for men?

Towards addressing the question above, we can consider the example of biological arguments about the differences between male and female brains, and how these can be used to justify discrimination towards women (Bing, 1999). Bing asserts that research findings about such differences are misrepresented by writers and simplified or exaggerated (generally distorted) by the media, in ways that make differences between men and women appear as inherent and unchangeable. Difference is then often reinterpreted as deficiency, which is used as an explanation or justification for women being biologically unsuited for certain 'male preserves'. Another example can be found in the 1996 court case in North America, in relation to Virginia Military Institute's resistance to becoming a co-educational academy. The arguments used in this case to prevent women's access to this prestigious military institution relied largely on generalizations about women being 'more emotional' and 'less aggressive' than men, and unable to endure the 'psychological trauma' involved in that particular programme (Shields, 2000). The key point here is about gender polarization, whether it is based on biological arguments, or arguments around women's and men's socialization. The problem with any binary generalizations is that they do not put forward neutral views about individual women and men, but rather perpetuate strongly held ideologies that, in a circular manner, find their way into curricula, legislation, and social policy – both informing them and being invoked by them. Moving beyond difference involves an increasing awareness that gender is not a characteristic of individuals but a symbolic system:

> a set of ways of thinking, images, categories and beliefs which not only shape how we experience, understand and represent ourselves as men and women, but which also provide a familiar set of metaphors, dichotomies and values which structure ways of thinking about other aspects of the world [...] [H]uman characteristics and endeavors are culturally divided into those seen as 'masculine' and those seen as 'feminine' (e.g. mind is opposed to body; culture to nature; thought to feeling; logic to intuition; objectivity to subjectivity; aggression to passivity; confrontation to accommodation; war to peace; abstraction to particularity; public to private; political to personal; realism to moral reflection, etc.), and the terms coded 'male' are valued more highly than those coded 'female'.
>
> (Cohn and Ruddick, 2004: Chapter 21)

Further examples of the effects of gender polarization, such as on the position of women teachers, on attitudes surrounding feminist pedagogies and women's studies programmes, and on women's access to decision-making on matters of war and conflict, can be found in Litosseliti (2006). Anti-war feminists have suggested that national security paradigms and policies are distorted by the devaluation and exclusion of 'the feminine', to the point where it becomes extremely difficult for anyone, female or male, to take the devalued position, to express concerns or ideas marked as 'feminine'. There is also a related discussion on women being excluded during times of conflict from newspaper pages and television screens, or generally restricted to the 'softer' areas of the news (e.g. features and domestic stories) which are associated with the private rather than the public sphere (Holland, 1987; Litosseliti, 2006). Finally, for a detailed discussion of the 'symbolic' association of women with emotion and irrationality (the discursive construction of emotion as gendered) in public contexts, see Litosseliti (2002, 2006).

To sum up, we need to be vigilant about claims of 'difference'. In the next chapter we will see that, to start addressing and redressing systematic gender ideologies, with their related gender imbalances, we need to examine their masking in *discourse* and the interests served as a result. The past theoretical models examined in this chapter have been criticized for underplaying the role of context, for ignoring the similarities between women and men and for over-emphasizing difference. A combination of those approaches would be more useful, to ensure a multi-dimensional view of gender and language (Uchida, 1992). In the late 1980s and 1990s, the shift away from gender as a binary and from views of women's language as lacking, powerless or simply different, towards discursive and post-structuralist perspectives, has led to asking more critical and more nuanced questions. One of the key questions now tends to ask in what ways gender is an effect of language use, rather than a determinant of different uses of language.

Discourse approaches to gender and language are based on a conceptualization of language as social practice, and assume that:

■ We don't *have* gender, but we *do* gender in interaction.
■ Gender is complex, variable, dynamic, a site of (re)positioning and struggle.
■ Gender, and gender identities, are socially constructed through language use.
■ Power relations are an effect of discourse, not of individual intentions.
■ Other social parameters and relations, not just gender, are important.
■ Gender is culturally constituted and context-dependent; all meanings are situated.
■ Gender needs to be studied in relation to localized contexts and specific communities, as well as more globally.

These issues are discussed in detail in the next chapter.

SUMMARY

■ 'Dominance' and 'difference' models are products of the political climate for women in the 1970s and 1980s. They are also a reaction to 'deficit' approaches, which treat women's language as lacking, weak, hesitant, and trivial.
■ There is no straightforward connection between linguistic form (e.g. a type of question) and communicative function (e.g. to express uncertainty). The use of any form depends on many contextual and social parameters.
■ Early theories have reinforced the female–male dichotomy by asking questions that assume the existence of a binary, and also effectively support the perception of women as deficient.
■ Despite its shortcomings, Lakoff's work has been important for initiating a discussion of key issues from a feminist perspective, and for contributing to the expansion of linguistic theory.
■ As part of a more political climate, 'dominance' approaches in the late 1970s and 1980s aimed to extend the notion of patriarchy to language. The conversational division of labour – found in women and men's use of features such as questions, interruptions, qualifiers, back-channelling and topic control – is seen to reflect and perpetuate male dominance.
■ Fishman argued that female speakers are skilled communicators, but are the ones responsible for providing conversational support and keeping the interaction going – and this reflects their inferior social position, rather than their social training or inherent ability. Male speakers assert an asymmetrical right to interrupt women and control the topics of conversation, without evident repercussions.
■ Criticism of dominance theories has focused on the problematic correlation of gender with specific forms of speech behaviour, on locating the source of domination through these forms, and on their view of women as victims.

■ 'Difference' theorists have been interested in analysing women's talk within their speech communities, and in re-evaluating it in positive ways. They have theorized differences as the result of people participating in different male and female 'subcultures' from an early age, and being socialized into different gender roles.

■ Tannen, in particular, argued that miscommunication between women and men is a result of their different socialization, which involves different conversational expectations (such as 'rapport' and 'report' talk).

■ Difference theories do not really account for similarities, for the diversity of styles within gender groups, and for social conditions and power relations between women and men.

■ Past approaches have been valuable at a theoretical level (leading to more complex questions on gender) and at a political level (foregrounding feminist issues around language use). But they have also promoted a simplistic conceptualization of gender (where other variables have been less important or ignored), and their assumption of difference has reinforced gender polarization.

■ Gender polarization puts forward mutually exclusive scripts for being male and female, which shape strongly held ideologies about gender, and typically translate into female disadvantage.

■ Current thinking in gender and language research is more likely to ask questions about gender as an effect of language use, rather than as a determinant of different uses of language.

FURTHER READING

Cameron, D. (1990) *The Feminist Critique of Language*. London: Routledge (especially Chapter 2).

Cameron, D. (1992) *Feminism and Linguistic Theory*, 2nd edn. New York: St Martin's Press (Chapters 7, 8 and 9).

Coates, J. (1993) *Women, Men and Language*. Harlow: Longman (especially Chapters 2 and 3; also Chapters 6, 7 and 9).

Coates, J. and Cameron, D. (eds) (1988) *Women in Their Speech Communities*. Harlow: Longman (Chapters 1, 2 and 6).

Goddard, A. and Patterson, L.M. (2000) *Language and Gender*. London: Routledge (see the activities).

Graddol, D. and Swann, J. (1989) *Gender Voices*. Oxford: Blackwell (especially Chapter 6).

Talbot, M. (1997) *Language and Gender: An Introduction*. Cambridge: Polity Press (Chapters 2, 3, 7 and 8).

Tannen, D. (1990) *You Just Don't Understand*. New York: Morrow (especially Chapters 1 and 2; also Chapters 3, 4, 5 and 7).

Uchida, A. (1992) When 'difference' is 'dominance': a critique of the 'anti-power-based' cultural approach to sex differences. *Language in Society*, 21(4): 547–68.

The shift to discourse:

the discursive construction of gendered identities

> At any moment we are using language, we must
> say or write the right thing in the right way while
> playing the right social role and (appearing) to
> hold the right values, beliefs and attitudes. Thus
> what is important is not language and surely not
> grammar, but saying – (writing) – doing – being –
> valuing – believing – combinations.
>
> (Gee, 1989: 6–7)

In order to outline current concerns and frameworks in feminist linguistic research, this chapter concentrates on discourse(s), discourse analysis, and the discursive construction of gendered identities. The emphasis here is on the interplay between language, gender, and social structures. We will see that gender is produced in discourse, in variable, dynamic and context-situated ways; this is illustrated through various examples.

DISCOURSE AND DISCOURSES

The term *discourse* has been alluded to in previous chapters. In Chapter 1, there was discussion of potentially sexist discourses, as distinguished from sexist wordings. It was suggested that the ways in which people and groups are represented (i.e. described, defined, as well as potentially discriminated against) in discourse may not be at all obvious; rather, most of the time, these representations – or constructions, as we will see later – are subtle, and typically rely on (often stereotypical) assumptions. Because of this, it was put forward in Chapter 1, while raising awareness about sexist language is an important step towards change, it is crucial to be both aware of and prepared to change our discourses and discourse practices. Along the same lines, it was claimed in Chapter 2 that we need to be vigilant about the masking in discourse of gender ideologies and the interests they may be serving.

The term discourse is used widely and in different ways across academic disciplines, and is often left undefined, vague or confusing (Mills, 1997; Wodak, 1997). Although most analysts see discourse, at a basic level, as some stretch of connected sentences or utterances, thereafter they differ. There are those who treat it linguistically, as text with patterns and rules of coherence; those who treat it sociologically, as conversational interaction with certain social functions; those who treat it from a social and critical theory perspective as the manifestation of cultural ways of thinking and doing (Antaki, 1994); and many who draw on a combination of these perspectives, by varying degrees, as reflected in the following definitions of discourse as:

- language which communicates a meaning in a context, that is, constitutes inter-action between people and groups of people in real social situations (Cameron, 1998);
- 'spoken and written language', 'situational context of language use', 'interaction between reader/writer and text' (Fairclough, 1992: 3);
- 'text in context' (van Dijk, 1990: 164), i.e. both a specific form of language use and a specific form of social interaction;
- a social construction of reality from a particular perspective, a form of knowledge or social and ideological practice (as seen in post-structuralist social theories, largely influenced by Foucault, 1972).

Although rather general, these definitions point to some key aspects of discourse. To illustrate what they mean in relation to an example, let us consider the debate on the 'pay gap' that exists between females and males in the same professional roles, across the professions. Discussions on this topic are often underpinned by equal opportuni-ties or feminist discourses, which are context-situated, for example, in interaction among politicians, in media debates, in protests by women's groups, in academic and legal documents. These discourses also see the world from a particular perspective: both women and men being in paid employment, inequalities being unacceptable or undesirable, and so on. Linguists interested in social and critical theory point out that it is more appropriate to talk about multiple *discourses*; in the example above, not only is it not possible to talk about a unifying or homogeneous feminist discourse, but also any given discourse about women must include and relate to other discourses: about men, about employment, the workplace, and so on. It is similar discourses that we have to be able to recognize, in order to make sense of expressions such as 'proper mother' (see Extract (1B) in Chapter 1).

We can then think of discourses as a web of social themes, voices, assumptions, and explanations – what Gee describes as 'saying – (writing) – doing – being – valuing – believing – combinations' (1989: 6–7). Discourse theories interpret and examine this web in a variety of, not always converging, ways (see Analysing discourse, p. 54), but generally agree that discourses have particular characteristics:

Discourses are recognizable and meaningful

A range of gendered discourses, for instance, are available to people (in both a histor-ical and systematic sense) when the arrival of a new baby is announced: 'It's a boy/girl!' People's responses about little boys' strength and little girls' beauty, as well as the related choices of toys and clothes for children, draw on discourses about gen-der that are recognizable by and meaningful for the language users (i.e. they pre-exist their users). Other dominant discourses that are recognizable may include a 'female emotionality' discourse (Litosseliti, 2006), a 'part-time father' discourse (Sunderland, 2004), or a 'compulsory heterosexuality' discourse (Rich, 1980); more resistant discourses may include those promoting gender or sexual diversity.

Discourses can be supporting as well as competing or conflicting

Discourses are in flux and not necessarily coherent. Some discourses are mutually supporting. For example, Hollway (1984) examines discourses of heterosexuality, two of which she describes as the 'have/hold' discourse (i.e. sexual relations within a monogamy and family life ideal) and the 'male sexual drive' discourse (i.e. men can't help themselves). In one sense, these can be seen as supporting discourses, for example, in women's and men's lifestyle magazines, where it is precisely the assumption of a 'male sexual drive' discourse that facilitates the 'manipulative female' in her mission to have and hold her man. Alternatively, these discourses may be seen to be conflicting or paradoxical for the men (see also Sunderland, 2004).

In the same vein, Coates describes two competing discourses of femininity: a dominant maternal discourse, which involves mothers' sharing of their pride and positive feelings about their children, and a competing or 'subversive' maternal discourse, which includes expression of their negative feelings about their children (1997). Baxter (2003) also discusses various competing discourses within mixed-sex classrooms and business meetings involving senior managers. And in Chapter 6, we see examples of an 'equal opportunities' discourse competing with a 'practical considerations' discourse, when the topic of employment opportunities is discussed (Wetherell *et al.*, 1987; see Extract (6J) in Chapter 6).

Discourses represent and constitute ways of thinking and doing

According to post-structuralist and social constructionist theories, in particular, discourses construct or give meaning to how we see the world (see Litosseliti and Sunderland, 2002, for a discussion). The discourses mentioned above do not simply represent ways of seeing the world; at the same time, they articulate, maintain, constitute, re-constitute, negotiate, and even resist some of these ways. Discourse is a potential site of struggle, and participants are neither helplessly controlled by dominant discourses, nor 'rational' individuals who make free choices. In resisting and contesting dominant discourses and the assumptions embedded in them, we are part of a process of changing perceptions of experience, as well as roles and identities (see Weedon, 1987; Fairclough, 1992).

Discourses are ideological and social power is acted out through them

Discourses are inherently ideological, in that they put forward certain viewpoints and values at the expense of others – as may be seen in the marginalization of women's writing in dominant discourses within literature departments (Gee, 1990). Moreover, positions are created and social power relations are acted out, as well as challenged, through discourses. Gee quotes the discourse of successful 'mainstream', 'middleclass' interviewing as an example of this (1990). Litosseliti (2006) looks at how discourse of 'female emotionality' helps construct unequal positions for women, in terms of limiting their access to the public debates and decisions that matter most. In other words, discourses systematically construct positions of power and powerlessssness for participants. It is, however, important to also bear in mind that a speaker may 'be positioned as relatively powerful within one discourse but as relatively powerless within another, perhaps competing discourse' (Baxter, 2003: 9).

Discourses exist in relation to other discourses

As mentioned earlier, discourses exist in relation to other discourses. Feminist discourses exist in relation to discourses about patriarchy, men's domination of public life, discourses of domestic violence, and many more. Discourses about the crisis of masculinity exist in relation to discourses about boys' under-performance at school, the phenomenon of the 'ladette', fathers' rights to the custody of their children, and feminism, to name but a few. Some of these relationships will be opposing, others causal, and others supporting (as we saw above). In addition, any text, spoken or written, is characterized by 'interdiscursivity': discourses appearing within discourses and the mixing together of discourses (Kristeva, 1986; Fairclough, 1992; Chouliaraki and Fairclough, 1999), as seen in Extract (3A) opposite. This phenomenon is also variously described as 'multi-voicedness', 'heteroglossia', or 'polyphony', and illustrates that people do not have their own words, but the words 'given to them by the discourses and genres of which they have had experience' (Kress, 1989: 49). Any given discourse will be instantiated in various texts in different ways, reproduced to a different degree and to different effect, not only by different people but also by the same people in different contexts.

Discourses may also be part of a network or 'order' of discourse, by which poststructuralist theories refer to a larger, shifting complex of discursive/social practices (see Fairclough, 1995). To go back to a previous example about fatherhood discourses, Sunderland (2002) identifies a 'part-time father' order of discourse, 'supported' by three discourses of 'father as baby entertainer', 'father as mother's bumbling assistant' and 'father as line manager'. She analyses textual evidence of these discourses (e.g. address features, references to fathers and 'shared parenting', absences of fathers, as well as visual and other features) in contemporary parentcraft literature, and concludes that, in addition to a dominant 'part-time father' discourse, this literature offers a highly 'feminine', 'mother-friendly' environment, which addresses primarily mothers (a feminine bias) even if it appears to be formally gender-neutral.

Let us now consider some of the characteristics of discourses mentioned in this section, with reference to examples. The newspaper extract below is from an article in *The Guardian*, by Gary Younge, following a forum on being British and Muslim, organized in the UK by the newspaper.

Extract (3A)

From *The Guardian*, 1 December 2004

'No offence, but why are all white men so aggressive?'
Turn round the questions asked of black people and you may get the point

By Gary Younge

… It's time to flip the script, to lay bare just a hint of the assuming subconscious that infects the most common questions I have either been asked or heard. To ask the kind of questions of white, British people (some are just for Christians) that they often pose to 'others' but are never asked themselves. …

Do you think of yourself as white or British or both? Does it worry you that you got your job just because of your race? Where are you from? No, but really? Since this is where you live, don't you think you should try and integrate with other races more? Is your first loyalty to your God, or to your country? Is it true what they say about white guys? Given the genocide, slavery and colonialism unleashed in the name of Christianity over the last two centuries, do you feel your religion is compatible with democracy? Mr Grant, do you think of yourself as a white actor or an actor who happens to be white? I don't mind white people, but if they want to live here then why shouldn't they have to fit in with our traditions? Shouldn't the police be doing more to tackle white-on-white crime? Given the objectification of women in your culture and the rise in teenage pregnancies, don't you think it's time to ban young girls wearing make up? What do you make of the tribal conflict in Ukraine? I thought you asked for flesh-coloured tights? Don't you feel that this politically correct belief that we have to respect white people's feelings has stifled honest discussion and debate? Isn't it a shame that white people cannot pick more responsible leaders? What do you mean, you can't Morris dance? Don't you ever worry about being pigeonholed as a white person? Why aren't you doing more to check the rise in Christian fundamentalism? Who are your community leaders? Why should we balance our belief in human rights with our tolerance for Christians? What do white people think about Jews? How would you define 'white' style? Mr Amis, why do you write about white people all the time? Don't you find that limiting? What are you doing for your people? Have you seen what the Bible says about women? Are you the token white guy? Don't take this personally, but why are white men so aggressive? Now the Olympics are over, can we finally admit that white people are genetically equipped to excel in archery and rowing? What is it with white people and homophobia? You know what white women are like, don't you? I understand that as a white person you come at this from a particular place, but can't you try to look at it objectively for a moment? Why do you people have such a chip on your shoulder? Don't get offended, I was only asking.

First, it is necessary to point out that sometimes the term 'discourse' is used to refer to a discourse type based on some notion of genre, setting, subject matter or social situation (e.g. newspaper discourse, classroom discourse, interview, TV news). Used in this way, the extract can be described as 'newspaper discourse' – an understanding that implies a set of conventions associated with this linguistic activity, and some specified positions for those involved (such as the journalist's role in putting forward a polemic against racism). Sunderland (2004: 6) calls such a discourse 'descriptive', while the focus on 'discourses' in this book (in line with the characteristics of discourses outlined earlier) is on what she terms 'interpretive' discourses (ibid.; also see Potter *et al.*, 1990).

It would be an impossible task to try and identify all the discourses being drawn on in a text such as the above. Then there is the question of whether, and how, we can identify discourses. Sunderland claims that discourses are describable and nameable, through a process of identifying their 'traces', discourse 'cues', and linguistic features (2004: 28). She rightly points out that this process of spotting the recurrent features that echo discourse elsewhere – first, traces in terms of the content of a spoken or written text, then traces to do with the actual interaction – is a highly interpretative one. More on this later, and in the following section on analysing discourse, but in relation to Extract (3A), it is possible to say that at least the following interpretative discourses can be traced in the text:

- race/racial discourses: a 'racial differences' or 'battle of the races discourse'; 'racism discourses' and 'anti-racism discourses'; and further, discourses of 'positive discrimination/affirmative action', and 'political correctness';
- discourses around religion, ethnicity and nationality: a 'religious differences discourse', discourses of 'cultural integration and segregation', and of 'immigration';
- gendered discourses: a 'gender differences discourse'; 'sexism discourses' and 'anti-sexism discourses', discourses about 'gender and sexual behaviour', and about 'sexuality'.

These discourses are recognizable and historical, which is why the readers of this newspaper text will have no difficulty making sense of the layers of the text (articulated as well as assumed) and identifying its sources of both humour and unease. In this case, such recognizability is accentuated by reference to presuppositions, preconceptions or stereotypes, e.g. the associations of race with particular activities, such as sport and dance, and particular attitudes, such as the objectification of women. It should be emphasized that a process of interpretation is at work here, on the part of those who produce, re-produce and challenge these stereotypes, as well as on my part, for describing them from my perspective as 'stereotypes' in this paragraph. Discourses are highly contextualized, complex, and interpretative; and further:

> Discourses are systematically-organised sets of statements which give expression to the meanings and values of an institution [by providing] a set of possible state-

ments about a given area, and organis[ing] and giv[ing] structure to the manner in which a particular topic, object, process is to be talked about.

(Kress: 1985: 6–7)

The manner in which the topic of race is talked about in this text is organized and shaped by the discourses around race, religion, gender, etc. mentioned above; and in particular, by the relationships between discourses, and the juxtaposition, in ironic and subtle ways, of dominant and resistant discourses. These include competing discourses about racial equality having and *not* having been achieved; and discourses of 'equal opportunities', 'affirmative action', and 'political correctness' compete with 'racism discourses', as in 'Does it worry you that you got your job just because of your race?' Which of these are dominant and which resistant will largely depend on the particular context in which discourses are articulated and negotiated. For instance, 'resistance' will mean different things for *The Guardian* and *The Sun* (in the UK context), as these media will have different agendas for embracing or resisting 'otherness'. In addition, these discourses will also have different realizations in different communities of practice and different cultural contexts (e.g. the above are relevant in a particular 'western' context). It is, then, more useful to think of discourses, not simply as dominant or resistant, but as part of a complex ongoing political struggle among different interest groups and in competition with other, established, discourses (Ashcraft and Mumby, 2004).

The extract indeed illustrates how difficult it is to view any discourse as separate from other discourses (also see Chapter 1, Question 3). The question, 'Given the objectification of women in your culture and the rise in teenage pregnancies, don't you think it's time to ban young girls wearing make up?' ironically (re)produces a number of gendered discourses (e.g. 'women as sex objects', 'sexual permissiveness') that exist in relation to religion discourses, such as those contested in parts of the world about women's right or obligation to wear Islamic headscarves. Similarly, discourses of 'black males as aggressive' and 'black-on-black crime' often appear within or alongside discourses around immigration, asylum seekers, violence, and terrorism. Not only do such discourses create specific subject positions for people and groups, but they also constitute and re-constitute ideologies which in turn shape a whole range of broader social practices. Some recent examples of social practices include the banning of headscarves in French schools and of youths wearing hooded clothing by a shopping centre in the UK, as well as anti-terrorist policies in many European countries.

Question 1

Re-read Extracts (1A) and (1B) in Chapter 1.

What discourses do you think are evident in the texts?

Would you describe some of these discourses as 'sexist', and do any of them draw on sexist wordings (see Chapter 1)?

This question is intended as a reminder of the discussion on sexist language in Chapter 1, and the idea that sexist discourses may or may not draw on sexist language items. We can now look at the texts more broadly: the linguistic forms used are not sexist in themselves, but people's multiple meanings and multiple choices with language (which are the result of the discourses available) do reflect and contribute to the maintenance of traditional or discriminatory views of women and men (McConnell-Ginet *et al.*, 1980). Intervention with regard to sexist discourses becomes much more difficult than intervention towards changing sexist language. The indeterminacy of discourses means that some may find them damaging (and not necessarily damaging in the same ways), others may recognize and resist them, while others may become empowered by them (Sunderland, 2004). In addition, as Mills (2003) argues in her analysis of professional feminist women's choice of titles and surnames, people often appropriate 'sexism', 'anti-sexism' and 'political correctness' discourses, making them work for them, thus potentially changing how they are viewed in general.

The question above is also useful for revisiting the texts and asking more complex questions about gender: in particular, what gendered discourses are assumed and put forward in the extracts, and how men and women are positioned through them. These questions are properly explored later in this chapter.

ANALYSING DISCOURSE

Like discourse, *discourse analysis* is a broad term used across disciplines, which encompasses many different and overlapping approaches to discourse, from linguistic, sociological, and social theory perspectives. The analysis of discourse has been the focus of theoretical and methodological frameworks that include: Discourse Analysis (as an umbrella term for variously critical approaches to DA), Critical Discourse Analysis (CDA), Conversational Analysis (CA), (Critical) Discursive Psychology, Pragmatics, Interactional Sociolinguistics and Ethnography. Discourse Analysis, in other words, does not describe a particular or coherent set of frameworks.

This wealth of approaches is usefully and critically overviewed in a number of recent publications. Among the books published in the five years prior to this book, useful references are Cameron's *Working with Spoken Discourse* (2001), Wetherell *et al.*'s *Discourse as Data: A Guide for Analysis* (2001), and Renkema's handbook *Introduction to Discourse Studies* (2004). The following books, all published in 2005, also offer critical and up-to-date introductions: Gee's *An Introduction to Discourse Analysis*, Blommaert's *Discourse: A Critical Introduction*, and Wooffitt's *Conversational Analysis and Discourse Analysis: A Comparative and Critical Introduction*. An extended list of recommended readings in this area can be found at the end of this chapter.

While it is not within my scope here to review different frameworks, it is important to consider the relevance of some of them for the study of gender and language. All the frameworks mentioned above share an interest in the ways in which we give meaning to experience through language, and, broadly speaking, in the contextual and social aspects of language use. They also value self-reflexivity on the analyst's part and acknowledge the impossibility of impartial research. Moreover, they demonstrate a critical awareness of what we *do* with language; in some cases this involves critically examining the relationship between form and function (as in Pragmatics), in others, revealing the 'connections which may be hidden from people' (Fairclough, 1989: 5) and which help maintain particular power relations and ideologies (as in CDA). From a feminist linguistics perspective (see Chapter 1), all these elements are important.

There is continuous debate and disagreement about the merits of different discourse analytic frameworks, and this extends to their contribution to the study of gender and language. The debate has largely focused on the advantages and limitations of CA and CDA approaches (see Schegloff, 1997, 1998, 1999a, 1999b; Wetherell, 1998; Billig, 1999a, 1999b).

CA usually involves a detailed and systematic micro-analysis of spoken extracts, in particular, their conversational organization and participants' 'orientations' to them. It focuses on the details of the interaction and on analysis of only those social categories (such as gender) that are manifestly oriented to by the speakers in their discourse (Chouliaraki and Fairclough, 1999: 7). For instance, in a conversation between a man and a woman, the analytical category of gender will be used only if the participants in the interaction orient to it. Some argue that such an approach is useful but insufficient for an analysis of gender and language where social structures are paramount (Weatherall, 2002a, 2002b; Sunderland, 2004; though also see Kitzinger, 2002).

In contrast, CDA approaches explicitly go beyond the text itself in their analysis, to examine the related discursive practices, social issues and social relations of power. In such analysis, the theoretical preoccupations and informed insights of the analyst are important, and indeed a common criticism of CDA is that it can impose (as part of its political mission) its own preoccupations on the discourse (Chouliaraki and Fairclough, 1999). In general, most criticism has been levelled against the CDA emphasis on sociological perspectives, over micro-linguistic ones (Widdowson, 1995; Stubbs, 1996). For other critiques of CDA, see Schegloff (1997) and Wetherell (1998), and Widdowson (1995) and Chouliaraki and Fairclough (1999) for a reply; also Antaki *et al.* (2002) and Burman (2002). Despite criticisms, CDA is particularly useful for the analysis of less obvious and implicit meanings behind spoken and written texts (as well as visuals and gestures); moreover, it draws on work from different disciplines (in terms of the questions it asks and the analytic categories it uses) and on a wide range of analytical levels/foci, such as words, utterances, turns, and discourses (Lazar, 2005).

Much feminist research in recent decades has increasingly focused on post-structuralist social constructionist approaches to discourse, including CDA. As Wodak argues, 'many proposals and basic assumptions of feminist linguistics relate to and overlap with principles of critical linguistics and critical discourse analysis' (1997: 7; see also Kotthoff and Wodak, 1997; Lazar, 2005). CDA is concerned with complex questions about the power people activate whenever they produce meaning, about social inequality and struggle, and about institutionalized dominance. It has an explicit interest in making transparent the 'hidden agenda' of discourse – which, for instance, may be responsible for creating and sustaining gender inequalities. Like a feminist linguistics, a critical analysis (like CDA) can thus never be descriptive or neutral (Wodak, 1989). Let us consider the following example, found on the website of a cookery school in England:

Extract (3B)

From www.ashburtoncookeryschool.co.uk/gentrel2.html (August 2005)

Gentleman's Relish
Cooking confidence for men

Gentleman's Relish is a cookery course for men who enjoy good food, who want to learn more about the kitchen end of the country pursuits or simply a fantastic gift for that special man in your life.

It's a modern take on traditional British cookery, like a cross between Mrs Beeton, Gary Rhodes and Hugh Fearnley-Whittingstall.

The course focuses on game, meat and freshwater fish, as well as fundamental techniques like making the best steak sandwich or the perfect omelette. It's very much a 'hands-on' course – we'll have a butchery demonstration; home smoking; sausage-making; plucking, drawing and preparing game birds; old school puddings, and the Ultimate Roast!

© Ashburton Cookery School

According to Fairclough's tri-partite CDA framework (Fairclough, 1992, 1995; see also van Dijk, 1998), the analysis of a *text* such as this must take into account the associated *discursive practices* and broader *social practices*. In terms of discursive practices, CDA may ask how the text is produced to also appeal to men's partners and spouses ('a fantastic gift for that special man in your life'), and how the text is consumed, for example, by men who are more likely to respond to 'hands-on' action-packed descriptions of the cookery course in question. There are also wider socio-economic practices that are relevant here: class associations of food with leisure activities ('the country pursuits'); the existence of celebrity chefs in the UK context; the fact that while everyday cooking remains largely a female domain, chefs at the higher levels of their profession are overwhelmingly male; and that it is more acceptable for many men to be seen to be involved in the more 'masculine' elements of a traditionally 'non-masculine' activity (making a steak sandwich or plucking game). Sunderland and Litosseliti (2002) similarly discuss this framework with reference to the example of the *Harry Potter* children's books.

The synthesis of such discursive and social practices as well as textual features is necessary for an analysis of discourses in the extract. A discourse of 'male ineptitude for cooking' or 'men's lack of involvement in the kitchen' can be traced to the use of words 'learn' and 'more' in 'learn more about the kitchen end of the country pursuits', as well as phrasing that points out the need for 'Cooking confidence for men'. A 'progressive discourse' can be traced in the parallels drawn between 'modern' and 'traditional' cookery. A 'men as active' discourse is at work in lexical choice ('hands-on', 'butchery demonstration', and verbs such as 'plucking', 'drawing', 'preparing') and in associations of men with hunting and fishing. Similarly, the use of pronouns is revealing: women are as much (if not more) the implied readers of this text as men ('that special man in *your* life').

At text level, CDA examines lexico-grammatical choices: vocabulary, the use of modal verbs, the use of the passive voice, who is included and excluded in discourse, and so on. But ultimately such analysis goes beyond the text, to look at the relationship between text, discursive and social practices as mutually dependent and mutually constitutive – a dialectical relationship (see Litosseliti, 2002, for an illustration of analysis). What is said has a function in context and as social practice involving speakers, hearers, groups and institutions. As Lazar puts it, CDA offers a productive demystification of discourse as social practice and its 'role in constructing and maintaining dominance and inequality in societies' (1993: 447). So, for instance, analysis of the meanings of 'more' above ('learn more about the kitchen end'), can help demystify discourses of female domesticity that may have become 'naturalized', that is, taken as given and non-changeable, thus serving and undermining particular interests (Cameron, 2001; Litosseliti and Sunderland, 2002). CDA can problematize this process further: it is not simply the case that such discourses straightforwardly serve men's interests and act against women's; in other contexts (e.g. fathers' custody rights), men's assumed lack of involvement in domestic activities may work against them, limiting their options. CDA is precisely the analysis of the 'effects' of power on people, groups and societies, and how this impact comes about (Blommaert, 2005). Such focus on the 'effects' of power and on inequality implies that

> unlike other domains or approaches in discourse analysis, CDA does not primarily aim to contribute to a specific discipline, paradigm, school or discourse theory. It is primarily interested and motivated by pressing social issues, which it hopes to better understand through discourse analysis … Unlike other discourse analysts, critical discourse analysts (should) take an explicit sociopolitical stance: they spell out their point of view, perspective, principles and aims, both within their discipline and within society at large.
>
> (van Dijk, 1993: 280)

The principled taking of an explicit sociopolitical stance certainly underpins the constantly developing feminist approaches to discourse analysis, such as Feminist Post-Structuralist Discourse Analysis (FPDA) and Feminist Critical Discourse Analysis. Feminist Post-Structuralist Discourse Analysis (Baxter, 2003) draws on a combination of analytical concepts and assumptions, shared by social constructionist feminism, post-structuralist feminism, as well as CDA work. Along similar lines, Feminist

Critical Discourse Analysis focuses 'on how gender ideology and gendered relations of power are (re)produced, negotiated and contested in representations of social practices, in social relationships between people, and in people's social and personal identities in texts and talk' (Lazar, 2005: 11). The emphasis of such approaches is on critically examining the ways in which women and men *do* gender, or *construct* particular gendered relations and identities through discourse (see the following section). But because of the emphasis of discourse analyses on the articulation of such construction within texts, rather than looking at women's material conditions, they have also been criticized for an over-emphasis on the discursive, and for paying insufficient attention to the connections between discourse and feminist political action (Crawford, 1995; Gill, 1995; Wilkinson and Kitzinger, 1995; Billig, 2000).

GENDERED DISCOURSES, GENDERED IDENTITIES

Extract (3A) earlier illustrated some of the relationships between discourses – most notably, about race, religion and gender. *Gendered discourses*, in particular, are discourses that say something about women and men, girls and boys, and about their – in certain ways gendered – actions, behaviours, positions, choices, relations, identities. More specifically, gendered discourses are discourses that represent and (re)constitute, maintain, and contest gendered social practices. For example, a 'gender differences discourse' in Extract (3A) may represent or resist representations of men as aggressive; hypothesized 'sexism discourses' ('what white women are like', 'why are white men so aggressive?') are juxtaposed with 'anti-sexism discourses' ('the objectification of women') and discourses about women's sexual behaviour ('ban young girls wearing make up'). Further, we see in Extract (3B) more specific gendered discourses, about men as active ('hands-on', likely to appreciate 'plucking, drawing and preparing game birds') yet inept at or uninterested in cooking ('learn more about the kitchen end of the country pursuits'), and about women's role in reversing such a state of affairs ('a fantastic gift for that special man in your life').

Rather than being associated with the gender of the person who articulates them (as studies of gendered language have done in the past), gendered discourses are articulated by both women and men, in different ways and different situations. Women are as likely to produce sexist or anti-women discourses as men are to produce anti-sexist or feminist ones. Yet, despite the fluidity and flexibility of discourses, it should also be said that there are constraints on the discourses that women and men are allowed to articulate and participate in; this depends on their social positions and on institutional structures (as we will see in relation to the 'double bind' that women often face in the workplace, see Chapter 6).

Gendered discourses *position* women and men in certain ways, and at the same time, people *take up* particular gendered subject positions that constitute gender more widely. In this sense, discourses can be *gendered* as well as *gendering* (Sunderland, 2004: 22). Some gendered discourses were mentioned earlier in this chapter, to illustrate that they are recognizable, historical, ideological, interconnected, and complex. The examples included broader discourses of parenthood, femininity, heterosexuality, feminism; and specific gendered discourses, such as those about 'female emotional-ity' or a 'crisis of masculinity'. In her discussion on the – highly interpretative – issues of discourse identification and naming, Sunderland (2004) overviews a range of gendered discourses that have been identified, and which include:

- discourses of *gender differences*, which may produce a 'male as norm' discourse or a 'mutual incomprehension of the sexes' discourse, but which can also take a critical view of gender differences (as discussed in Chapter 2);
- *heterosexuality* discourses (see Hollway, 1984), mentioned earlier, including a 'male sexual drive', a 'have/hold', and a 'permissive' discourse; also *compulsory heterosexuality* discourses (Rich, 1980), which constitute heterosexuality as normative, desirable, and hegemonic;
- discourses of *gender and employment opportunities* (Wetherell *et al.*, 1987), such as 'equal opportunities', as well as a limiting 'practical considerations' discourse (see Chapter 6, for examples and discussion);
- discourses of the *menopause* (Coupland and Williams, 2002), which involve competing 'pharmaceutical' and 'alternative therapy' discourses, but also an 'emancipatory feminist' discourse;
- discourses of *self-disclosure* or *consciousness-raising* (Coates, 1999) in girls' talk;
- Discourses of *fatherhood* (Sunderland, 2002, 2004), involving, apart from a 'part-time father discourse', discourses of 'traditional family fatherhood', 'new fatherhood', 'shared parenting'; and a wider 'progressive discourse' and 'discourse of diversity'.

Discourses of 'gender differences' (often of 'gender polarization') are particularly widespread, with various effects, in classrooms, magazines and advertisements, and the workplace. We will see examples and discuss some of the implications of this in each chapter of Part II. In addition, we will examine other gendered discourses in the following chapters:

- discourses around girls' and boys' learning and achievement, and those around co-operative and competitive talk (see Chapter 4);
- discourses of consumer femininity, female emotionality, a crisis of masculinity, feminist discourses, traditional and progressive discourses of masculinity, discourses of popular post-feminism, discourses of conservative and egalitarian gender relations, and new sexism discourses (see Chapter 5);
- discourses of femininity, of motherhood, of female emotionality, of equality and discrimination in the workplace (see Chapter 6).

Gendered discourses such as these can be identified (to follow Foucault, 1972):

> because of the systematicity of the ideas, opinions, concepts, ways of thinking and behaving which are formed within a particular context [and in line with which] women and men behave within a certain range of parameters when defining them-

selves as gendered subjects. These discursive frameworks demarcate the boundaries within which we can negotiate what it means to be gendered.

(Mills, 1997: 17–18)

The discourses listed above set boundaries for gender behaviour and offer particular, obvious and less obvious, positionings of women and men (e.g. positioning men as the norm, or women as mothers). An analysis of gendered discourses begs the question: What identities are created as a result of different positioning through different discourses, in different contexts and situations? And what opportunities as well as gender inequalities are created and maintained as a result?

I use the plural term *identities* to suggest that our sense of who we are – as professionals, parents, partners, members of different groups in terms of gender, age, ethnicity, race, sexuality, and so on – is neither singular nor fixed. Our identities are at the same time individual and social, as we make ongoing choices about ourselves from the ideas, beliefs, and possibilities available in our social contexts; in other words, they are shifting as our relationships with other people and social groups are changing. Our identities mark the ways in which we identify with people and social groups, as well as the ways in which we see ourselves as different from them. In other words, identity formation is an active process of affiliation as well as differentiation and resistance – but also involves attribution of identities by others (see Sunderland and Litosseliti, 2002, for a discussion; also Jaworski and Coupland, 1999).

To understand this better, consider the example of 33-year-old Scottish mountaineer, Alison Hargreaves, who was killed in August 1995, during her attempt to climb K2 in Pakistan, the world's second highest mountain. Hargreaves had gained respect in the international climbing community for becoming the first woman to climb Mount Everest alone without oxygen. She was variously described in the press as a 'tough', 'energetic', and 'ambitious' mountaineer, but even more often as a 'mother of two', 'mother of two small children', and 'outspoken mother'. Her case is of interest for the criticism she received, unlike her male colleagues in the sport, for leaving her children at home while taking 'selfish' risks on big mountains. As one of the writers of a book on her life and achievements put it:

> Alison's death threw into a stark and very public arena the moral dilemmas surrounding women who take risks. It struck at something visceral within society, provoking outrage and sorrow in equal measure. It's fine, it seems, for men to do these things, to take exceptional risks, even if they have children, but for mothers, the public's approval is far more equivocal.
>
> (Press release, 2000, nationalgeographic.com)

One could speculate about how Hargreaves may have negotiated her identities as mountaineer, female mountaineer, mother, wife, and (it appears) sole breadwinner; and how she may have managed their potential conflicts and contradictions. She was reported to have told friends that she loved the feeling of controlling danger, of being tested and staying calm. Also, she had written from K2 base camp: 'It eats away at me – wanting the children and wanting K2. I feel like I'm being pulled in two.' In her talk and writing, she was thus constructing a range of different identities. Yet, the media coverage of her death concentrated disproportionately on her role as a mother (attribution of identity), and this role was then dissected from a particular prescriptive, moralizing perspective.

If different identities are in the foreground and in the background at different times, this also applies to our gendered identities, our sense of self as women and men. We can then talk about a whole range of *femininities* and *masculinities* that become salient within individuals and within social contexts – an ongoing social process based on statement and restatement (Johnson, 1997). From a feminist post-structuralist perspective, our sense of self and our sense of self as women and men are dependent on the various subject positions created in discourse (Simpson, 1997: 202). Put differently, we *produce* or *construct* our multiple gendered selves through the choices we make from different discourses available. Most current research in feminist linguistics makes the fundamental assumption that people *become* gendered, or *do* gender (to use a concept from ethno-methodology) through discourse (Eckert and McConnell-Ginet, 1994; West and Fenstermaker, 1995; Coates, 1996; Cameron, 1997a). This process is variously described as a *discursive accomplishment* of gender (and other) identities: 'Accomplishment suggests that people, through their linguistic (and non-linguistic) behaviour, produce rather than reflect *a priori* identities as "women" and "men" in particular historical and cultural locations' (Lazar, 2005: 12).

'Accomplishment' also suggests that becoming gendered/doing gender is a dynamic process that is never complete; and it is a process where people are active agents, who can also disrupt particular (normative) constructions of gender identity. Finally, accomplishment helps us see more clearly the links between femaleness and femininity. Kiesling (2004), for example, states that the former is about what individuals do, while the latter is about social constructs (including stereotypes) that individuals must deal with. He suggests that the power that men as a group have over women as a group is not necessarily felt by men as individuals (see also Griffin, 1991). Galazinski (2004: 7) also elaborates on a dual understanding of masculinity: first, as 'an accomplishment in the local situation', a gender identity as a discursive construct, provisional and in flux; and second, as 'a system of practices', a more abstract social construct or ideology, society's way of associating certain practices with gender. In other words, in the local context of interaction, individual men will construct themselves as men by taking on or resisting the *normative* social constructs or ideologies about what 'makes' a man more or less masculine (e.g. engaging in activities such as hunting vs. cooking, to refer back to Extract (3B)).

Contrary to essentialist frameworks, where gender, race, class, etc. are taken as a given set of traits, constructionist approaches view identity as a process through which categories are actively constructed (Lorber and Farrell, 1991). While it is beyond the scope of this book to look in detail at the theoretical underpinnings of the idea that gender identities are *constructed* in discourse, it must be stressed that the term 'construction' is often used unquestioningly. Sunderland (2004) undertakes a good discussion of the term, reminding us that it includes construction of self and others, and may involve speakers, interlocutors, over-hearers and social/institutional structures. In this chapter, I have referred to the idea of construction of gender identities in discourse in a number of ways: people *do*, *produce* or *accomplish* different femininities and masculinities. These verbs help emphasize the multiplicity and fluidity of identities, where 'gender is continually realised in interactional form' (Wodak, 1997: 13), as well as the notion of individual agency. In addition, gender may be *represented* (see Chapter 5), *indexed* (e.g. gender, and sexuality, signalled through dress or voice pitch), as well as *performed* (see below).

When we talk about the construction of gendered identities, we necessarily refer to a two-way process: discourses (in people's own talk and in the talk of others) constitute multiple identities; and people's identities (such as gendered, racial, sexual identities) give rise to particular discourses. To give an example, a woman is not only constructed – in her talk and in how she is spoken about – as, say, a feminist, business woman and mother, but she also contributes to shaping the recognizable discourses surrounding these positionings. 'Shaping' here may mean negotiate, and often modify, the possibilities and the boundaries of being positioned in a certain way. The same woman who positions herself as a capable and successful businesswoman may seek to downplay her (competing) identity as a mother, while at the workplace. This may be, for example, because she questions or doubts the consequences of her positioning as a working mother, when compared to that of working fathers.

A way of describing the active and intentional production of gender identity is – to use a post-modernist concept – as *performing* identity. The conceptualization of gender as performative, which has been influential since the 1990s, was theorized by Butler (1990) as the repeated performance of specific ritualized acts (both bodily and discursive) which constitute gender identity. Examples of gender performance often mentioned in the literature include the drag queen's exaggerated performance of femininity (Barrett, 1999), and the example of female telephone sex workers in California, who use a 'feminine' 'powerless' language style to perform the kind of femininity they think their customers expect (Hall, 1995). Recent work on language and masculinity also draws on the notion of gender performance. For example, Pujolar i Cos (1997) discusses how working-class males in Barcelona perform masculinity through their choice of Spanish or Catalan. Cameron (1998b) looks at how a group of young men (American college students) use so-called 'feminine' linguistic features (e.g. 'gossip' and other co-operation and solidarity features) in order to perform heterosexual masculinity and to construct homosexuality as alien, thus dissociating themselves from it as a group. These examples usefully illustrate the problem with fixed and binary understandings of gender, and the significance of the dynamic, recursive ways in which we 'do' and 're-do' gender. At the same time, the notion of performance seems to be putting more emphasis on the individual and on individual agency, and less on power relations and the materiality of gender (see Cameron, 1997b). Readers will find useful discussions of gender identity as performance in Cameron (1998a), Hall and Bucholtz (1995), and Litosseliti and Sunderland (2002), among others. (While Butler's work is a key point of departure for discussions of 'performance' and 'performativity', I would first direct those who are unfamiliar with her work to one of her interviews (1993), where many of the terms she uses are clarified.)

Question 2

Re-read Extracts (1A) and (1B) in Chapter 1.

What gendered discourses do you think are evident in the texts?
How are women and men positioned through them?

What identities is Heather Clark producing in Extract (1B)? What identities are attributed to her by the interviewer?

FEMINIST LINGUISTICS: CURRENT TRENDS

This chapter has addressed the shifts of emphasis within gender and language study towards more complex questions about language, discourse(s), gender, and the role of discourse in doing identity work. As a result, current theorizations of these questions and relationships make a number of assumptions, which can be summarized as follows:

■ Discourses reflect and constitute (i.e. create, maintain, resist, modify) social 'realities', practices, relationships, identities. There is a dialectic relationship between any text (spoken or written), its associated discursive practices, and the broader social and institutional context in which it exists.

■ The discursive (i.e. social and linguistic) construction of gender identities is accomplished through an ongoing process of selection, negotiation, appropriation, and restatement. Identity work involves making choices from the discourses about femininity and masculinity that are available and appropriate in our social contexts. These choices are not free choices, but shaped by the highly contextualized enabling and constraining potential of 'doing' gender appropriately.

■ Rather than a set of attributes or simply a social category, gender is conceptualized as a process: something we do, produce, accomplish, perform. Gender identity is then a communicative achievement, an *effect* of discursive practices, 'rather than an *a priori* factor that determines linguistic behaviour' (Christie, 2000: 34).

■ (Gender) identities are multi-layered, variable, diverse, fluid, shifting, fragmented, and often contradictory or dilemmatic.

For feminist linguists, these new, more complex and nuanced ways of looking at the relationships between gender and language entail a wider re-thinking of the notion of 'gender differences', in ways that acknowledge an engagement with feminist political aims; and, in addition, they entail a sharp focus on the dynamics of the particular sites and communities where gender is enacted. Let us look at these in more detail.

In terms of 'difference', it becomes obvious that current theories make it difficult to make global statements about women's and men's linguistic behaviour. If gender identities are in flux and come into being in actions, then their construction in discourse will also vary from one situation to the next (Johnson and Meinhof, 1997). Whereas 'difference' and 'dominance' models assumed 'that "women's language" is, in essence, the language characteristically used by women' (Cameron, 1997b: 27), discursive and social constructionist models have a broader, and much less clear-cut, view: they allow for the possibility of women and men producing both similar and different gendered discourses; and of women and men constructing their gendered identities (and being constructed by others) in a range of ways. In their recent work, for instance, Holmes and Schnurr (2004) observe that women managers with a secure gender identity in the workplace feel free to enjoy and exploit stereotypical, and even hyperbolic ways of doing femininity. Similarly, women may respond in a range of ways to the femininities available in magazines and advertising: recognize, embrace, perpetuate, resist, criticize, or exploit them in their own gender performances.

The notion of gender differences is still important, but instead of assumptions about *a priori* binary differences, current approaches focus on the difference gender makes. Differences are also relevant in the sense that it is important to examine how we talk about them and what we do with them. If we are constructing women and men in discourses differently, and if we are being positioned as women and men differently, then feminist linguistics needs to examine the significance and consequences of such difference. Does it mean that different opportunities are made available for women and men, and systems of inequality are being maintained? What linguistic and social practices are appropriate and legitimate for women and men to participate in? Who benefits and who is disadvantaged by this? To give an example, the discursive construction of women as more suited than men for certain jobs – on the basis of 'linguistic superiority', high communication skills, caregiving abilities, or whatever – helps to ensure that women stay in low-status low-pay jobs, such as call centre jobs (Cameron, 2000). Clearly, the question of how discursive practices relate to broader social practices and struggles, such as those regarding equal access to jobs and education, is important (even if difficult to address). As long as feminist linguistics seeks to identify, demystify, and resist certain gender divisions and inequalities, it has to ask how the enactment and maintenance of gender relations in discourse are connected to power and status (Crawford, 1995). A consideration of differences, then, must be part of a social critique that serves feminist ends – something that past questions about how women and men speak differently have, in themselves, not achieved (ibid.).

Much of 'third-wave feminism' (see Chapter 1) conceptualizes power, in a Foucauldian sense, as a complex web of relations acted out and managed locally in interaction (Mills, 2002) – which brings us to the second point about gender being enacted within specific sites and communities. New theorizations are more concerned with paying attention to gender enactment at both the micro- and the macro-levels, while all the time considering the relationships between them. As Gal (1995) observes, the study of language and gender is very much enhanced by focusing, on one hand, on everyday practices, and on the other, on the ideologies about women, men and language that frame these practices and render them sensible within social contexts and institutions. The web of power relations created by these ideologies operates on the macro-level of institutional processes (e.g. within organizations or classrooms) and on the micro-level of practices, where individuals in specific contexts (e.g. managers, students, teachers) accommodate or resist them. The challenge for current and future studies that approach gender and language from a critical discursive and feminist perspective would then be 'to ensure that a study compromises neither in its close analysis of [a particular] discourse, nor in its work to relate this to wider, invariably gendered, and potentially damaging, social arrangements' (Sunderland and Litosseliti, 2002: 33).

As we have seen, the analysis of discourse at the micro- and the macro-levels is based on an understanding of texts and meanings in context, as inseparable from the discursive and social practices pertaining to them. This understanding has led to an interest in how gender is intertwined with other aspects of identity (such as race, ethnicity, age, religion, class, status, sexual orientation); and to an interest in women and men in specific settings, communities, institutions, and cultures.

First, as Cameron (1997b) rightly observes, a woman's race, class, or ethnicity will affect her gender relations (for economic exploitation of women differs among social classes) as well as the symbolic representations of femininity to which she has access (cultural models for 'feminine' behaviour may not be the same for white and black women). At the same time, we cannot talk about other identity categories independently of gender. It has been argued, for example, that lesbians experience greater discrimination than heterosexual women, because normative gender identities are implicitly heterosexist (Lazar, 2005; Butler, 1990), and also that white women enjoy privileges that black women do not (McIntosh, 1989). The possible interconnections among different social categories depend on different power relations among people and groups, and on the various social positions (as parents, lovers, professionals, friends) that people regularly occupy at different times and places (Cameron, 1997a).

Second, as regards the examination of gender within specific settings, the current emphasis in gender and language study is increasingly on particular *communities of practice* (Lave and Wenger, 1991). A community of practice (henceforth CofP) is 'an aggregate of people who come together around mutual engagement in an endeavour', in the course of which certain 'ways of doing things, ways of talking, beliefs, values, power relations – in short, practices – emerge' (Eckert and McConnell-Ginet, 1992b: 464; see also 1992a). We participate in multiple CofPs, as members of a family, students in a classroom, employees in a given workplace, members of a political party, choir, club or other group formed around an endeavour. A CofP differs from a traditional community in being 'defined simultaneously by its membership and by the practice in which that membership engages' (Eckert and McConnell-Ginet, 1992b: 464). And 'mutual engagement', 'a joint negotiated enterprise' and 'a shared repertoire of negotiable resources accumulated over time' are key elements of such a community (Wenger, 1998: 76). As individuals grow up performing the practices around which the community is formed, these practices become part of their everyday life or 'habitus' (Bourdieu, 1984; Joseph, 2004). This is how individuals develop a national, ethnic, and religious identity (see, for example, Joseph's (2004) discussion of identity in the new quasi-nation of Hong Kong, as well as Christian and Muslim identities in Lebanon).

Gender identity is accordingly formed, produced, and reproduced – as well as resisted and contested – through women's and men's participation in multiple CofPs, as they define themselves in relation to other women and men. In particular, we become gendered through our engagement with gendered practices in our CofPs, and also through our differential gendered participation in them (see Holmes and Meyerhoff, 1999, for a key discussion). One example of this would be a group of language learners who are learning gendered practices in the classroom (Sunderland, 2000; see also Chapter 4), such as those around 'disruptive boys' and 'neat girls'. Another example would be the 'masculinization' of talk by women in positions of power, when participating in male-dominated institutions and CofPs (Lazar, 2005). Similarly, Bergvall (1996) describes how women as a minority in the CofP of engineering students constantly shift and struggle between multiple gender positions, and argues that these women feel disempowered as a result, and unlikely to pursue further education and a career in this area.

In line with a focus on gendered discourses and gendered identities, the notion of CofPs is particularly useful in helping us distinguish between speakers' assumed gendered behaviour and the range of identities available in the gendered communities that speakers inhabit. In a study of two all-female institutions (a police station and a feminist crisis intervention centre) that address violence against women in Brazil, Ostermann (2003) found that the co-operative strategies feminists used when interacting with victims (e.g. providing responses) were less valuable, indeed were counterproductive, for the police officers in their 'habitus'. Co-operative or affiliative interactional patterns, rather than being 'natural' to women, reflect the gendered CofPs in which these professional women participate. (In this respect, see also Erlich (1999) for an example of the differential behaviour of a female tribunal judge and a female complainant in a sexual harassment/date rape trial.) In sum, the notion of CofPs allows for an examination of both the 'fluidity and complexity of identity and social participation', which has the advantage of moving researchers away 'from the temptation to "pigeon-hole"' participants in interaction (Eckert, 2000: 39). (For detailed discussions of the CofPs' framework and gendered CofPs, I would refer the reader to the June 1999 issue of *Language in Society* (vol. 28, no. 2), edited by Holmes and Meyerhoff; see also Bergvall *et al.*, 1996; Hall and Bucholtz, 1995; Pavlenko *et al.*, 2001.)

To conclude, the theories and analyses of the relationships between gender and language have come a long way. Their scope has become wider, increasingly interdisciplinary, more diverse, more specific, and more nuanced. The ongoing debate and critical re-evaluation of ideas mean that the field is constantly developing, and a combination of methods and approaches is flourishing. This is evident in the diverse literature produced in the past decade (see a list of key texts below). It is also evident in academic fora, such as the International Gender and Language Association (IGALA) conferences, which reflect the widening of the field towards non-essentialist models of gender and discourse, as well as the study of masculinities and sexualities. (The role of language in the constitution of sexuality is beyond the scope of this book. Those interested in this area will find in-depth discussions in Cameron and Kulick (2003; and 2005), Leap (1995), Livia and Hall (1997), Hall and Bucholtz (1995), and Bucholtz and Hall (2004).)

SUMMARY

- Discourses represent and constitute a web of social themes, voices, assumptions, explanations, and practices – in short, ways of seeing the world, manifested in texts.
- Discourses create specific subject positions for people and groups, and they also constitute and re-constitute ideologies which in turn shape a whole range of broader social practices.
- Discourses are context-situated; recognizable; ideological; supporting, competing or conflicting; and meaningful in relation to other discourses.
- The analysis of discourse has been the focus of a range of theoretical and methodological frameworks. In particular, the aims of Critical Discourse Analysis to demystify the role of discourse in maintaining social inequality, overlap with those of feminist linguistics.
- Gendered discourses represent, (re)constitute, maintain, and challenge gendered social practices. Rather than being associated with the gender of the person who articulates them, gendered discourses are articulated by both women and men, in a range of ways and contexts.
- Gendered discourses position women and men in certain ways, and at the same time, people take up particular gendered subject positions that constitute gender more widely. Their examination involves asking what identities are created as a result of different positioning through different discourses; and what gender inequalities are created or maintained as a result.
- Identity formation is an active process of affiliation and differentiation, and also involves attribution of identities by others. People *produce* or *construct* their multiple gendered selves (femininities, masculinities) through choices from different discourses that are available and appropriate in their social contexts; they *become* gendered, or *do* gender through discourse. This is a dynamic, ongoing process of negotiation and restatement, and one which is influenced by the enabling and constraining potential of doing gender appropriately.
- Current thinking in feminist linguistics points to a re-thinking of the notion of 'gender differences', in ways that acknowledge an engagement with feminist political aims, and a sharp focus on the dynamics of the sites and communities where gender is enacted.

■ The notion of 'gender differences' is important, but instead of assumptions about *a priori* binary differences, current approaches engage with a feminist critique of the difference gender makes. In what ways do people draw on discourses around gender differences, and what are the significance and consequences of this? What linguistic and social practices are appropriate and legitimate for women and men to participate in? Who benefits and who is disadvantaged by this?

■ In turn, these questions entail an analysis at both the micro- and the macro-levels: of how gender is enacted through everyday interactions and practices, and of the gender ideologies that frame these interactions and practices, and render them sensible within social contexts.

■ Individuals grow up performing the practices of different *communities of practice*, where people engage in an endeavour together. Their gender identities are formed, produced, and reproduced through engagement with gendered practices in such communities, and through differential gendered participation in them.

■ The scope of theoretical and analytical frameworks of gender and language has become wider and interdisciplinary, more diverse, more specific, and more nuanced. New approaches benefit from ongoing debate and critical re-evaluation of ideas, and from a fruitful combination of methodologies.

FURTHER READING

Recent introductory books on discourse and discourse analysis

Blommaert, J. (2005) *Discourse: A Critical Introduction*. Cambridge: Cambridge University Press. A new introduction, focusing on the theory and methods of Critical Discourse Analysis. Includes discussions of language and inequality, and ideology and identity.

Gee, J. (2005) *An Introduction to Discourse Analysis: Theory and Method*, 2nd edn. London: Routledge. An accessible introduction to discourse analysis, as both a theory of language-in-use and a method of research. Includes perspectives from different approaches and disciplines and many examples of spoken and written language (group discussions, interviews, academic texts, policy documents, etc.).

Locke, T. (2004) *Critical Discourse Analysis*. London: Continuum. An introduction to Critical Discourse Analysis as a research methodology. Includes an overview of the key terms and theories, and examples of how they can be applied to texts. An excellent resource for students and those new to CDA.

Renkema, I. (2004) *Introduction to Discourse Studies*. Amsterdam: John Benjamins. A very comprehensive textbook in discourse studies. With detailed explanations of all the key concepts, it is best used for reference purposes and for an overview of what is a very diverse field. Part IV, in particular, focuses on discourse from a social perspective.

Wooffitt, R. (2005) *Conversation Analysis and Discourse Analysis: A Comparative and Critical Introduction*. London: Sage. A book that examines the merits of conversational analysis and discourse analysis, while championing the analytical strengths of the former. An excellent resource for those teaching discourse studies.

Some other texts on discourse and discourse analysis

Antaki, C., Billig, M., Edwards, D. and Potter, J. (2002) Discourse analysis means doing analysis: a critique of six analytic shortcomings, *Discourse Analysis Online*, www.shu.ac.uk/daol/articles/v1/n1/a1/antaki2002002.html

Cameron, D. (2001) *Working with Spoken Discourse*. London: Sage.

Fairclough, N. (2003) *Analysing Discourse: Textual Analysis for Social Research*. London: Routledge.

Wetherell, M., Taylor, S. and Yates, S.J. (eds) (2001) *Discourse as Data: A Guide for Analysis*. London: Sage/Open University.

Widdowson, H. (2004) *Text, Context, Pretext: Critical Issues in Discourse Analysis*. Oxford: Blackwell.

Wodak, R. and Meyer, M. (eds) (2001) *Methods of Critical Discourse Analysis*. London: Sage.

More advanced discussions on Critical Discourse Analysis

Chouliaraki, L. and Fairclough, N. (1999) *Discourse in Later Modernity*. Edinburgh: Edinburgh University Press.

Wodak, R. and Chilton, P. (eds) (2005) *A New Agenda in (Critical) Discourse Analysis: Theory, Methodology and Interdisciplinarity*. Amsterdam: John Benjamins.

Key texts on discourse, gender and gender identities from the past decade (1995–2005)

Baxter, J. (2003) *Positioning Gender in Discourse: A Feminist Methodology*. Basingstoke: Palgrave.

Bergvall, V., Bing, J. and Freed, A. (eds) (1996) *Rethinking Language and Gender Research: Theory and Practice*. London: Longman.

Bucholtz, M., Liang, A.C. and Sutton, L.A. (eds) (1999) *Reinventing Identities: The Gendered Self in Discourse*. New York: Oxford University Press.

Cameron, D. (ed.) (1998) *The Feminist Critique of Language*, 2nd edn. London: Routledge.

Cheshire, J. and Trudgill, P. (1998) *The Sociolinguistics Reader*, vol. 2: *Gender and Discourse*. London: Arnold.

Christie, C. (2000) *Gender and Language*. Edinburgh: Edinburgh University Press.

Coates, J. (1996) *Woman Talk: Conversation between Women Friends*. Oxford: Blackwell.

Coates, J. (ed.) (1998) *Language and Gender: A Reader*. London: Routledge.

Coates, J. (2002) *Men Talk: Stories in the Making of Masculinities*. Oxford: Blackwell.

Coates, J. (2003) *Women, Men and Language*, 3rd edn, extensively revised. London: Longman.

Crawford, M. (1995) *Talking Difference: On Gender and Language*. London: Sage.

Eckert, P. and McConnell-Ginet, S. (2003) *Language and Gender*. Cambridge: Cambridge University Press.

Hall, K. and Bucholtz, M. (eds) (1995) *Gender Articulated: Language and the Socially Constructed Self*. New York: Routledge.

Holmes, J. and Meyerhoff, M. (eds) (2003) *The Handbook of Language and Gender*. Oxford: Blackwell.

Johnson, S. and Meinhof, U. (eds) (1997) *Language and Masculinity*. Oxford: Blackwell.

Kotthof, H. and Wodak, R. (eds) (1997) *Communicating Gender in Context*. Amsterdam: John Benjamins.

Lazar, M. (ed) (2005) *Feminist Critical Discourse Analysis*. London: Palgrave.

Litosseliti, L. and Sunderland, J. (eds) (2002) *Gender Identity and Discourse Analysis*. Amsterdam: John Benjamins.

Livia, A. and Hall, K. (eds) (1997) *Queerly Phrased: Language, Gender and Sexual Politics*. London: Cassell.

McIlvenny, P. (ed.) (2002) *Talking Gender and Sexuality*. Amsterdam: John Benjamins.

Mills, S. (ed.) (1995) *Language and Gender: Interdisciplinary Perspectives*. London: Longman.

Mills, S. (2001) *Beyond Sexism*. Cambridge: Cambridge University Press.

Pauwels, A. (1998) *Women Changing Language*. London: Longman.

Romaine, S. (1999) *Communicating Gender*. London: Lawrence Erlbaum.

Speer, S. (2005) *Gender Talk: Feminism, Discourse and Conversation Analysis*. London: Routledge.

Sunderland, J. (2004) *Gendered Discourses*. Basingstoke: Palgrave.

Talbot, M. (1998) *Language and Gender: An Introduction*. Cambridge: Polity.

Walsh, C. (2001) *Gender and Discourse: Language and Power in Politics, the Church and Organisations*. Harlow: Longman.

Weatherall, A. (2002) *Gender, Language and Discourse*. London: Routledge.

Wilkinson, S. and Kitzinger, C. (eds) (1995) *Feminism and Discourse: Psychological Perspectives*. London: Sage.

Wodak, R. (ed.) (1997) *Gender and Discourse*. London: Sage.

Other references

Extracts from *Gender as Performance: An Interview with Judith Butler*, interview by Peter Osborne and Lynne Segal, London, 1993, www.theory.org.uk/but-int1.htm

Regions of the heart: the triumph and tragedy of Alison Hargreaves, *National Geographic* Press Release, June 2000, www.nationalgeographic.com/events/releases/pr0006h.html

Gary Younge, No offence, but why are all white men so aggressive?, *The Guardian*, 1 December 2004

II GENDER IN CONTEXT

Gender and language research has incorporated a huge range of genres, sites, settings, and data. In addition to single-sex and mixed-sex talk, these include magazines, advertisements, newspapers, textbooks, fiction, meetings, sermons, parliamentary debates, political speeches, dictionaries, classroom interaction and materials, television debates, chat shows, soap operas, popular music, jokes, broadcast interviews, telephone conversations, computer-mediated communication, the internet, academic writing, letters, brochures, medical texts, courtroom discourse, and family interaction.

Part II concentrates on three broad areas where gender is salient: education, the media, and the workplace. These contexts are important, as they encompass continuously developing social experiences. A second reason is that a huge range of gendered norms, practices, relations, representations, and identities are (re)produced through institutions such as classrooms, workplaces and the mass media. And third, as we will see, there is ongoing debate and concern about the gendered practices produced within these contexts. Such concerns intensify if we consider the interpenetration of discourses, between these and other – public as well as less public – contexts.

In addition to examining the implications of research on gender and language in education, the media, and the workplace, this part also contextualizes the theoretical ideas and frameworks discussed in Part I. For example, the assumptions and consequences of the gender 'difference' and 'dominance' paradigms are illustrated through analysis of interaction in the classroom and in organizations; the notion of sexism is addressed in relation to media texts, such as advertisements; and gendered discourses and the discursive construction of masculinities and femininities are foregrounded throughout this second part of the book.

4 Gender and language in education

> Girls derive much more in the way of ligatures
> from the discursive practices of their education
> than boys do [while] boys seem to derive more
> options for themselves.
>
> (Corson, 1997: 142)

THE DEVELOPMENT OF GENDER AND LANGUAGE STUDIES IN THE CLASSROOM

Interactions that take place in educational settings enable students to develop sensitivity towards their own and others' rights and responsibilities as citizens in a community. Particularly important is collaborative and exploratory talk in classrooms, which allows students to construct knowledge together and negotiate their own and others' views (Mercer *et al.*, 1999). Educational settings also give students an understanding of their social identity in relation to each other and the institution (Freeman and McElhinny, 1996). In other words, they are important settings for the construction and enactment of gender.

There is a substantial and wide-ranging body of research in this area. Some studies have focused on teacher–student interactions – i.e. how the teacher's attention is distributed among girls and boys in class (Clarricoates, 1983; French and French, 1984; Kelly, 1988; Spender, 1982). Other studies have focused on student–student interactions – i.e., differences and inequalities in girls' and boys' language behaviour such as the amount of speech they produce in the classroom, or their turn-taking and interruption sequences (Gass and Varonis, 1986; Holmes, 1989; Swann and Graddol, 1988, 1995). More recent work marks a shift away from gender generalizations and differences, to examine the discourses and gender identities that are at work in educational settings (Norton and Pavlenko, 2004; Norton and Toohey, 2004; Pavlenko *et al.*, 2001).

Corson (1997) views schools as places where highly specialized discursive practices can be observed. He indicates that education enables people to have two types of life chances: 'options', which involves a great range of opportunities in their future, and 'ligatures', which involves the establishment of stronger bonds between individuals and groups as a result of people's experiences in education. He suggests that 'girls derive much more in the way of ligatures from the discursive practices of their education than boys do [while] boys seem to derive more options for themselves' (Corson, 1997: 142). Hence, instead of creating an environment that provides people with equal opportunities for participation in educational and extra-curricular activities, schools develop and reinforce gender segregation and stereotypes. That is, schools play an important role in the learning of the negative aspects of gender roles that occur in real-life situations (Sarah, 1988; Delamont, 1990).

Question 1
In what ways can classroom interaction be gendered?
What gender stereotypes are likely to be produced and reproduced at school?

Research focusing on 'dominance' in educational settings, during the 1980s and later, demonstrated that girls were at a disadvantage compared to boys in educational settings (Spender and Sarah, 1988; Swann, 1992; Swann and Graddol, 1988). A number of studies on teacher–student and student–student interactions revealed that boys' speaking styles enabled them to dominate most of the classroom time in a variety of ways, leaving girls with limited opportunities to contribute (Swann, 2003). Teachers asked more questions of boys than girls, and they often gave more chances to boys to take turns, to hold the floor longer, and to interrupt female and other male students in class (Kelly, 1988; Spender, 1988; Swann and Graddol, 1988; Swann, 1992).

An example where the teacher gives more opportunities to boys to take turns can be seen in Extract (4A) (Bayyurt, *in progress*). The extract is from an English-language lesson in an English-medium university in Turkey. The female teacher is facilitating a discussion among students on the topic of whether smoking should be banned in public places:

Extract (4A)

Female student:	[...] I'm not sure about banning smoking in places like [restaurants] but when you look from the [...] when you go to a bar or closed places you can't open your eyes [...] so it's really unpleasant for people who don't smoke and it really, hurting them because they are passive smokers –
Male student:	[*interrupts*] banning smoking in restaurants
Teacher:	[*to the male student*] go ahead X
Male student:	in a restaurant, you can't divide the places between smokers and non smokers but in a bar it's impossible [...] how can you allow, both the right [...] to have pleasure to smokers and also to non-smokers in the same place [*continues*]

(Bayyurt, in progress)

Bayyurt's analysis of the teacher's and the students' distribution of turns, and other interactional features such as interruptions, shows that the teacher holds the floor longer than the students, and also that the male students are given more chances to take turns than the female students. In terms of distribution of turns, 42 of the turns during the session were taken by the teacher, while female and male students took 7 and 30 turns respectively. The extract also illustrates a male student interrupting a female without any repercussions; however, the opposite was not observed in this particular study. In addition, elsewhere in the study, Bayyurt shows that the teacher tends to support male students by probing, while simply giving the female students their turn to speak without any initiating questions or further probing. In this case, the teacher, consciously or unconsciously, gives more opportunities to male students to participate in classroom talk, while leaving female students with limited options for doing the same. As Holmes suggests,

> opportunities to answer the teacher's questions and receive evaluative feedback, to ask the teacher for information and clarification, and to discuss material and issues with other students – these are all regarded as important educational strategies, each of which contributes to learning and understanding. If females are denied equal access to these learning resources, they are being educationally disadvantaged.

(1995: 199)

In her review of studies on teacher–student interaction, Kelly (1988) suggested that teachers tended to interact more with boys than girls in the classroom, despite their intention to treat girls and boys equally in terms of attention and interaction time. The findings of her study on a national sample of teachers illustrated that the majority of teachers disagreed with the statement 'Teachers often allow boys to dominate in mixed classrooms' (Kelly *et al.*, 1985). In reality, girls received approximately 44 per cent of instructional exchanges – i.e., teacher attention, questions, and response opportunities – while boys received approximately 56 per cent. The teachers who participated in Kelly *et al.*'s study were unaware of their biases in this respect.

Other studies similarly highlighted boys' dominance in classroom interaction (Clarricoates, 1978, 1983; French and French, 1984; Edelsky, 1981; Sadker and Sadker, 1985; Spender and Sarah, 1988). These were summarized in Swann (1992: 51–2) as follows:

- boys were more outspoken than girls in the classroom;
- boys interrupted more in conversations;
- topics and materials for discussion in the classroom were chosen in favour of boys' interests;
- boys had a tendency to hold the floor longer once they took their turn in the conversation.

More specifically, boys seem to get more 'blame, approval, disapproval and instructions than girls' (Sunderland, 1994: 148). Research findings show that boys dominate most of the classroom interaction time, while girls get involved in teacher–student interactions which support learning (Kelly *et al.*, 1985; Younger *et al.*, 1999). Even in classroom studies where girls outnumber boys, boys tend to take more turns. For example, in studies in Modern Greek, Ancient Greek and History classes in a Greek high school, Pavlidou (2001) focused on initiative turns, in the form of requests, disagreements, etc. in classroom interaction. She analysed two types of initiative turns, 'directive' and 'non-compliant' turns, and showed that both girls and boys preferred 'directive' turns to 'non-compliant' turns. She categorized 'directive turns' as 'requests for floor, requests for re content, other requests' and 'non-compliant turns' as 'those turns in which any sort of opposition to what the teacher is saying or doing is expressed, for example, protesting or complaining, disagreeing with the teacher, correcting the teacher and so on' (ibid.: 111). However, girls and boys differed in the type of 'directive' and 'non-compliant' turns they took. The main difference between girls and boys in terms of 'directive turns' was that boys preferred 'requests for floor' (19.8 per cent girls, 44.4 per cent boys) while girls preferred 'other requests' (47.5 per cent girls, 33.7 per cent boys). The distribution of the frequency of 'requests for re content' (i.e. requests that involve clarification of content) was 32.7 per cent for the girls and 21.9 per cent for the boys. This showed that although boys were not eager to participate in classroom activities, they still wanted to get the floor more often than the girls. As far as 'non-compliant' turns were concerned, girls were mainly interested in the management of class matters and the management of turn-taking, (67.9 per cent girls, 37.3 per cent boys), while boys preferred 'non-compliant' turns that concerned the 'content of the lesson or the topic of the current discussion' (30.2 per cent girls, 58.2 per cent boys). As Pavlidou shows, although girls do not initiate turns as much as boys do in class, they disagree with the teacher more than boys do and tend to challenge the teacher more often. Although boys also disagree with the teacher, this is not a challenge to the teacher's role and their relationship with the teacher, but tends to be a disagreement on a topic argued in class.

Question 2

Refer to Chapter 2, Conversational labour, p. 32. In what ways do the findings above correspond to those discussed by 'dominance' theorists in general?

From a 'difference' perspective, particularly in the 1970s and 1980s, research concentrated on the differences in choice of subjects, level of achievement, and interactional strategies of female and male students in the classroom.

In terms of subject choice, early studies revealed that girls favoured social sciences and languages, while boys favoured maths and science (e.g. Diamond, 1987). However, recent studies in the UK show that increasingly more girls are choosing maths and sciences, and more boys are choosing languages as subject areas of study (e.g. Francis, 2000). There also seems to be a difference in mixed- and single-sex schools in terms of the students' subject choices. While the majority of girls in mixed-sex schools prefer gender stereotypical subjects, girls in single-sex schools choose less stereotypical subjects and develop themselves in those areas (Elwood and Gipps, 1998; Dennison and Coleman, 2000).

In terms of achievement, while some studies focus on concerns about boys' under-achievement in a particular skill, such as reading (Brophy and Good, 1974), others focus on girls' position in school and in society, and how this affects their academic achievement (Wernersson, 1982). Educational achievement is a notion that varies from one sociocultural context to the next. In some societies, girls are not given opportunities (and may not be allowed) to go to school, in contrast to the opportunities given to boys; in others, girls are encouraged to study and achieve good results. In the UK context, there is some concern about boys' 'underachievement', compared to girls, in national examinations, such as the General Certificate of Secondary Education (GCSE) (Swann, 2003), and in terms of second/foreign language learning. We discuss this in the next section, but it is important to point out that discourses around boys' underachievement and girls' academic success must be considered in the context of the social positions they occupy and the goals they achieve later in life.

As we saw in Chapter 2, the study of differences between female and male interactional patterns has focused on women initiating and maintaining conversations, asking more questions, and generally facilitating interaction through back-channelling and other verbal and non-verbal clues that support the male speakers. Some of these patterns can also be observed in girls' and boys' speech in playgroup activities. For example, Goodwin (1980a, 1980b, 1998) illustrates how girls' and boys' conversational patterns in their playgroups vary in terms of the use of directives. Her findings suggest that girls mostly choose directives which imply a collective future action, in the form of auxiliaries and grammatical constructions such as 'let's do this/that'. In Extract (4B), Darlene and Pam are making plans for a joint task via the use of directives as follows:

Extract (4B)

All girls' group
Darlene: Let's play some more jacks.
Pam: Let's play 'one two three footsies'. First!
((Searching for turtles))
Pam: Let's look around. See what we can find.

(Goodwin, 1998: 129)

On the other hand, boys choose more explicit and direct imperatives/directives (e.g. 'do it!') to talk about future action, as illustrated in Extract (4C):

Extract (4C)

All boys' group

Michael: Now. *Remember* what I sai:d. And don't try to shoot till

Tokay: Like- like they in sight?

Michael: That's right.

Tokay: What if they ain't.

Michael: But if they- if they hidin in some bushes, don't you shoot. = You let them waste theirs. Count for the man how many he waste. Then after he waste as as many as you got you let him shoot his. But then you let him waste some more.

Goodwin (1998: 127)

In extract (4C), Michael, as the leader of his group, lays down the rules for working conditions and the division of labour, and decrees the group policy. Goodwin concludes that the boys' use of direct imperatives in playgroup activities is associated with the maintenance of a hierarchical social structure. In other words, the most powerful participants use direct imperatives to get things done. Male conversational patterns reflect the struggle and maintenance of power against others which enables them to hold positions of high status in society (Spender, 1982; Swann, 1992). Corson (1997) argues that in co-educational classrooms, girls tend to use the cooperative interactional modes of communication to which they are accustomed in their same-gender adult group exchanges, while boys opt for more competitive interactional styles, modelled on same-gender adult behaviour. In other words, male students' competitive conversational style may encourage them to practise power relations with their fellow classmates regardless of their gender, more freely than their female counterparts.

Similarly, as part of a project on secondary school students' argumentation skills, Sargeant (1993) has described male students' understandings of argument as dominance and female students' bridge-building approaches to argument. Her analysis of students' journals revealed that the girls showed

> far more appreciation of the different types of argument, of argument as a two-way process, as sometimes simply a sharing experience or a weighing-up in oneself; as something which may not necessarily result in winning or beating an opponent, as many of the boys saw it.
>
> (1993: 10)

On the other hand, boys' accounts were 'more reminiscent of a battle, a war to be won by confidence, boldness and expertise, a discourse missing from the girls' journals' (ibid.). We will return to these issues below.

As discussed in detail in Chapter 3, gender has now come to be seen as a site for struggle, a 'complex system of social relations and discursive practices, differentially constructed in social contexts' (Norton and Pavlenko, 2004: 504). Unlike past approaches that generally treated gender as a distinct group of different linguistic, behavioural and social characteristics attributed to female and male members of the community (teachers, students, school administrators), recent approaches view gender as constructed in interactions as part of participants' social identity. Since gender is only one part of social identity, it may be enacted in one situation but may not play a role in another. For example, a female university professor giving a lecture may be enacting her identity as a lecturer rather than as a woman. Depending on the situation of the interaction, participants may emphasize and de-emphasize their social identity as gendered in particular ways which will differ from one context to the next (Wodak, 1997; Sunderland, 2000a). It has been stressed that if earlier studies had focused more on the interaction contexts than on gender differences in those contexts, they would have found that it was those contexts that led the participants to enact their gender roles in particular ways (Crawford, 1995). Thus, current research in educational settings has been shifting from more '"static" models' towards 'differentiated and contextualised practices' where female and male students construct their identities differently (Swann, 2003: 640).

In her analysis of pupils' gendered discourse styles in small group discussions, Davies (2003) argues that classroom discourse provides an exceptional ground for observing how girls and boys perform gender in particular circumstances. When girls are engaged in a harmonious style of communication, this may be referred to as 'polyphony' (see also Coates, 1996). Boys' less harmonious discourse style is usually referred to as 'cacophony'. Girls' discourse style constructs collaborative and friendly learning environments that enhance and support their learning. Extract (4D) is taken from a session in an English class in a comprehensive school in the north of England, where 14-year-old girls are participating in speaking and listening activities. Rosa has been sharing her experience of her first day at school, when she was five:

Extract (4D)

All girls' group	
Rosa:	[...] /and my mum walked em into school/and she walked me into class and saw my teacher and I saw Lou/and I thought/oh she looks nice/You know when they say ah does anyone want to look after Rosa for the day and show her round?/
Lou:	Yeah/
Rosa:	Lou put HER hand up/and I sat next to her/and we were painting/
Lou:	Yeah/
Rosa:	we were doing finger painting and I grabbed all this paint and I just threw it at Ali and we started having a paint fight and I thought it was really funny because I made a new friend/
All:	<laughter>/
Rosa:	my first day of school/Ali. I've just told em about first day at school when me and you had a paint fight/you were my first friend/there is one about friendship for you/anyone else?/

All:	\<laughter\>
Rosa:	Right come on Jan/you've got to have something to say./
Jan:	I'm thinking/
Rosa:	now when Jan was a supermodel she learnt a very valuable lesson right/she will not forget her friends/cause you see we were all poor and she was rich/
Jan:	Thankfully then we sat down and talked about it and I realised my friends were more important/
Bel:	And she gave us a million quid/\<laughs\>/
Jan:	Well. not really a million/but I gave them all some money/and now I don't do modelling anymore so I'm poor./like THEM/
All:	\<laughing\>/

(Davies, 2003: 119)

As Davies indicates, 'the maintenance of amicable relationships seemed to be crucial to the process of learning support and the discussions tended to possess a highly positive aspect and to contain a high number of cohesive devices' (2003: 128). In other words, girls' cooperative learning style enabled them to create opportunities to learn the subject in an enjoyable and friendly manner, rather than in a competitive or individualistic way. However, for boys the situation is different. The societal norms and the task itself control the boys' choice of linguistic forms in classroom interaction (see Extract (4E)). Peer group expectations here are more important than the situation itself, and if they do not conform to the rules of the group, boys are singled out for not possessing the characteristics of 'real boys'. In the following extract from an English class (4E), Pierre wants to concentrate on the task in relation to the poem 'The Lady of Shalott'. He deconstructs the poem using elaborate lexical items, to show his appreciation of it; however, he is constantly distracted and scolded by his classmates, initially by Kirk and then by Andy.

Extract (4E)

All boys' group

Andy:	What are we on?/
Pierre:	Part three/\<high voice\>
Kirk:	Ooooh/ \<two tone high pitch in mockery of Pierre\>
Pierre:	The sun dazzling through the leaves ¦ like orange-/
Kirk:	¦ Pierre Pierre
Pierre:	¦ **and thinks its gorgeous**/
Kirk:	¦ shut up/I'm not bothered/\<high pitched mimicry\>
Pierre:	And the yellow gold/
Kirk:	You're just stupid you/
Pierre:	And a GOLDEN GALAXY/erm/
Kirk:	Shut up Pierre/

...

Andy:	Listen to him/Listen to him/oh God/
Kirk:	**He'll shut up now cause he's gonna smell it/**
Andy:	**Oh God!/**
Kirk:	Oh ⎸God
Pierre:	⎸**Like crystals like with all colours coming out of it/**
Kirk:	See?/do you HAVE to speak like that and moving your hands about like a <u>queer?</u> <laughs>/

(Davies, 2003: 126–7)

By showing persistence to complete the task despite his peers' distracting and scolding remarks, Pierre dominates the interaction in a way which would be unacceptable in the all girls' groups. Also in this example, the discourse of learning is in conflict with discourses of heterosexual masculinity. Davies shows that while girls deconstruct their story-telling experiences – i.e. retell and share their stories with the rest of the group – in an amicable environment, boys prefer to use 'distancing' tactics to complete similar tasks in class, such as criticizing one another and making disparaging remarks. In the first case, a co-operative climate for learning is created and maintained; in the second, learning is obstructed and boys' under-achievement is further sustained (ibid.).

Question 3

Refer to Chapter 2, Talking difference, p. 37. In what ways do the findings above correspond to those discussed by 'difference' theorists in general?

GENDER AND LANGUAGE IN THE FOREIGN LANGUAGE CLASSROOM

This section provides an overview of research on gender and language in the foreign language classroom. It concentrates on the areas of classroom interaction (teacher-to-student and student-to-teacher talk, as well as student-to-student talk), language learning and assessment, and language teaching materials.

Classroom interaction

Classroom interaction refers to teacher-to-student talk, such as initiating conversation, asking questions, giving directives; student-to-teacher talk, for instance, answering questions or asking for clarification; and student-to-student talk, during group work and pair work activities.

In the 1970s and the 1980s studies on teacher talk revealed that teachers not only talked more than the students in class but also gave unequal attention to boys and girls, such as more chances for boys to talk than for girls. Most of the time, this was unintentional. In her analysis of her own classroom sessions, Spender (1982) found that she spent more time with boys than girls, contrary to her own belief that she was treating both gender groups fairly. In her study, she reported that she was spending 58 per cent of her classroom time interacting with boys and 42 per cent with girls. Merrett and Wheldall (1992) also found that teachers in secondary schools gave more positive and negative responses (for example, praising and scolding) to boys than to girls – something which can be explained as a reaction to boys actually talking more in class (Brophy and Good, 1974). In her meta-analysis of 81 classroom interaction studies, Kelly (1988) stated that, across different age groups and a number of countries, girls obtained less of teachers' attention in class than boys, regardless of the gender of the teacher. She argued that the findings of these studies can be explained as signs of male dominance in society. Swann and Graddol (1988) have suggested that teachers giving more attention to boys is usually unintentional and should be considered as differential teacher treatment by gender rather than bias.

In addition, it is important to consider that teachers paying more attention to boys than girls may not necessarily help their learning. More importantly, it is the *kind* of attention that needs to be considered, in order to understand whether and in what ways it contributes to learning (Sunderland, 2000b). In some cases, boys may be given longer 'wait-time' opportunities than girls to answer a question (2000b), and the attention paid to boys may often have the function of disciplining them.

Question 4

In what ways can analyses of the quantity and of the quality of interaction produce different findings, as regards gender in the classroom?

In her study in a German as a Foreign Language classroom, Sunderland (1996) examined specific ways in which the teacher tended to treat the girls and boys differently. She used the concept of *solicit* which represented teachers' questions involving academic behaviour, such as 'What is the German word for "train"?', as well as non-academic behaviour, such as 'Could you please close the window?' She concluded that since many of the *non-academic solicits* were disciplinary, the teacher addressed the boys more often in order to tell them to behave themselves. At the same time, the teacher gave girls more chances to develop their academic abilities by allowing them to take longer turns and give their answers in German. In other words, the quality or the kind of teacher attention was more important than the quantity of teacher attention. The teacher interacted more often with the boys, but this interaction did not involve any academic exchanges. On the other hand, girls seemed to be more academically involved in the interaction. Other researchers, particularly those following early 'dominance' paradigms, would have interpreted the boys' taking up more classroom time as an educational disadvantage for the girls, and would have criticized the teacher for favouring the boys over the girls.

Student-to-teacher talk is another important component of classroom interaction. A number of studies conducted in classrooms in different subject areas illustrated that male students had a tendency to talk more to the teacher than female students (Spender, 1982; French and French, 1984; Sadker and Sadker, 1985; Swann and Graddol, 1988). In her meta-analysis, Kelly (1988) indicated that the girls were as willing as the boys to give answers to their teachers' questions, but the boys succeeded in calling out the answers much more than the girls. Specifically within foreign language classrooms, Batters (1987) found that male students were dominating oral and participatory activities, as well as conversation with the teacher in the target language. Such participation may be responsible for boys developing the self-confidence which enables them to become competent public speakers later in life. As Baxter (2002) found in her research in a secondary mixed-sex UK classroom, girls are positioned by competing classroom discourses as both powerful and powerless: discourses of 'collaborative talk' and of 'gender differentiation' construct girls in contradictory ways, as good, supportive listeners who conform to classroom rules, and at the same time as powerless.

> On one hand, girls appear to be powerfully located according to the discourse of collaborative talk because this values supportive speech and good listening skills. On the other, according to a discourse of gender differentiation, girls are stereotypically *expected* to be good listeners [...], which consequently might diminish a positive assessment of their contributions
>
> (Baxter, 2002: 16)

From a post-structuralist perspective, Baxter argues that, by obeying the rules, girls may occupy less powerful subject positions, provide more interactional support than they receive, and effectively serve the interests of the male students. This is even more important given that, as she further suggests, gender differentiation is deeply embedded in classroom discursive practices: in how boys and girls speak, listen, and interact in groups and in teacher–student relationships (ibid.).

In her classroom study of German as a Foreign Language in England, Sunderland (1996) also looked at student-to-teacher talk. She found that there were more similarities between girls' and boys' talk to the teacher than differences. She also found two kinds of statistically significant differences between girls' and boys' talk to the teacher: first, the average girl produced shorter solicits than the average boy, and second, when the teacher asked a question without naming a student to answer it, the average girl volunteered significantly more answers in German than did the average boy (ibid.: 163). This showed that girls were also participating in classroom activities as much as boys by volunteering to give answers to teachers' questions, to ask questions in relation to the content of the lesson and to improve their learning of German in general. Sunderland pointed out that teachers and researchers should be cautious with the 'more is better' interpretation when analysing interactions in the foreign language classrooms, and that we also need to look at what is done and achieved in that talk. For example, although at times boys talked more than the girls on some topics in her study, they talked less than the girls when it came to giving answers in German. The boys in her data showed willingness to volunteer for non-academic exchanges, such as 'Miss, can I open the window, it is hot in here?' or 'Miss, can I go out to fetch a piece of chalk for you?', more often than girls. On the other hand, girls asked questions relating to the content of the lesson, such as 'Miss, how can I say, "Can I open the window?" in German?' Sunderland summarized the implications of the findings of her study by saying that the femininity constructed in this class by the teacher and the girls themselves was a distinctly academic one, relative to the boys' masculinity.

Finally, classroom activities such as group work, pair work and seminars require students to interact with one another. These activities focus on collaborative talk that involves power relations among participants (Swann and Graddol, 1995). In her analysis of ESL (English as a Second Language) classroom discourse between adult students, Holmes (1994) found that men tended to openly disagree more than women did, and also men asked more questions than women. Gass and Varonis (1986) recorded classroom sessions of Japanese adult learners of English and observed that there was more negotiation in mixed-sex pairs than in single-sex ones. Although this was the case, in mixed-sex pairs men still had a tendency to dominate talk, with longer turns and overlapping speech. However, in same-sex pairs (male–male) the talk was equally distributed among the participants. In another EFL (English as a Foreign Language) classroom study in a Spanish secondary school, boys were found to interrupt girls and other boys more than girls interrupted each other (Alcón, 1994). In a study replicating Gass and Varonis, Provo (1991) found that male students were talking more. However, she observed that there was not much male overlapping speech, and in mixed-pair interactions female students were asking important questions – e.g. asking for clarification on a point that was made earlier in the discussion, probing into points made, etc. – as much as male students.

As can be seen from the above studies of classroom interaction – i.e., teacher-to-student talk, student-to-teacher talk and student-to-student talk – findings vary. In addition, studies conducted in primary and secondary schools often produce different findings, compared to those in tertiary education and university classrooms (see, for example, Mulac et al., 2001).

Language learning and assessment

In first language (L1) acquisition literature, some researchers have claimed that girls are inherently verbally superior to boys in the acquisition of some aspects of their L1 (Maccoby and Jacklin, 1974). Neurolinguistic studies investigating whether there is a connection between gender and linguistic development indicate that there may be sex differences in both development of linguistic ability and functional brain lateralization, and the two may be interconnected (Hirst, 1982). However, there are major problems with the analysis of biological sex differences in L1 acquisition, namely, the inconsistency of findings and the relative smallness of differences (Ekstrand, 1980). Ekstrand concludes that almost all the behavioural variation may be explained by cultural factors (1980), and others have similarly argued that gender differences in first and second language learning are socially constructed.

In terms of early second language (L2) acquisition/learning, Ehrlich (1997) discusses the importance of the setting where learners are exposed to new L2 forms. She indicates that naturalistic settings where language learning takes place – i.e. not classrooms, but settings such as the home, the street, and the playground – are often gendered. For instance, women are seen as the gatekeepers of maintaining traditional and/or standard language forms, and learners are being exposed to these traditional/standard language forms in naturalistic settings. In relation to second and foreign language learning, Ehrlich (1997) and Ogbay (1999) criticize earlier studies for disregarding the gendered nature of interaction in such classrooms – manifesting itself in teachers' unequal treatment of girls and boys, and in girls' and boys' different interactional strategies in class. More recent approaches to language learning and gender show how L2 acquisition can be seen as a social phenomenon to do with (gender) identity. As mentioned, Norton and Pavlenko (2004) identify gender as one of the important aspects of social identity which interacts with other factors such as race, ethnicity, class, sexuality, (dis)ability, age and social status – all of which influence students' language learning experience.

Motivation for learning a foreign language, including learners' attitudes towards the foreign language, plays an important role in female and male students' learning in L2 classrooms. Attitudes include those towards the language, the language teacher, the language learning materials, and the language learning activities. Perceptions include perceptions of the level of difficulty of language learning materials and seeing oneself as a language learner (Clark and Trafford, 1995; Harris, 1998; Sunderland, 2000b). Studies investigating whether female language learners are better motivated to learn foreign languages are numerous but inconclusive. Women learning a foreign language were found to be more instrumentally motivated, that is, motivated to learn languages for instrumental purposes such as meeting and communicating with people from the target language countries (Bacon and Finneman, 1992). Ludwig's (1983) study found no significant differences in terms of motivation among college learners of German, French and Spanish; however, women reported that they were not very happy when they could not produce correct linguistic forms in the target language and men said that they were discouraged when they could not understand the spoken language. The situation in primary and secondary schools was slightly different, compared to higher education settings. In a secondary school setting, Batters (1987) found differences between girls' and boys' attitudes towards language learning activities. While girls enjoyed classroom activities at all levels (speaking, reading, writing, and listening), boys seemed to enjoy speaking activities the most.

Language learning strategies are 'the specific behaviours that [language] learners employ, usually intentionally, to enhance their understanding, storage and retrieval of […] second/foreign language information' (Oxford, 1994: 140). Goh and Foong (1997) found that female Chinese ESL learners in Singapore used *compensation* strategies, such as guessing unknown words, and *affective* strategies, such as anxiety management, significantly more than the male students. It is important to note that individual inclinations towards learning strategies are not fixed, but are likely to vary across the same and mixed gender groups. Also, the majority of girls participating in a study by Arnot *et al.* (1998) adopted compensatory learning strategies, in response to male dominence in class, by approaching the teacher individually and asking questions after the lesson. Since foreign language learning needs constant building up of new linguistic forms and functions in addition to those already acquired, constant dedication to the study of these forms and functions is needed; this increases as students' L2 proficiency advances. If girls/women are more likely to commit themselves to building up on newly presented language forms, they may also be expected to be more successful as language learners. The reduced participation on the part of the boys/men may mean that they are expected to do less well. Teachers may actually reinforce a 'good' or 'bad' language learner identity, if they have such expectations. In addition, boys may see language study as a feminine practice (typically taught by female teachers and related to often assumed 'female' skills), and therefore something from which they are keen to distance themselves (Sunderland, 2000b).

The relationship between gender and language testing is an important one since test results are needed to partially explain girls' superiority as second and foreign language learners. There are three components of language testing that necessitate an understanding of the relevance of gender: the *topic* (or content), the *task* and the *tester* (or the interlocutor). A language test may contain gender stereotypes, such as women occupying the roles of secretaries, nurses, and housewives, and men being managers, doctors, or lawyers. When topics are 'female-oriented', such as fashion, beauty products, losing weight, and so on, girls/women may perform better on the test (Wood, 1978; Wedman and Stage, 1983; Carrell and Wise, 1998); and vice versa, if boys/men are given topics of their interest. In terms of tasks, boys have a tendency to do better in certain types of test, such as multiple choice items, and female students in others, such as free response items (Hellekant, 1994). Morris (1998) also stated that women ESL writers had a tendency to follow the guidelines when writing essays as part of written exams, and that as a result they were more successful than the men taking the same exam. Finally, the testers may have a positive or negative effect on the test outcomes in a number of ways. They may mark female and male students preferentially (Cheshire and Jenkins, 1991; Ferguson, 1994); the female and male markers may have different standards of marking tests, when not given a clear answer key; and the gender of the tester might influence how female and male students respond to questions during oral exams (Porter, 1991). As discussed in Sunderland (2000b), the above points highlight the need for further investigation into the impact of gender on language testing.

Language teaching materials

As Sunderland (2000a) notes, in the 1970s, 1980s and early 1990s, there was an abundance of studies in the area of language teaching textbooks. Some of these studies were related to L1 English teaching (e.g. Gupta and Lee, 1990); others were related to teaching modern languages such as French, Spanish, German as a first or second/foreign language (e.g. Cincotta, 1978; Hellinger, 1980); and the majority of studies focused on textbooks for the teaching of English as a second/foreign language (e.g. Stern, 1976; Hartman and Judd, 1978; Hellinger, 1980; Porreca, 1984; Pugsley, 1992). Overall, research showed that female characters in teaching materials were poorly represented in terms of their visibility, and negatively represented in terms of personal traits and occupational roles, both in text and illustration. At the same time, content analyses of language teaching textbooks revealed that male characters were overrepresented. Put simply, there were more male than female characters in the textbooks, and in addition, these male characters tended to have more powerful and varied occupational roles (e.g. bank manager, school principal, doctor) than the female characters, who occupied the more stereotypical roles of nurse, housewife, or secretary.

Hellinger's (1980) analysis of 131 passages from three ELT textbooks used in German schools revealed that 80 per cent of the speakers in the passages were men. Women characters in those passages rarely took part in any challenging or demanding activities, while men were represented as having a wide range of occupational and leisure interests. Women's roles in those language teaching textbooks were not only limited in variety, but also less powerful and influential in social terms (ibid.). In another study, analysing the illustrations in Longman's (1992) *Dictionary of English Language and Culture*, Jimenez Catalan and Ojeda Alba (2000) found that men appeared in illustrations more often than women. They also found many more prestigious jobs in the illustrations of men (66 jobs), compared to 21 lower status jobs for women.

In addition to content analyses of textbooks, linguistic analyses have shown that female characters in textbooks seem to give more encouraging verbal feedback to their conversational partners, interrupt less in mixed-gender conversations, introduce common topics to keep the communication channels open, participate less in conversations, apologize more often, and agree more with others (Holmes, 1995). Analysis of texts for teaching Greek as a foreign language has found women to be asking for information and making requests, and men to be giving information and performing directives (Poulou, 1997). Other studies, however, found no significant differences in representations of female and male gender roles in textbooks for teaching English as a foreign language (Jones *et al.*, 1997), indicating that this may be a reflection of increased awareness of gender issues in recent years. Further research in this area would be necessary, in addition to research on reader reception of such texts. (The above studies are discussed in detail in Sunderland, 2000b.)

In line with the difficulty of identifying sexism discussed in Chapter 1, it is also difficult to make a connection between gender bias in teaching materials and learning. In an unpublished study of gender bias by the 'Women in EFL Materials' group, examining the illustrations and texts in the Streamline Departures series (1978), one particular representation of female and male characters has been subject to much criticism. The male character in the text and illustrations is crashing his car because he is distracted by a female character in a mini skirt. It is still difficult to say in what ways a representation such as this may impede girls' and women's language learning. In their study, Jones *et al.* (1997) indicate that, despite its sexism, the Streamline series has been a success with both female and male learners, for example, in terms of improvement of the learners' oral fluency. In this case, although gender bias in language teaching texts may have no impact on learning, it may nevertheless contribute to shaping learners' social attitudes and expectations around issues of gender. Teachers may sometimes exacerbate the gender bias in the text by adding their personal views, or by just focusing on teaching points while ignoring the bias. Nevertheless, as Sunderland *et al.* (2002) suggest, teachers need to be vigilant about problematic representations of gender in teaching materials, and can 'rescue' these in talk, in line with more progressive pedagogic practices.

Question 5

What are possible responses to perceived sexism in language learning materials, on the part of teachers and education policy-makers?

Responses to bias on the part of teachers and policy-makers may include explicit discussions and guidelines against gender stereotyping, reversal of stereotypes in order to illustrate and demystify sexism, and implicit discussions centred around role-play and role-reversal activities that encourage students to think critically. Policy – with the aid of research – can support and promote the use of gender-inclusive materials, a range of curriculum topics and texts that appeal to both girls and boys, as well as gender-awareness information and training for teachers. Ultimately, teachers and policy-makers can have broader, critical pedagogic aims, where the focus is not just on raising gender awareness in relation to specific classrooms, subjects, or materials, but on the interactions among these, and the whole range of discourses and practices that frame them.

SUMMARY

■ Educational settings are important settings for the construction of gender and the (re)production of a range of gendered norms, practices, relations, representations, and identities.

■ Research studies on language and gender in education have focused primarily on teacher–student and student–student interaction, as well as on language learning and language teaching materials.

■ 'Dominance' theories demonstrated that girls were at a disadvantage compared to boys in educational settings. Boys tended to dominate the classroom time. Teachers, despite their intentions, asked more questions of boys than girls, and they often gave more chances to boys to take turns, to hold the floor longer, and to interrupt other students. Topics and materials for classroom discussion often favoured boys' interests.

■ 'Difference' theories concentrated on gender differences in girls' and boys' choice of subjects, level of achievement, and interactional strategies in the classroom. Subject choice and achievement depended on a number of contextual factors. Differences in interactional patterns involved girls facilitating and maintaining interaction, and supporting other speakers. Also in playgroup activities girls used directives which imply a collective future action, whereas boys chose more explicit and direct imperatives. Further, girls' discourse style established collaborative learning environments that supported their learning, whereas boys' distancing tactics obstructed learning.

■ Research on interaction in the foreign language classroom has looked at teacher-to-student talk (e.g. initiating a discussion), student-to-teacher talk (e.g. answering questions), and student-to-student talk (group and pair work).

■ It is important to consider the opportunities and constraints created by a gender differences discourse, and how it influences classroom practices. Issues of power in interaction are not straightforward, and researchers need to consider the kind of attention teachers give to boys and girls in the classroom, and whether and in what ways it supports their learning.

■ In terms of foreign language acquisition, findings are inconsistent and depend on various factors, such as the setting where learners are exposed to a new language; the motivation for learning a foreign language; the learners' perceptions and attitudes towards the language, the language teacher, and the language learning materials and activities.

■ Language testing may involve gender stereotypes (e.g. women and men occupying particular roles), gender-oriented topics, and tasks where girls or boys tend to perform better. In addition, testers may mark female and male students preferentially, and the tester's gender may influence students differently.

■ The majority of studies on gender in language teaching materials have focused on textbooks for the teaching of English as a second or foreign language. Females in those materials were under-represented, as well as negatively represented in both texts and illustrations. Male characters were over-represented, and generally occupied more powerful and varied roles than the female characters.

■ Linguistic analyses of textbooks have also shown that female characters in textbooks give more encouraging verbal feedback to their conversational partners, interrupt less in mixed-gender conversations, introduce common topics to keep the communication channels open, participate less in conversations, apologize more often, and agree more with others.

■ Teachers need to be vigilant about problematic representations of gender in teaching materials, and more generally. Addressing gender bias in the classroom is, however, a demanding task that poses difficulties.

ACKNOWLEDGEMENTS

This chapter was written collaboratively with Yasemin Bayyurt, at Bogazici University, Turkey. <u>Citation details</u>: Bayyurt Y. and Litosseliti L. (2006) Gender and language in education, in Litosseliti L. *Gender and Language: Theory and Practice*. London: Hodder Arnold, pp. 73–89.

FURTHER READING

Baxter, J. (2002) Competing discourses in the classroom: a Post-structuralist Discourse Analysis of girls' and boys' speech in public contexts, *Discourse and Society*, 13(6): 827–42.

Corson, D. (1997) Gender, discourse and senior education: ligatures for girls, options for boys, in R. Wodak (ed.) *Gender and Discourse*. London: Sage, pp. 140–64.

Kelly, A. (1988) Gender differences in teacher–pupil interactions: a meta analytic review, *Research in Education*, 39: 1–24.

Rogers, R. (2004) *An Introduction to Critical Discourse Analysis in Education*. Hillsdale, NJ: Lawrence Erlbaum.

Sunderland, J. (2000a) New understandings of gender and language classroom research: texts, teacher talk and student talk, *Language Teaching Research*, 4(2): 149–73.

Sunderland, J. (2000b) State of the art review article: gender, language and language education, *Language Teaching*, 33(4): 203–23.

Swann, J. (2003) Schooled language: language and gender in educational settings, in J. Holmes and M. Meyerhoff (eds) *The Handbook of Language and Gender*. Oxford: Blackwell, pp. 624–44.

Swann, J. and Graddol, D. (1988) Gender inequalities in classroom talk, *English in Education*, 22(1): 48–65.

5 Gender and language in the media

> The world of the magazine is one in which men
> and women are eternally in opposition, always in
> struggle, but always in pursuit of each other.
>
> (Ballaster *et al.*, 1996: 87)

This chapter examines media discourse in general and questions around gender and
language in the media, before concentrating on the discursive construction of gender
in magazines and advertisements.

MEDIA DISCOURSE

In past decades, profound changes to media markets have altered the face of the mass
media around the world. These changes can be summarized as increasing *competition,*
globalization, tabloidization, and *centralization* (Thompson, 1998). They are evident,
for example, in the proliferation of tabloid sections and colour magazines as part of
broadsheet newspapers; in the profusion of commercial television channels; in the
entertaining treatment of news, current affairs, history, and science; and in the general
trend for confessional, increasingly personalized stories and programmes. As the
media have to operate on a market basis and respond to commercial pressures and
increased competition, there is now a greater emphasis on entertaining readers and
viewers. This results in a 'tension between the objectives of giving information and
entertaining' (Fairclough, 1995: 5) or a combination of these: 'infotainment'
(Thompson, 1998: 93).

The implications for contemporary media language can be seen in the media's
increasing 'conversationalisation' (Fairclough, 1995: 10), the mixture of public and
private talk, and the use of ever more sensationalist as well as adversarial language
(see Tannen, 1998, for examples from the UK and US media). The conversationalization of media language can be subtle, for example, in magazine articles and TV programmes that present a science topic in a conversational way, in terms of rhythm and
intonation, and in terms of colloquial and idiomatic vocabulary. It can also be more
pronounced, as in rhetorical, attention-grabbing features (seen particularly in newspapers in the UK) such as melodramatic vocabulary, sensational disclosures as headlines,
metaphors, direct questions, personal narratives, and dramatic stories. These arguably
illustrate the media tendency to sensationalize, personalize, and even demonize, in
their eagerness to attract attention (Tester, 1994; Thompson, 1998; Litosseliti, 2002).

Apart from the pervasiveness of the media as a form of mass communication that reaches very large audiences, there are good reasons, from a critical and feminist linguistic perspective, why the analysis of media language is a worthy enterprise. As discussed by Fairclough (1989, 1995):

- The media have *signifying* power, that is, the power to *represent* things in particular ways – largely (but not only) a matter of language use.
- The media are not simply representational, but can be seen as sites for the discursive *construction*, and *contestation*, of knowledge, beliefs, values, social relations, and social identities.
- Media discourse works *ideologically*: the meanings produced serve a system of power relations, and all representation involves decisions about what to include and what to exclude, what to foreground and what to background.
- Media discourse assumes/creates *subject positions* for an ideal reader, viewer, or listener; actual readers, viewers, or listeners have to negotiate a relationship with the positions offered.

Feminist linguists are interested in the possibilities within media texts for the negotiation of particular femininities and masculinities and the proliferation of gendered discourses and ideologies. Research in this area has focused on media texts which are targeted at and consumed by women (Winship, 1987; Tetlow, 1991; Mills, 1994, 1998; Talbot, 1995; Macdonald, 1995; Thornborrow, 1998), and more recently by men (Benwell, 2002, 2003; Crewe, 2003; Jackson *et al.*, 2000). The questions that are pertinent for feminist linguists follow from the points above, and can be summarized thus:

- How are women and men represented in media texts and images (e.g. as passive or active, and in specific roles and domains)?
- What femininities and masculinities, and what gender relations, are constructed for women and men in the texts?
- Who is the ideal reader and what subject positions are available in the texts?
- What power relations, particularly unequal power relations, are created through certain inclusions/exclusions?

Question 1

Refer to Extract (1A) in Chapter 1. Consider the questions above, in addition to the questions asked in Chapter 1, in relation to the extract. In what ways are the questions above more critical and more helpful for an analysis of media texts?

First, questions about representation are important because, in addition to women being under-represented across the media, the actual representations of women and men are often stereotypical and limiting. The United Nations Fourth World Conference on Women in 1995 outlined these areas of concern and proposed two strategic objectives: (1) to 'increase the participation and access of women to expression and decision-making in and through the media'; and (2) to 'promote a balanced and non-stereotyped portrayal of women in the media' (FWCW Platform for Action). The media portrayal of women with an emphasis on their physical attributes – physique, beauty, sexuality – to the exclusion of other characteristics, is well documented (see, for example, McCracken, 1993; Macdonald, 1995) as a manifestation of their unequal power positioning in relation to men. Despite profound changes in social expectations and gender roles, women are still disproportionately represented as sex objects, as mothers and wives (in relationships with others, rather than independently), in passive or supportive roles, and as victims. Men are overwhelmingly depicted as strong, active, independent (often isolated), and sexually confident. At the same time, however, the ways in which women and men are constructed in media language, images, and discourses are also changing, becoming less coherent, more subtle, and potentially more insidious (an idea introduced in previous chapters, and developed in the next section).

The construction of gender identities and relations in media discourses (for example, 'consumer femininity', the 'new man', or heterosexual identities and relations – see below) is complex. The femininities and masculinities established and reinforced therein exist in relation to an assumed audience or, in the case of newspapers and magazines, an ideal reader. While media producers construct the ideal reader, viewer or listener as addressee, those on the receiving end typically negotiate or position themselves in relation to that ideal subject (Fairclough, 1989). We may hypothesize that 'an actual reader who has a great deal in common with the imaginary ideal reader inscribed in a particular text is likely to take up the [subject] positions it offers unconsciously and uncritically' (Talbot, 1995: 146); on the other hand, distancing oneself from an ideal reader may involve raising the reader's awareness of the positioning, and perhaps one's critical ability. However, distancing may be made more difficult to achieve by the fact that the mass media try to address the audience or reader as a 'unified, natural subject' (Thompson, 1998: 78) or a unified 'general public' with shared values and characteristics (Watney, 1987: 84). Particularly in the case of newspaper stories, this typically means a reader who is treated (and constantly reassured) as 'normal', 'healthy-minded', 'right-thinking', law-abiding, commonsensical, part of a society in 'consensus' (ibid.; also see Hall *et al.*, 1978). In the case of women's magazines, the ideal reader is addressed as a single unified community by virtue of its femaleness: 'the world of women' (Ferguson, 1983: 6; Weedon, 1987).

It is unclear whether media producers are concerned about or interested in the implications of gender representations, beyond an interest in gender as newsworthy, or beyond an appropriation of gender for profit, as in the case of advertisements. But the fact that media texts 'are authored by teams of people addressing targeted audiences' may provide less scope for clear critique by individuals within that production team (Mills, 1998: 196). In addition, there are further constraints. Newspapers, for instance, will have different criteria about selecting what to report and in what ways, according to their sense of their audience, their editorial policies and (re-)drafting processes, the newspaper's personality, and the newspaper's line on issues (Mills, 1998; Thompson, 1998). Reporters also typically choose a particular 'frame' (Goffman, 1974; Tannen, 1993) or point of view when discussing events and issues. To illustrate this with an example of newspaper reports on sexual harassment, Bing and Lombardo (1997) have shown that different media frames have different effects, both in terms of defining harassment and in terms of dealing with it. A *judicial frame* matches behaviours to legal policies and suggests reactive strategies, such as legal actions; a *victim frame* emphasizes harm or injury to the victim(s), suggesting social change and social responsibility regarding sexual harassment, while an *instigator frame* defines the (mis)behaviour as socially acceptable and leads to inaction; finally, a *social science frame* integrates the other approaches, allowing for changes in attitudes, knowledge, and legal grounds. A close analysis of these can provide insight into the arguable media influence on both public debate and public attitudes (ibid.).

In addition to the above, a media text is shaped by the community of practice in which it is produced. For example, while members in an academic community take a stance in their texts as legitimate members of that community, journalists tend to distance themselves from the text (e.g. in news reporting), and in the advertising community the author stance is not important (Scollon, 2004). Along the same lines, the production formats in journalism and in advertising mean that it is not one and the same person who authors a text, physically produces it, and takes responsibility for it (Goffman, 1974, 1981; Scollon, 2004).

Then there are broader questions about the social production of media views, for instance, the issue of what constitutes primary news value. In their influential work, Hall *et al.* (1978) describe a variety of factors for the selection of primary news value, ranging from the individual reporter's hunch about a 'good story', to 'giving the public what it wants', to structured ideological biases. The process of selection also involves 'resignification', i.e. the rephrasing of news items seen as lacking primary news value by the news definers (government ministers, academics, official organizations). Key news values dictate an emphasis on particular events: extraordinary and/or dramatic ones, those that concern elite persons or groups, those which can be personalized so as to point up essentially human characteristics (e.g. of sentimentality, humour, etc.), events with negative consequences, and those that are part of an existing newsworthy theme (Hall *et al.*, 1978: 52; see also Aitchison and Lewis, 2003, for a more recent discussion). In this light, it may be easier to understand why, although disease takes a hundred times as many lives as homicide in the USA, newspapers contain three times as many articles on death from homicide as death from disease (Slovic *et al.*, 1980). Similarly, we can begin to explain why ideas and findings about the 'essential difference' between men and women are over-reported, simplified and exaggerated, while similarities tend to be overlooked (see Chapter 2, Beyond difference, p. 40).

Any analysis of media texts needs, then, to be cautious of the media tendency

> to shape their treatments of events, however rare, according to conventional formats [and] in terms of existing discourses, reflecting an assumed or already

constructed public opinion, which in reality may be nothing more than a figment of the media's own imaginative capacities or worldview

(Thompson, 1998: 100)

The publicizing of an issue in the media can often 'give it a more "objective" status as a *real* (valid) issue of public concern than would be the case had it remained as merely a report made by experts and specialists' (Hall *et al.*, 1978: 61). At the same time, the media may be claiming to be speaking for the public, thus enlisting public legitimacy for any views expressed.

The notion that the media are sites for under-reporting, mis-reporting, and myth-making (Greenslade, 2004), is perhaps especially problematic for any analysis that is concerned with the *reception* and impact of media texts. As much as media producers can be selective with what to report, what to highlight, and in what frames, readers can also be selective. As mentioned above, readers typically negotiate their position in relation to the subject positions of an ideal reader. And while there are limits to the possible meanings and ideologies that are inherent in positions, different readers will respond to the same text differently (van Zoonen, 1994; Christie, 2000). A reader may understand or misunderstand, agree or disagree with any part of a text, and with the writer's framing of the issues at hand. Often, readers are selective of particular frames, reading what reinforces their world-view and already held opinions, while rejecting what may contradict or challenge their world-view – something that has been described as 'cognitive dissonance' (Schaff, 1984; see also Bing and Lombardo, 1997). Other readers may be aware and critical of particular frames, discourses, and subject positions, and therefore may resist them, appropriate them for their own ends, contest or reject them (Cosslett, 1996; Sunderland and Litosseliti, 2002). As we saw in Chapter 3, there is some scope for this kind of negotiation and agency in our con-stant engagement with discourses.

It is clear that we cannot assume that the producer and the receiver understand or interpret a text in the same way. Media and cultural studies analyses since the 1980s have turned their attention to how real audiences use texts, to show that they 'are not as passive, as easily fooled, or as inexorably positioned by texts, ideologies or state forces as was once thought' (Burn and Parker, 2003: 65; see also Hermes, 1995). But while such analyses may be able to address the question of reception, or more specif-ically, the relationship between the *encoding* of meaning (by the producers of media texts) and its *decoding* (by audiences), textual analyses are limited in this respect (Mills, 1994). As mentioned in Chapter 3, there are methodological problems with connecting micro-discursive and macro-sociological perspectives in general; and in this case, with connecting the language of media texts and the audience reception and interpretation of these texts. Some have asserted that the hybrid micro- and macro-perspectives of CDA approaches, in particular, have led to an under-analysis or a watering down of the micro-element (Widdowson, 1995; Stubbs, 1996; see also Chapter 3, Analysing discourse, p. 54). But although ethno-methodological approaches like CA (that focus on micro-perspectives) can be used to assess reception, for example, through interviews with magazine readers, they are limited in terms of recreating the original context of reading (Benwell, 2005). A combination of methods is therefore more likely to be productive, so that the discourses identified in readers' talk can be linked to other, intersecting, communicative contexts, such as media debates and everyday talk (ibid.). CDA is certainly useful in explicitly allowing for such links to be made (see the list adapted from Fairclough at the beginning of this section; also Chapter 3 for a more detailed discussion). However, it also needs to take into account the fact that analysts sometimes impose on a (media) text 'a much wider variety of interpretations' than would ever have been possible for those participating in its production and reception (Brown and Yule, 1983: 12).

In short, the analysis of media texts must take into account the fact that they are polysemic (Christie, 2000): they have a range of (not necessarily coherent) meanings, a range of audiences, and a range of interpretations. This is also true of the visual images and sounds (for the mass media are multi-modal) used in a synergistic relationship with language. A combination of theoretical and analytical approaches to the analysis of media texts should incorporate semiotic analyses, alongside discussions of discourse, design, production and distribution; in sum, it needs to incorporate some key elements:

- ■ a systematic approach to signification – to how texts make meanings, and how these meanings may be carried by a variety of different communicative forms, such as language, image, sound and gesture;
- ■ the capacity to integrate textual analysis with an analysis of audiences and their engagement with the texts under scrutiny;
- ■ the capacity to integrate textual analysis with the political, economic and social contexts in which texts are produced.

(Burn and Parker, 2003: 3–4)

For key discussions of theories of multi-modality and social semiotics, see particularly Hodge and Cress (1988) and Kress and van Leeuwen (2001).

Finally, analysis also needs to be extended from traditional media, such as newspapers, magazines, and television, to 'new' media, such as the Internet, the World Wide Web, email, SMS, etc. New media create a new, specific language, new interaction rules, new social rules, uses, and communities. For example, communication on the Internet is a hybrid of traditional and new communicative features; web advertisements are more similar to chats and assume an active involvement and interactivity with the addressees, compared to traditional ads; and although online ads, emails and SMS are written texts, they use spoken language elements, such as questions, imperatives, and simplified, abbreviated language (Aitchison and Lewis, 2003; Janoschka, 2004). Some of these new issues and implications are explored through recent research, seen for example in an e-journal on language and the Internet, which states that

technical and pragmatic conditions of use [of the Internet] have given rise to uses of language in a new mode that, while related to both written and spoken language, appears in many ways to represent a new language medium in its own right, in competition with the two other language media, and certainly with new communicative genres.

(Language@Internet Journal, www.languageatinternet.de)

GENDER IN THE WORLD OF MAGAZINES

The range of magazines targeted at women is extraordinary: from glossies, style and fashion magazines (like *Marie Claire*, *Cosmopolitan*, *Vogue*), to general interest (such as *Woman and Home*, *Executive Woman*, *Good Housekeeping*) and celebrity magazines (*Hello!*, *OK*, etc.). The UK market, for example, is saturated with magazines aiming to cover every stage of a woman's life. A sample from the past five years includes almost every age group, from *Barbie* (aimed at 5–10-year-olds) and *Mizz* (10–14-year-olds), to *The Lady* and *People's Friend* (aimed at 45+), with a whole range in between. Some magazines are global brands across the world and published in local editions (e.g. *Vogue*), some are country- and culture-specific (e.g. *Woman's Era* in India, or *Hints* in Nigeria), and some have online versions.

To survive in a very competitive market, each one tries to attract readers by distinguishing itself from other publications. The images used (e.g. of women executives, of women with children), the layout, and the texts appearing on the cover are key for attracting the reader's attention, building up their anticipation and encouraging them to purchase one magazine instead of another (McLoughlin, 2000). Magazine covers are striking, in that they immediately label the assumed or ideal reader, as the following examples illustrate:

Cosmopolitan	The World's No. 1 magazine for young women
She	For women who know what they want
B	Everything you want
Woman's Own	For the way you live your life and the way you'd like to
Company	For your freedom years
Minx	For girls with a lust for life
Femina (India)	For the woman of substance
Executive Woman	For women who really do mean business
Wench	Where women are, where they are going, and where they should be already

The use of personal pronouns, such as 'you' and 'your' above as well as 'we', is a common feature of the language of magazines, which assumes a set of shared views and values between the reader and the text producer (McRobbie, 1978; Winship, 1987). Crucially, these views and values are not only assumed to be the same, but they also remain implicit and unquestioned. Also, such personalization is a key element in the maintenance of a code of femininity in women's magazines. Consider the following extract from an editorial:

Extract (5A)

From *Good Housekeeping* editorial, February 1999

By Pat Roberts Cairns

> Most of us try not to think too much about fitness and diet right now, as we haven't shifted those few extra pounds from Christmas. But Rosemary Conley will get you into that leotard before you can say chocolate! Her philosophy is that we can all look better and feel fitter (... and look what it did for her!). But it has to be done at your own pace, which is why we've devised a healthy diet and exercise routine that anyone can follow. If you think that you've tried them all, try ours. The Hay Diet, the F-plan – you name it, we've done it too – so we're well placed to create a weight-loss and well-being plan that will work for you.

Here, common ground and solidarity with the reader are established through using pronouns as 'in-group' markers of inclusiveness ('most of us', 'we can all look better', 'we've done it too') and to directly address the reader: 'you' and 'your'. Contact with the reader is also maintained through words like 'anyone', imperatives ('try ours'), and colloquial expressions that mimic the speech patterns of the ideal reader ('look what it did for her!'). This synthesis of simulated solidarity or two-way friendly interaction between readers and magazine writers has been described as *synthetic personalization* (Fairclough, 1989: 62) or, in the case of women's magazines, *synthetic sisterhood* (Talbot, 1995). Further, magazine texts such as the above construct 'a confiding personal relationship with the individual reader, encouraging her to identify with the feminine community' (Eggins and Iedema, 1997: 169). This 'feminine community' is actually an idealized social setting, where economic and social differences, or differences in terms of ethnicity or race, are not made explicit. What matters is making the reader 'believe she is an autonomous individual, a voluntary member of a classless community of beautiful and successful women' (ibid.).

In addition, appearance is crucial in the 'feminine community', as seen in Extract (5A), and overwhelmingly in women's magazines. Femininity is hard work for women, and consumerism of beauty-enhancing products is promoted as the way to achieve the ideal feminine appearance. *Consumer femininity* (Talbot, 1992) is constructed in magazines (and advertisements and other media), as well as by women themselves:

> Women actively participate, spending on it their creative energies and time, as well as their money. Fashion and beauty standards are shaped by the manufacturing, advertising, fashion and magazine industries, which offer a range of material and symbolic resources for creating femininity. In participating in consumer femininity, a woman constructs herself as an object requiring work, establishing a practical relation with herself as a thing. This work is always required: no one can approximate the kinds of appearance offered without effort and expense.
>
> (Talbot, 1998: 172)

There is a presupposition in magazines, also seen in Extract (5A), that 'beauty work' is something that women necessarily undertake, and that it is a worthwhile enterprise. These are presented as shared or common-sense values. The ideal reader of women's magazines has been transformed over the years: 'woman' has become an 'individual' consumer (Winship, 1987; McCracken, 1993; Mills, 1995) involved in the ongoing project of becoming feminine – a project seen to be realized successfully through products. The point is stressed through instructional, 'how to' discourse that is structured as 'problem + solution', on virtually every topic. For example:

Vogue (UK)	Do you dare bin black? Here's how …
J17	Don't conform to uniform. Take a lesson from our style crew
Bella	How to get a beautiful bedroom (and solve your storage problems)
Hair	We show you how to get your guy looking like a Latin Lover
Bliss	40 ways to get his attention
Zest	If your body offends you, mild plastic surgery might make you feel happier

Linking desire to consumerism in general (McCracken, 1993), and femininity to consumption in particular, is central to the magazines' existence, given that their revenue comes primarily from advertising. Editors are under intense pressure to relate the magazine's content to advertising. Such pressures guide the large number of advertisements in the magazines, as well as the proliferation of genres such as advice columns, interviews, and 'advertorials' – where products are promoted less explicitly, as part of 'advice' to readers. In addition, consumer femininity is not restricted to the fashion, style, and health sections of magazines. In their analysis of two Australian magazines, Eggins and Iedema (1997) found that the workplace is turned into another domain where traditional femininity is strong, through business women's preoccupation with colour of furnishings or clothes and hairstyle; and through the sexualization of work relations (see also Chapter 6). A good illustration of both of these can be seen in the following example, taken from *Style*, a fashion supplement magazine to *The Sunday Times*:

Extract (5B)

From *Style* magazine, *The Sunday Times*, 19 September 2004
WHAT THEY [*name of fashion designer*] SAY:

> We empower women in the workplace and beyond by injecting sexy, sensuous curves into our tailoring. And when you take off the jacket, we have sexy tops – ideal for socialising after office hours.

Although the role that lifestyle magazines play in sustaining traditional notions of femininity has been widely criticized as patriarchal and limiting for women (Gilbert and Taylor, 1991; McCracken, 1993; Macdonald, 1995), it must also be acknowledged that they are pleasurable for many women (Caldas-Coulthard, 1996). Studies of reader reception show that women seek out bits of knowledge from magazines, rather than reading them from cover to cover, and they accumulate practical and aesthetic tips for transformation (Hermes, 1995). One can expect that some of the discourses populating the magazines will be assimilated, some appropriated, and some resisted by reluctant readers. It is difficult to know what reception processes are at work, not least because women are often reluctant to admit reading them, or construct themselves as distanced from the target readership.

The more interesting questions are, what discourses are available to women and what subject positions are set up for them in the magazine texts and images etc.? As Talbot (1998: 177) observes, magazines are multi-voiced and diverse. They draw on a range of genres (such as advice columns, advertisements, fictional narratives, letters, and other features) and on a range of discourses (journalism, economics, family, fashion, beauty, health science, even feminism). In addition to primarily setting up women as consumers continuously engaged in feminizing practices, discourses in magazines also construct the female readers as universally heterosexual, sexually passive/confident/manipulative, and primarily responsible for relationships. The apparent contradictions in some of these discourses arguably give editors, writers and readers room to move in terms of their ideas of femininity, so that they are not restricted to stereotypical or subordinate gender positions (Ballaster *et al.*, 1996; McRobbie, 1999).

Discourses of universal or 'compulsory heterosexuality' (Rich, 1980) constitute heterosexuality as desirable and normative, as in the example above from *Bliss* ('40 ways to get his attention'). Women are positioned as actively pursuing heterosexual relationships, preparing themselves for them physically and emotionally, dealing with them through a series of 'steps' and guidelines, analysing and discussing them. Sex generally takes up a large proportion of different magazine genres, and is particularly evident in advice columns, letters, and instructional and information-giving features. A 'male sexual drive' discourse (Hollway, 1984), according to which men cannot help having a high sexual drive, is prominent. It is taken for granted in the following examples:

Cosmopolitan	'What?' my doctor asked. 'You don't feel randy anymore? Your boyfriend must be desperate.'

(from a feature on sex therapy)

B	It's in their genes. Men (yes, even the nice ones) like naked women.

(from an advice column on the topic of pornography)

Here, the texts construct specific gender identities, clearly defined and differentiated; the examples reinforce the presupposition that women and men are biologically (and categorically) different – a presupposition presented as common sense and devoid of ambiguity or complexity. As Benwell observes, biological accounts of gender represent an enduring orthodoxy in women's and men's lifestyle magazines, their whole ethos being 'entirely predicated upon the assumption that men and women occupy exclusive sub-cultures which are polarised in terms of values, behaviours and styles, and that such differences, whether emotional, linguistic or lifestyle, are entirely natural and essential' (2003: 17). However, while 'male sexual drive' (in the examples above) is rarely explained or questioned, the discourses in magazines of women as sexual beings are multi-faceted and conflicting: women are encouraged to be on the receiving end of 'male sexual drive', be accommodating and accepting; at the same time, they are increasingly positioned as sexually confident; other times, as sexually manipulative or simply far too confident. Usually, we find a combination of these:

Extract (5C)

Is that it? And six other ways you fuel his first-night nerves.

[…] It'll be a hard thing [for him] to handle if you are [more experienced than he is]. It'll make him feel small in every sense.

(Company, March 1999; aimed at 18–26-year-old readers)

Girls on top
Too many commands ('Do this, Don't do that') can be off-putting and may make him feel like a bad lover or a sex toy. You won't get everything you'd like the first time, so it's best not to try. Giving him positive encouragement works best; just say, 'Mmm, I love that, don't stop!' … For ecstasy, you have to let go.

(19, February 1999, aimed at 17–19-year-old readers)

Even with a recent conquest, march into the bedroom reeling off a list of orders and you can guarantee his weapon won't be firing tonight.

(She, January 1999, aimed at 30–35-year-old readers)

What we find in examples such as these, is that men are also objectified in the magazines in ways that women have always been (consider also: 'Men: The Ultimate User's Guide', *New Woman*, January 1991). It is also common to construct male sexuality in magazines in competing ways, as both powerful and fragile (Seidler, 1992), and here we see examples of the latter. At the same time, a careful look at the examples illustrates that women's newly-found sexual confidence is framed in particular ways, from the perspective of the male partner and the effect of their confidence on the men. Eggins and Iedema (1997) also found that women's magazines maintain the notion of responsible heterosexuality, where women take responsibility for the success or failure of heterosexual relationships. This is seen especially in problem pages, where, similarly to the 'beauty project', women are the ones who actively pursue the 'relationship project', i.e. improving the communication and other aspects of relationships.

In addition, the examples above depict women 'on top', but not in positive ways to be aspired to. Women's assertiveness is depicted as potentially off-putting; there are limits, beyond which women are seen as aggressive, manipulative and threatening. (As we will see in Chapter 6, women are often faced with a double bind situation, where they are negatively evaluated, whatever their behaviour.) In other words, as others have suggested (Winship, 1987; Macdonald, 1995; Eggins and Iedema, 1997), magazines continue to mark non-traditional behaviour of women as marginal. This is also illustrated in the following extract, from an advice column in *Cosmopolitan* where a woman's sexuality is pathologized as a psychological disorder:

Extract (5D)

From *Cosmopolitan*, 'In the session' advice column, January 1999

> **Q:** I find it difficult to stay faithful to a man. When I embark on a relationship, I make it clear I want it to be 'open'. I don't think I could ever be monogamous, even though I'm sure that's what I should be in the future. Is there any way I can change?
>
> (Marion, 28)
>
> **A:** Marion is allowing her early, unpleasant experiences to colour her view of all men, so now she only attracts men who subsequently confirm her prejudices. If she stopped being so manipulative she might find that a different kind of man would start showing an interest.
>
> (Dr Raj Persaud)

When not marginalized, magazine representations of atypical women (as in the above extract) are appropriated on a surface level. For example, feminist terminology may be adopted, but 'without taking on board the ideology that underpins it' (Macdonald, 1995: 91). As Winship also put it, in relation to the notion of the 'superwoman', a woman having it all in professional, domestic, maternal, and romantic roles: 'Superwoman is only the elitist and individual success story – "I'm all right sisters" – which leaves untouched the deep problems for most women of how to satisfactorily combine "home" and "work" without being made to suffer for it' (1987: 157).

In this understanding, both the greater variety of magazines and the more pronounced changes in women's lives have not necessarily led to a greater range of femininities available through those media. Further, even the femininities available can be problematic, given that many of the magazine representations may bear no relation to women's and men's actual experience, for example, representations of the 'perfect' woman as very thin and attractive, and the 'perfect' man as strong and athletic. If we accept that magazines play a role in processes of social and cultural change, then we need to question both the representations and their effects. One of the obvious effects is the pressure on women and men to live up to unrealistic representations of their bodies, of their relationships, and so on – a pressure which may exacerbate or at least contribute to problems such as anorexia.

Question 2

Refer to any of the extracts included so far in this section.
(Alternatively, choose a text from a women's magazine, e.g. an article on health or beauty, an interview, an advice column, etc.)

Who is the ideal reader in the extracts?

In what ways are women/men positioned in the extracts? What femininities and masculinities are constructed? Why?

What kind of power relations are assumed/created?

What are some possible ways in which readers can respond to the various positionings in the texts?

How do the cultural practices in the texts compare with those in other cultures?

In addition to women's magazines, feminist accounts of gender and language have more recently also turned to men's lifestyle magazines. The advent of men's lifestyle magazines is a relatively recent phenomenon. Magazines that were targeted at young professional affluent men – such as *Arena, GQ, FHM, Esquire* – emerged in Britain in the late 1980s, and became popular over the past two decades. With them came a new form of masculinity, the so-called 'new man': arguably a media creation, with an unembarrassed interest in fashion, health, leisure, style and appearance, as well as in more serious and even feminist-friendly issues (Benwell, 2002). This marked a new relationship between masculinity and previously 'feminine' endeavours around desire and commodity consumption (Nixon, 1996). The 'new man' was built on the assumption that men's 'transformation' is both desirable and possible; and, as in women's magazines, something that can be achieved through consumer products. In addition to this kind of consumer masculinity (Edwards, 1997), the 'new man' is decidedly heterosexual, professional, middle class, and typically white. Above all, he is someone men can aspire to be. In the words of Lee Eisenberg, editor-in-chief of *Esquire* magazine: 'There are two kinds of men – the good and the bad. If you've got the first, buy him a copy of *Esquire*. If he's the second, there's help at hand.' This aspirational, transformed man is also the ideal reader of advertising in these magazines. Ads such as the one for Loake shoes overleaf neatly combine the elements of being a 'new man'.

The last phrase in this ad which makes reference to unwanted sexual advances ('If you think she means "yes" when she says "no"') emphasizes the purportedly anti-sexist discourses espoused by the 'new man'. In many ways, however, the 'new man' is a contradictory development: on the one hand re-packaging an old, traditional (or 'hegemonic' – see Connell, 1995) masculinity, based on male success, wealth, power, heterosexual desire; and on the other, entertaining progressive and anti-sexist discourses to approach relationships and family life. Similarly to representations of the 'superwoman' above, ideas of 'breadwinner' masculinity and new fatherhood do not

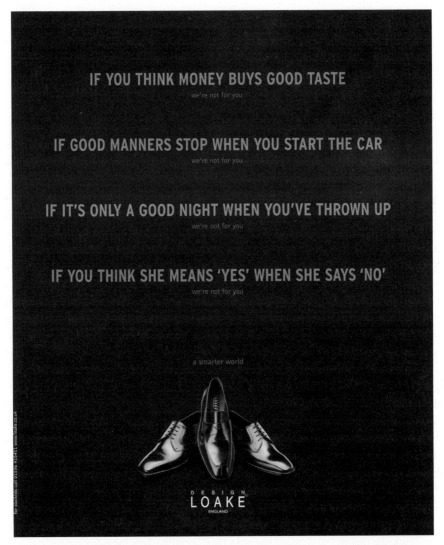

Fig. 5.1 Loake advertisement from 2001. Reproduced with permission.

sit comfortably together. It is suggested that the more progressive ideas about a 'new' masculinity are simply echoed at a surface level, while leaving the existing gender practices unchanged (see also Chapter 6, Moving forward, p. 127, for similar arguments in relation to the workplace). In parallel to conflicting traditional and progressive discourses of masculinity, there is also a tension between the celebration of a heterosexual masculinity and the promotion of 'female-oriented' beauty and grooming products in the magazines. Benwell, for example, shows how the images of such products are heterosexualized by including an admiring woman, and through the use of irony and humour, as in the following example (2002: 164):

> Water for Men: This isn't some fancy, foreign water, full of poncy minerals. This extra-butch bottled water contains just one mineral: salt, and plenty of it. And because it's oestrogen-free it won't turn you into a eunuch like tap water does.
>
> (*GQ*, June 1997: 29)

This kind of description ensures that a distance is achieved between the reader/consumer and both femininity and homosexuality (see also Edwards, 1997). This distance is further pronounced in the more recent and more defensive magazines for men, such as *Loaded*.

In 1994, the launch of *Loaded* magazine in Britain precipitated the creation of an alternative male identity, deliberately opposed to the 'new man', and reverting to a more traditional type of masculinity: the 'new lad'. The 'new lad' is a more mid-market, reactionary, badly behaving type, who celebrates his interest in sport, sex, drinking and male bonding (Edwards, 1997; Jackson *et al.*, 2001; Nixon, 2001). *Loaded* claims to be targeting the average man, constructing this type of masculinity as more 'real' than, and an antidote to, the feminist-friendly, sensitive 'new man'.

The discursive construction of the 'new lad' draws on certain key elements: an exaggerated emphasis on the certainty of gender and the need to re-assert traditional masculinity through the exclusion of 'the other'; irony-as-knowingness; ambiguity, ambivalence, contradiction; and strategic negotiation of oppositional discourses such as progressive or feminist ones (Benwell, 2003). The re-assertion of traditional masculinity involves addressing women as sexual objects, celebrating exclusive male friendship, as well as drawing on working-class values. Exclusion of 'other' identities is accomplished through the magazines distancing themselves from homosexuality, and ignoring issues of ethnicity, as well as work and fatherhood. In addition, the magazines are full of irony, humour, ambiguity and ambivalence – all of which provide a distancing effect from potentially objectionable ideas – allowing for claims that they are used in an ironic way, and thus as 'harmless fun'.

A good example of this irony-as-knowingness can be found in a series of advertisements for TEAC hi-fi systems that appeared in *Loaded* (1999). One of these ads is dominated by the image of a scantily-clad smiling young woman, facing the reader in a provocative posture and a state of half-undress. At the bottom of the ad, the product, a small hi-fi system called *The Reference 3000 Micro System*, is pictured. At the top of the ad, the headline reads: 'It's Amazing What You Can Get Out Of A Small

Body'. In another ad for the same line of products, which is entitled 'Toys for the Boys', we see a man at the centre of the page, undressed from the waist up, surrounded by three made-up women in provocative black dresses, with exposed cleavage. The small product, this time three hi-fi separates, is pictured at the bottom of the page. The ad claims to be

> Introducing a system designed from the outset for the discerning man … Each component is a true hi-fi separate on its own and you can mix and match them to achieve your own ideal system using CD, tape or MiniDisc. Whichever you choose, with its champagne metal finish, it looks simply gorgeous.

This text is followed by: 'It is the definitive *toy for the boys*. Unless you prefer one dressed in black.'

Finally, the same idea is reproduced in a similar ad for TEAC products, where the man, who is in the process of removing his shirt, is again surrounded by three attractive sexily dressed young women. At the top of the page, the first thing a reader sees is a thought bubble linked to the man: 'I Want To Have All Three …'; and then, towards the bottom of the page the word 'Systems!', next to the pictured three products. This is a typical arrangement in advertisements, where the top section is there to 'promise', and the lower section to provide the information needed (McLoughlin, 2000). Also, like many advertisements, this one establishes primarily visual contact with the reader; the image takes precedence over the text in both catching the reader's attention and telling the story of the advertising message (see Janoschka, 2004, for more on the interplay between text and image).

Of course, it is extremely common, as we will see in the next section, for women's bodies to be used in advertisements to sell products. However, in these examples, the objectification of the women, i.e. their identification with the product and something 'boys' can play with ('what you can get out of a small body', 'toys for the boys', 'I want to have all three …') is so unmistakable that it can only work if read as a knowingly ironic and humorous intention on the part of the producers of the ad. Such intention arguably operates as an invitation for readers to share the joke and as a pre-emptive disclaimer, which makes the ads immune to criticism for being sexist (see also Mills, 1998; Christie, 2000). The ads cleverly leave open the less questionable interpretations of the ads: that 'a small body' and 'toys' refer to the micro hi-fi system, and that 'to have all three' refers to purchasing all three products. Although this is somehow undermined by the fact that the ads are dominated by close-up images of women's bodies, while the product takes very little space at the bottom of the page, it nevertheless remains a possible interpretation. Benwell describes this well as

> a cheeky knowingness and self-reflexiveness (commonly glossed as irony), which enables [the text or message] to simultaneously affirm and deny its values [and] allows a writer to articulate an anti-feminist sentiment, whilst explicitly distancing himself from it, and thus disclaiming responsibility from or even authentic authorship of it.

(2002: 152)

Sexism, in other words, is taking different, new forms in these and other media (see later). As Mills (2002) also maintains, in relation to the British television programme *Men Behaving Badly*, exaggerated sexism cannot be objected to as sexist, but rather is perceived as intentionally humorous or playful, and consequently unchallenged. The same may apply to some of the television programmes aired on British TV at the time of writing (e.g. *Wife Swap*, *Ladette to Lady*, *Britain's Worst Wife*).

The reasons for the 'new lad' phenomenon in *Loaded* and similar magazines (*FHM, Front, Maxim*) are complicated, and beyond the scope of this chapter. However, a brief consideration of suggested reasons may clarify our understanding of the dominant discourses and the masculinities and femininities evident in these magazines. A relatively straightforward reason is that the 'new lad' formula of consumerism, drink, sport and sex has been very successful in terms of sales, and increased readership brings increased revenue to the magazines. As a result, more magazines for men are becoming more 'laddish' in their approach. It has also been suggested that the celebration of 'laddishness' is a (not necessarily systematic or coherent) response to the instability in gender roles precipitated by feminism, and to an alleged loss of the power of traditional masculinity (Stevenson *et al.*, 2000). The reassertion of traditional masculinity may be seen in frequent 'crisis of masculinity' discourses, such as in 'Let him put down his foot for a change' (see p. 113); and in the accommodation and appropriation of feminist discourses in ways that eventually undermine women (Talbot, 1997; Jackson *et al.*, 2001; Benwell, 2003). We will see examples of these later. While such reassertion may be damaging for women, it is also doubtful whether it actually does any favours for men, in terms of addressing their emotional and relational needs with women and family (Stevenson *et al.*, 2000).

THE CONSTRUCTION OF GENDER IN ADVERTISEMENTS

On the cover of a humorous book of postcards with the title *The Woman's Place in the Classic Age of Advertising* (2000), we find an image (from the early twentieth century) of a woman next to a bottle of the product being advertised. It asks a question: 'You mean a woman can open it …?'; and offers an answer: 'Easily – without a knife blade, a bottle opener, or even a husband!' Other ads from around the same period include, for example, an ad for *Gillette* razors:

Keep an eye on your wife
– possibly she isn't as happy as she seems […]

Is she worrying about you? After all, most wives are loyal and proud, and rather reluctant to speak up. This may be miles from the fact – but there's a chance she's distressed because you aren't as careful about shaving as you were in times past.

an ad for a cereal:

A romantic moment
Alone at last the newly-weds pledge their love anew.

[Woman's speech bubble reads]: 'Hubby, darling. From now on, you get a cereal that has food value'

[Man's speech bubble reads]: 'Angel wifie, if it doesn't have flavor I'll go straight home to mother'

and an ad for a food processor:

The Chef does everything but cook
– that's what wives are for!

Advertising reflects the social and cultural trends of the time, and although we may nowadays view these examples as exaggerated, incredible, or even ridiculous, they did fit the gender roles and sensibilities of the time. Advertisements, like other media genres, contain patterns of textual choices and paralinguistic features, like images, gestures, facial expressions, etc. In the spatially constrained genre of advertising, these choices and features have informative as well as persuasive functions. The AIDA (Attention, Interest, Desire, Action) concept describes persuasion in advertising as a series of mental processes, where the first crucial step is to attract the addressee's attention; this is followed by establishing an interest in and desire for the product advertised, thus leading to action, i.e. the purchase of the product (Janoschka, 2004). In addition to the various textual and non-textual features, advertisements also carry multiple voices, associations from other texts, discourses and systematic beliefs or ideologies (Myers, 1994, 1998). In constructing particular subject positions for the readers or viewers, advertisements play a role in constituting identities.

Similarly to other genres in women's magazines, women are placed primarily in the subject position of consumer in the ads. This is not surprising; women currently buy or influence the purchase of 80 per cent of consumer goods, including products such as cars. The early twentieth-century car advertisements were neither subtle nor sarcastic in their attempt to attract women buyers through lines such as 'Ladies! Here's the key to your driving problems' or (attached to an image of a terrified woman driver) 'The mini automatic. For simple driving'. And although the car ads of that time, such as the one that includes the following text, may now be seen as outdated, the use of such gender stereotypes (in subtler ways) has been persistent.

Ladies' dept: what she looks for –

Comfort and roominess, smart gay colours, really large luggage trunk, easily adjustable seat, sensible doors (– safe for children), easy gear change

Mainly for men: what he insists on –

More miles per gallon, good acceleration, safe braking, visibility, efficient springing, handling

In recent years, this kind of approach has been replaced by an emphasis on consumer femininity discourses, where buying a car is linked by advertisers to ideas of femininity and women's bodies. One such ad consists of the close-up image of a woman's breast, pierced by a key ring exhibiting the logo and name of the car being advertised, and the line 'EXTRAORDINARY what young ladies are getting into these days'. Another ad, for Renault cars, plays with images of a young, attractive, made-up woman in two similar postures: first sitting in a hairdresser's chair having her hair done, and then sitting in the driving seat of the car advertised. The reader is told: 'Stay beautiful' and then 'Drive the safest car in its class', accompanied by text which includes the extract:

> As you know, beauty should be more than skin deep. That is why our new Renault Mégane not only looks stunning, it also features our most effective, personalised safety system ever … So if you want to stay beautiful, use your head and call … for details of your nearest dealer.

This is a good example of using a theme that is expected to appeal to women, in order to sell the idea of car safety, alongside a car's looks.

A considerable number of ads are targeted to a *specific* female consumer: young, professional, attractive, well-groomed, single and independent. This is the woman targeted, for instance, in the various texts and ads of *Cosmopolitan* – and its 44 different national versions. As Hermes (1995) found, the typical *Cosmopolitan* reader has a disposable income, wears expensive clothes and make-up, and tends to have a job. Machin and Thornborrow (2003) show that *Cosmopolitan* creates a fantasy world, where women acquire power through the clothes they wear and places they frequent, but also through sex, seduction, and social manoeuvring. Pictures of sexy, seductive, made-up women similarly furnish the receiver 'with a temporary fantasy of an ideal self' (Hermes, 1995: 39). These elements can be seen, for example, in one of the print and screen ads for 17 cosmetics, where an over-sized lipstick is depicted as a missile, with the caption 'Be afraid boys, be very afraid' and the strapline 'IT'S NOT MAKE-UP … IT'S AMMUNITION'.

Feminists have long objected to ads that portray women as sexual objects, a state of affairs that neither the impact of feminism nor a climate of 'political correctness' has affected significantly. Images of women's sexuality and physical attributes are used to sell countless numbers of products, very often when the appearance of women's bodies is both irrelevant and unnecessary. We have seen examples of this in the hi-fi ads in *Loaded* magazine above. Another example is an ad by British Telecom for a BT EasyReach pager. The scene for the ad contains a close-up of a blonde young woman in a low-cut dress and make-up, sitting at a restaurant table holding a glass of wine. She is shown gazing adoringly into, we presume, the eyes of a man across the table. The man is not visible in this close-up picture, but we can see his fingers holding the restaurant menu, and on top of it, in capital letters, the words: 'ALRIGHT STEVE? … WE'VE JUST GONE 1-0 UP. HAVE YOU SCORED YET? CHEERS, BRIAN.' Here, the punning use of 'scored' refers to both football and getting closer to the woman. This ad appeared in many newspapers and magazines in Britain, rather than just being restricted to magazines with a 'new lad' readership. It is also easy to find other similar examples in advertisements for a range of financial services, such as the one on p. 111.

An identical image to the one opposite (but with a different woman) also appears in an advertisement for Cheltenham and Gloucester mortgages, advertising a mortgage at a discounted rate. In this example, the script next to the woman's bare back reads: 'Mine's incredibly low', a pun referring to the woman's dress and to the rate offered. In both cases, the image is of a woman in a sexually suggestive and passive pose, with a fixed smile, as the object of the 'male gaze' (Goffman, 1976). In addition to appearing willing and ready to provide sexual pleasure, women also typically appear 'pieced up' in advertisements, with the focus on their breasts, legs, or (as above) back. In contrast, when men are the object of the viewer's gaze, they tend to be active and non-sexual; and when they occupy a subject position by gazing out at the reader, they tend to appear as hostile and unsmiling, often with arms crossed or legs apart (Benwell, 2002).

We also often find advertisements where the objectification and the domestication of women go hand in hand. An ad for Wonderbra depicts a blonde young woman posing in her bikini underwear, with the caption 'I can't cook. Who cares?' The woman appears to be confident and sexually assertive. Nevertheless, the implication in the text is that there are two key achievements for women – being good at cooking and being sexy/attractive – and in the absence of one, the other will suffice. Also, in 2000, the supermodel Naomi Campbell posed in a black bikini, stiletto heels, and silver rubber kitchen gloves for a magazine advertisement for Persil washing-up liquid. The text in this ad asked 'What does it take to get me into rubber?' and the answer: 'PERSIL WASHING UP LIQUID'S FREE DESIGNER GLOVES'. This ad appeared in women's glossy magazines, men's upmarket lifestyle monthly magazines, as well as men's 'laddish' magazines. Feminists have argued for a long time that images of women's bodies, which are presumed to be playful and harmless, may actually help solidify the objectification of women, and in some cases contribute to a wider climate of violence against women. The link with violence may be seen in some more offensive examples of advertisements, such as an ad where a nude female model advertises chocolates with the slogan 'You say No; We hear Yes', and an ad for a brand of cream with the words 'Even whipped or beaten, [X] stays creamy' (where X constitutes a pun for a woman's name as well as the brand name).

Although such images of women as sexual objects in ads (and popular culture in general) persist, there have also been certain changes. First, the Advertising Standards Authority (ASA) in Britain reports an increase in complaints about the use of sexual titillation to sell products. The ASA has upheld complaints, for example, for an ad for industrial cleaning equipment, which pictured a woman in a bikini pulling against a motorized cleaner with the slogan: 'Chained to your old scrubber? Not any more, ride-on scrubbers made easy.' Although complainants' objections tend to be more about the offensiveness of ads, and less about their sexism, when complaints do focus on sexism, they do so about both the language and images of the ads, and about both women's and men's portrayal (Cameron, 2004). This is the second thing that has been changing in recent years, namely, that men are often also objectified in advertisements – something

Fig. 5.2 © Cantor Index.

perhaps also reflected in the sharp increase of men complaining to the ASA about the way they are depicted by advertisers. Examples of this include a Coca Cola TV ad, where the body of a half-naked man with model looks and a job cleaning office windows is the object of women's gaze; an ad for Lee jeans, depicting a woman resting her stiletto heel on the naked prostrate body of a man, with the slogan 'Put the boot in'; and an ad for Club 18–30, with a close-up picture of the front of a man's pelvis, in boxer shorts, with the caption 'Girls. Can we interest you in a package holiday?' Male complainants to the ASA have objected to being depicted in ways similar to those in which women have always been (*The Observer*, 2001): not only as sex objects (with unfeasibly muscular and lean bodies), but generally as objects to be consumed, as seen in a Lambrini sparkling wine ad in which a woman tells a friend that she has lost a lot of 'useless fat', and her friend's reply is the line, 'So you dumped him then?'

In addition, complaints focus on the portrayal of men as incompetent and stupid in advertisements, an idea often left unquestioned. In an ad with the title 'At last an oven men can use', readers are told that the oven 'does the thinking for you': it 'will set the right cooking combination' [...] 'You don't have to weigh the food or set the cooking time. This leaves loads of time for more important "man things" like surfing the net, shelf fixing or concentrated Sports Channel watching'. A range of gendered discourses are drawn on in this ad, and from a receiver's point of view, are necessary in order to make sense of this message. The producers are careful not to alienate either male or female audiences. The ad appeals to a male ideal reader by emphasizing the labour-saving qualities of an essentially domestic and traditionally 'female' product. A distancing from both femininity and homosexuality, coupled with a gentle mockery of men, is achieved through the listing of those 'important "man things"'. It also appeals to females by emphasising their alleged superiority in the mastery of cooking appliances: 'Females (who naturally think for themselves) will be pleased to know that they can take control' of the product's functions and 'create their own culinary masterpieces'. What is absent from these discourses is a mention of men being interested in and enjoying cooking (see also Extract (3B), Chapter 3), and of women who can benefit from more time to do other, presumably 'woman' things.

Moreover, what is striking about many advertisements, including the one discussed above, is the 'gender differences' or 'gender polarization' discourses that they draw on and perpetuate. We have discussed this in various parts of the book and earlier in this chapter. Media texts, and ads in particular, emphasize the 'otherness' of men and the 'otherness' of women, in various positive, negative, and humorous ways. Sometimes, this is articulated explicitly, as in the example of an ad for the fruit drink J_2O (in 'Man-sized Bottles' as a stress on manliness is deemed necessary to sell a 'soft' product) with the caption 'US MEN LOVE MAPS AND WE LOVE J_2O'. It reads:

Few books are as interesting to a man as a road atlas. That's because we love roads. Stop off in any service station in the land and you'll hear one bloke telling another how he got to the M1 via the A414–A12 North Circular, then bypassed Birmingham with the M45–A45–A499...

Most of the time, however, gender polarization works on the level of assumption or presupposition, as in the Persil detergent ad depicting a man with a baby pram, and the slogan 'Of course he's sensitive. He cried when Millwall lost.' In this example, discourses of traditional masculinity (strong silent men) first appear to be disrupted, an idea then undermined through irony, with the end result of reasserting the traditional masculinity stereotype. Consider also the example in Figure 5.3 (p. 114).

This ad is playing with various gender stereotypes: the strong, silent, active man; the emotional, relational, talkative woman; and the idea of the male provider, an idea in which women are constructed as being complicit and which they are keen to exploit. The ideal reader of the ads is male, in a heterosexual relationship, with disposable income; and someone who appreciates traditional rituals of courtship and marriage. Polarized and traditional notions of gender appeal directly to such a reader and likely consumer of diamond jewellery. It becomes clearer that the ideal reader in this case is male, once we consider more of the advertisements produced for the same range of products (Figures 5.4 and 5.5, pp. 115 and 116).

The texts assume that a proposal of marriage is something anticipated and pursued by all women, that men are responsible for the proposing and women for the receiving, that women will indeed accept the proposal, and that a diamond is the most appropriate manifestation of that kind of love and commitment. In line with compulsory heterosexuality discourses (see earlier), women and men are expected to progress from being a couple to being a married couple, and in the world of ads such as these, women and men deal with this prospect differently. The 'tearful acceptance speech' draws on discourses of women as emotional (discussed elsewhere in the book), while the warning not to keep a woman waiting alludes to the stereotype of women being strident or difficult (and by extension, of men being henpecked). This stereotype holds strong in various cultural representations used for selling products; for example, this can be seen in its crudest form in the message 'Beware of the wife', printed on a doormat found in a South London market. Macdonald (1995), among others, has suggested that the negative depictions of 'real' women in magazines (wives, girlfriends) may be an indirect response to the threat of women's increased participation in public life and the workplace.

Another way in which the threat of women is made salient in advertisements is in 'crisis of masculinity' discourses, and generally in how feminist discourses are accommodated and appropriated. In an example of an ad for leisure racing, with the title 'FORGET EQUALITY. LET HIM PUT DOWN HIS FOOT FOR A CHANGE', we find the following text: 'Inside every man there's a boy racer trying to get out. So, this Christmas, why not let him? [...] And should you want to challenge his manhood, you can always join in yourself'. As we have seen in the section on magazines, the ambiguity and irony of advertisements such as this can gloss potentially unpalatable messages. The ambiguity in this example is achieved through a pun: 'let him put his foot down', which can refer to racing as well as to the release of pent-up frustration and the assertion of power over another. While the sentence

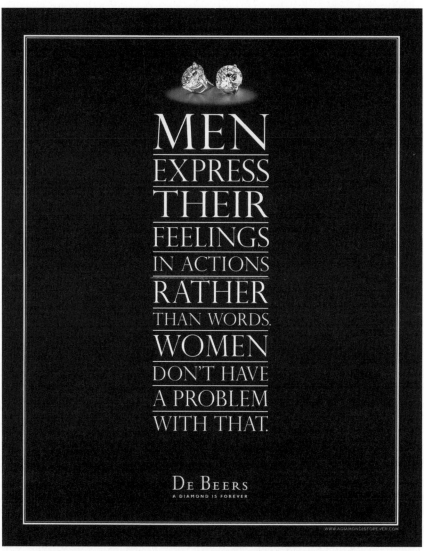

Fig. 5.3 © De Beers, 1994–2000. Reproduced with permission.

Fig. 5.4 © De Beers, 1994–2000. Reproduced with permission.

Fig. 5.5 © De Beers, 1994–2000. Reproduced with permission.

'And should you want to challenge his manhood, you can always join in yourself' entertains a feminist discourse, the ad on the whole appropriates such discourses at a surface level. More specifically, the use of imperatives ('forget equality', 'let him'), questions ('why not let him?'), and lexical choice as in the phrase 'for a change', constructs gender equality as something complete and achieved, a thing of the past. Lazar (2005) refers to this as a discourse of 'popular post-feminism' or a 'global neo-liberal discourse of post-feminism', which states that, once certain gains have been met, feminism has achieved its purpose. These constructions of alleged equality, or even reversal of gender roles, pay superficial lipservice to feminism yet obscure actual gender inequalities and the differences in women's and men's experience, in terms of their roles, expectations, and power positions in society. Moreover, representations of the 'superwoman' in magazines ('having it all'), as well as those of men in various contradicting roles, have the same misleading effect. The appropriation of feminism and feminism values for commercial gain often 'entails an insidious subversion of feminism as a political force' (Lazar, 2005: 15).

Discourses of 'popular post-feminism' in advertising are usually in conflict with women's and men's actual experiences and social roles, thus supporting new forms of sexism. As Williamson (2003) elaborates, the concept of sexism has fallen into disuse in recent years, and social imagery in ads – of men at home and women in the boardroom – has airbrushed away the real day-to-day sexism that women still face. She writes:

> 'Social' advertising has achieved a gender revolution before the fact, creating an implicitly post-feminist world in which women are powerful and men compliant (or, if not, about to get their comeuppance). It is a depiction of gender relations that fuels sexism, while banishing it: the portrayal of contemporary society as female-dominated generates powerful sexist feelings which, however, cannot 'innocently' be expressed in this imaginary present.
>
> (*The Guardian*, 31 May 2003)

Williamson asserts that sexist feelings are now channelled into 'retro-sexist' imagery, where overtly sexist scenarios are couched in outmoded presentation or styling, 'to imply that it's knowingly done, self-aware, even kitsch'. She describes retro-sexism as 'sexism with an alibi: it appears at once past and present, "innocent" and knowing, a conscious reference to another era, rather than an unconsciously driven part of our own'. This kind of highly ironized and tongue-in-cheek sexism is disarming feminist critique and leaves open few possibilities for contestation (Mills, 2002).

To conclude this chapter, many of the points made so far can be thrown into sharp focus by examining two different versions of the same advertisement. Consider the following two advertisements for the same product, which appeared in the same issue of *Living South* magazine (a magazine distributed to residents of parts of South London, in the UK).

Then consider the questions at the top of p. 119:

Fig. 5.6 © John Corby Limited.

Fig. 5.7 © John Corby Limited.

> ### Question 3
>
> Refer to the Corby Trouser Press advertisements.
>
> Who is the ideal reader of each of the ads?
>
> Can you identify any of the linguistic features discussed in the first section of this chapter?
>
> In what ways are women/men positioned in each of the ads? What femininities and masculinities are constructed? Why?
>
> What kind of power relations are assumed/created?
>
> What are some possible ways in which readers can respond to the various positionings in the ads?
>
> How do the cultural practices in the ads compare with those in other cultures?

In addition to the notion of the 'superwoman', mentioned previously, one of the points raised by the ads above, and not discussed so far, is the idea that women are assumed to be achieving an identity through their relationships with partners, husbands, and children – something not necessarily assumed of men. Lazar describes this as women's 'other-centredness', which she illustrates through analysis of a government advertising campaign in Singapore. She argues that 'women's energies in realising their personal interests, including the pursuit of a career outside the home, are channelled towards seeking fulfilment almost entirely in and through others' (2002: 112); and that this feminine self-identity through other-centredness in the ads is rooted in a 'discourse of conservative gender relations'. Lazar's analysis, more particularly, illustrates that this discourse co-exists in the ads with a 'discourse of egalitarian gender relations', which appears to support women's personal and career choices. This is necessary for the ad to be able to reach the large numbers of modern, educated women – and this would seem to also apply to the ideal reader of the Corby Trouser Press ads above. What is problematic, however, is the asymmetry which can be seen in both ads above, in terms of who uses the product, to support whom, in what ways, and with what consequences. As Lazar argues, 'Men's involvement with women and children does not entail a suppression of their own self-interests. Indeed, heterosexual masculinity thrives upon the other-centredness of women, as it helps men further their own personal and career goals' (ibid.: 113).

SUMMARY

- ■ Changes to media markets, such as globalization and increasing competition, have also led to changes in media discourse: 'infotainment', 'conversationalization', and a tendency to use sensationalist, personalized, and adversarial language.
- ■ The media are sites for the representation, construction, and contestation of

knowledge, values, social relations, identities and ideologies – including gendered ones.

■ The media address an ideal reader, viewer, or listener. Actual readers, viewers, or listeners have to negotiate a relationship with the subject positions offered in media texts and images.

■ Women are often portrayed in the media through their physical attributes, as sex objects, as mothers and wives, in passive or supportive roles, and as victims. Men are overwhelmingly depicted as strong, active and independent – but also often objectified too. Media representations of gender are changing, becoming less coherent, more subtle, and potentially more insidious.

■ Mass media addressees (e.g. women in magazines) are typically treated as a unified community with shared values and characteristics.

■ Media texts are produced by teams and shaped by a range of editorial processes, policies, agendas, production formats and decisions. Key news values dictate an emphasis on particular events, and on particular 'frames' or points of view.

■ The reception of media texts is multi-faceted, and their interpretation is not necessarily shared by producers and addressees.

■ Analyses of media texts need to combine textual/discursive, semiotic, and audience perspectives; to consider their design, production and distribution, and the social and political contexts in which they are embedded; and to extend to 'new' media and their rules, uses, and communities.

■ Personalization (e.g. through the use of personal pronouns) is a key element of the language of magazines. It both assumes shared values between producer and receiver, and helps establish a simulated solidarity or two-way interaction with the receiver. In women's magazines, such personalization encourages women to identify with an idealized, unified feminine community.

■ Linking desire to consumerism, and femininity to consumption, is central in women's magazines, where revenue comes primarily from advertising. In addition to consumers continuously engaged in feminizing practices, women are also depicted as sexually passive, or confident and manipulative, and as responsible for relationships. Atypical women are marginal, and feminism is appropriated at surface level.

■ Other discourses in the magazines include 'compulsory heterosexuality', 'male sexual drive', and 'gender differences'.

■ Men's magazines also construct men as consumers. The masculinities available in these magazines, the 'new man' and the 'new lad', are conflicting as well as characterized by contradictions. Progressive and feminist discourses are simply echoed in both cases, and a distance is achieved in the texts and images between the readers and femininity, as well as homosexuality.

■ The discursive construction of the 'new lad' is characterized by an exaggerated emphasis on the certainty of gender and the need to re-assert traditional masculinity; and by irony-as-knowingness and ambiguity, which deflect criticism of objectionable or sexist sentiments.

■ Advertisements make use of linguistic and non-linguistic features, and draw on a range of voices, discourses and ideologies, in their effort to inform and persuade.

■ Feminists have criticized the use of women's sexuality and physical attributes to sell almost any product, for contributing to a general view of women as objects that can be used. Such objectification can also be found nowadays in some advertisements' portrayal of men.

■ 'Gender differences' or 'gender polarization' discourses are widespread, explicitly and implicitly, in advertisements. Women are stereotypically constructed as emotional, strident or difficult; men as suffering, in crisis. Conservative and progressive gender discourses often co-exist. These, like discourses of 'post-feminism' that claim that feminism is now redundant, can, however, obscure the actual gender inequalities in society, and perpetuate new forms of sexism.

FURTHER READING

General references

Fairclough, N. (1995) *Media Discourse*. London: Arnold.

Gauntlet, D. (2002) *Media, Gender and Identity: An Introduction*. London: Routledge.

Hollows, J. (2000) *Feminism, Femininity and Popular Culture*. Manchester: Manchester University Press.

Macdonald, M. (2003) *Exploring Media Discourse*. London: Arnold.

Talbot, M., Atkinson, K. and Atkinson, D. (2003) *Language and Power in the Modern World*. Edinburgh: Edinburgh University Press (Chapter 1).

van Zoonen, L. (1994) *Feminist Media Studies*. Newbury Park, CA: Sage.

Magazines

Ballaster, R., Beetham, M., Frazer, E. and Hebron, S. (1991) *Women's Worlds: Ideology, Femininity and the Woman's Magazine*. London: Macmillan.

Benwell, B. (ed.) (2003) *Masculinity and Men's Lifestyle Magazines*. Oxford: Blackwell.

Crewe, B. (2003) *Representing Men: Cultural Production and Producers in the Men's Market*. Oxford: Berg.

Hermes, J. (1995) *Reading Women's Magazines*. Cambridge: Polity Press.

Jackson, P., Stevenson, N. and Brooks, K. (2001) *Making Sense of Men's Magazines*. Cambridge: Polity Press.

Macdonald, M. (1995) *Representing Women: Myths of Femininity in the Popular Media*. London: Arnold.

Talbot, M. (1998) Multiple voices in magazines, in M. Talbot *Language and Gender: An Introduction*. Cambridge: Polity Press, pp. 176–84.

Winship, J. (1987) *Inside Women's Magazines*. London: Pandora.

Advertising

Cook, G. (2001) *The Discourse of Advertising*, 2nd edn. London: Routledge.

Goffman, E. (1976). *Gender Advertisements*. London: Macmillan.

Myers, G. (1994) *Words in Ads*. London: Arnold.

Romaine, S. (1999) *Communicating Gender*. Mahwah, NJ: Lawrence Erlbaum. (Chapter 9).

Talbot, M. (2000) Strange bedfellows: feminism in advertising, in M. Andrews and M. Talbot (eds) *'All the World and Her Husband': Women in 20th-Century Consumer Culture*. London: Cassell.

Vestergaard, T. and Schrøder, K. (1985) *The Language of Advertising*. Oxford: Blackwell.

Other references

FWCW Platform for Action – Women and the Media, www.un.org/womenwatch/daw/beijing/platform/media.htm

Language@Internet Journal, www.languageatinternet.de

Style magazine, *The Sunday Times*, 19 September 2004.

Postcards: *The Woman's Place in the Classic Age of Advertising* (2000), Prion.

John Arlidge, Men fight back over sexist TV adverts, *The Observer*, 9 December 2001.

Judith Williamson, Sexism with an alibi, *The Guardian*, 31 May 2003.

6 Gender and language in the workplace

> It is simply not possible to make meaningful
> generalisations about the behaviour of 'women'
> vs. 'men' at work which ignore the complexities
> of the influence of their particular roles,
> professional identities and specific goals, and the
> social contexts in which they are operating.
>
> (Holmes, 2000b: 10)

This chapter critically examines research on so-called distinguishing features of male and female communication in the workplace (such as direct-indirect speech, aggressive-conciliatory speech, competitive-facilitative speech). In addition to difference perspectives, the chapter covers dominance perspectives of gender and language in the workplace, but it ultimately concentrates on research that contradicts binary and simplistic theorizations of gender. Dynamic approaches are discussed and examples of gendered discourses in the workplace are examined. In addition, broader political issues that are highly relevant to feminist linguistic inquiry in this area, namely the 'double bind' and the 'glass ceiling', are discussed, and ways forward are explored.

DIFFERENCE AND DOMINANCE IN THE WORKPLACE: A BRIEF HISTORY

Early research examining language and gender in the workplace was heavily influenced by the popular theoretical paradigms of the time, the power/dominance and culture/difference approaches (seen in Chapter 2). As women began to enter the workplace in greater numbers, language and gender research in this area started to grow, and a number of key studies were produced. All these early studies take gender difference as given. In a review of language and gender studies in the workplace, Kendall and Tannen (1997) make the point that the majority of initial work at their time of writing focused on professional–lay person interaction. This has changed in recent years, as there has been a huge growth in work which examines gender and communicative strategies among colleagues, particularly in businesses (Holmes, 2000a, 2000b; Baxter, 2003; Mullany, 2003, 2004a, 2004b, forthcoming; Holmes and Marra, 2004; McRae, 2004; Holmes and Schnurr, 2005).

In order to introduce the field, initial research focusing on professional–lay person interaction will be examined. These studies tended to focus on the domain of medicine, particularly doctor–patient interaction (West, 1984, 1990; Ainsworth-Vaughan, 1992). Pizzini (1991) examined midwife–patient interaction along with doctor–patient interaction, and similarly, Fisher (1993) compared doctor–patient to nurse–patient interaction. To illustrate the theoretical alignment of these medical studies to the dominance and difference approaches, we will focus in particular on the findings of West (1984, 1990) and Ainsworth-Vaughan (1992).

West (1984) argues that male patients' interruptions of female doctors display their dominance and control in mixed-sex medical encounters. Consider Extract (6A), where doctor and patient have been discussing possible ways of reducing the patient's weight. One suggestion offered by the physician was to slow down while eating; but the patient has just countered that suggestion with the complaint that he does not like cold food.

Extract (6A)

Patient:	And they take twenty or thirty minutes to eat
Physician:	Well what you [could DO]
Patient:	[And then by the] time they get through their food is cold and uh-they likes it you know
Physician:	[engh-hengh-hengh-hengh-hengh] .hh=
Patient:	[And th' they enjoy that] =but I- I don't like cold food (.2)
Physician:	One thing you could d[o]
Patient:	[spesh'ly] food that's not supposed to be cold=
Physician:	= okay h = is to eat say the meat first you know but if you have a salad to eat to save that till after you eat the meat (.) cos the salad's supposed to be cold

West (1984: 92)

In this data extract, the male patient repeatedly interrupts the female doctor while she is trying to articulate her suggestions for treating his condition, thus dominating and controlling the conversation, despite the fact that the doctor is of a much higher status and an authority figure in this context. According to West, the power that men have over women in society more widely is reflected in such workplace encounters.

West's (1990) later work is strongly influenced by the difference approach. Although West does not explicitly align herself with this framework, her work examines the effectiveness of different strategies that women and men doctors adopt in single- and mixed-sex settings. The following extracts are taken from single-sex encounters where doctors are meeting patients for the first time: Extract (6B) is between a male doctor and a male patient, whereas Extract (6C) is between a female doctor and a female patient.

Extract (6B)

Physician:	You can drop your trousers, fact, why don't you just take them off. (.6)
Patient:	((leans forward on the examining table, looking at the physician))
Physician:	Take your trousers off

West (1990: 103)

Extract (6C)

| **Physician:** | Okay so: what do you think, =maybe we'd just take the top of your-your dress off? |

West (1990: 103)

West draws upon Goodwin's (1980) definitions of directives (see also Chapter 4) to analyse her data. Goodwin (1980: 157) outlines directives as 'speech acts that try to get another to do something'. Goodwin draws a distinction between 'aggravated' and 'mitigated' directives. Aggravated directives are where orders or demands are issued in the most direct, explicit way possible. In contrast, mitigated directives are where speaker intentions are expressed in a less obvious manner, for example, through proposals or suggestions. In Extract (6B), West reports that the male physician uses two aggravated directives, followed by an explicit demand, in contrast to the female physician's utterance, which West (1990: 99) describes as 'a proposal for joint action', expressed as a question: asking the patient for her opinion. Whereas the male physicians prescribed to their female and male patients what they 'had to' do, the female physicians constructed their statements as suggestions for co-operative action with female and male patients. They tended to use 'we' instead of 'you' in their directives, and mitigated them by using modals such as 'can' or 'could'. West discovered that the female physicians in her data were far more likely to gain the compliance of their patients with their use of mitigated directives (the compliance rate was 67 per cent), as opposed to the men's use of aggravated directives (a compliance rate of 50 per cent). Indeed, in Extract (6B) the male doctor did not gain the compliance of his patient, whereas in Extract (6C) the female doctor immediately gained the compliance of her patient. Overall, West concludes that the more aggravated the directive, the less likely the doctor was going to be in gaining the compliance of the patient. The different speech styles that West draws attention to show how the female doctors' style is more effective, and thus can be seen as a good example of the manner in which work influenced by the difference paradigm celebrated women's speech styles.

Ainsworth-Vaughan's (1992) study focuses on the way in which topic transition occurs in single- and mixed-sex doctor–patient encounters. As was the case with West (1990), Ainsworth-Vaughan does not overtly align herself with the difference approach, but its influence is clearly observable in her findings. She draws a distinction between symmetrical and asymmetrical ways of controlling a topic. She termed the symmetrical changes *reciprocal*, whereby control of topic is shared and jointly negotiated. In contrast, asymmetrical topic changes are termed *unilateral*, defined as when speaker topic change occurs without gaining overt consent. Ainsworth-Vaughan found that female doctors enact their interactional power in very different ways by avoiding unilateral topic changes with both female and male patients. On the other hand, the male doctors favour unilateral topic transitions. This leads her to argue that unlike their male colleagues, the female doctors are not viewing the encounters as power struggles. She also suggests that the strategies of female doctors benefit the patients more, pointing to evidence which suggests that if patients feel included and are able to assert themselves they are more likely to experience better health care.

Despite the main focus on professional–lay person interaction in early language and gender workplace research, a few studies did examine professional–professional interaction, including work in educational settings. Eakins and Eakins (1979) found that men talk more often than women in university faculty meetings, and Edelsky (1981) found the same in meetings where there was an expectation that one speaker would speak at a time. Woods (1989) set a precedent for later research by investigating office interaction, along with Tannen's (1994) work on corporate businesses, and Case's studies (1988, 1995) focusing on the interactions of managers in a management school. Whilst Case's investigations showed patterns such as men interrupting more than women, she did question the findings of studies that focused on gender differences, and her work has influenced more recent, theoretically advanced approaches. It will thus be discussed further in the next section.

In her analysis of mixed-sex interactions of individuals with differing status, Woods (1989) found that male subordinates still dominated, holding the floor longer than their female bosses, interrupting on more occasions, and also giving less assent to women speakers. This evidence led her to argue that gender overrides status in the workplace, with men still being dominant, regardless of women's positions of power. (For a detailed discussion of dominance in interaction, refer to Chapter 2.)

From the perspective of the culture/difference approach, Tannen (1994) examines professionals talking to their status equals, and superiors interacting with their subordinates. Extract (6D) gives an example from this work:

Extract (6D)

Marge:	Oh, but you've still got Mitch and Evan in the same office you know!
Secretary:	Are you kidding? Oh, darn.
Marge:	[*laughing*] You know, it's hard to do things around here, with all these people coming in!

Tannen (1994: 180)

In this extract, Tannen argues that the speaker with the superior status, Marge, saves face for her female secretary when drawing her attention to the fact that she had made a mistake. She further suggests that, due to differences implemented during the socialization process, women are far more likely to mitigate criticisms and save face in this way than men. (Again, refer to Chapter 2, for a detailed discussion of the difference paradigm.)

MOVING FORWARD: DYNAMIC APPROACHES

In the mid to late 1990s, social constructionist approaches to language and gender began to develop. In addition to the notions of 'doing gender' in discourse and of communities of practice (see Chapter 3, and below), some of these dynamic approaches, such as Kendall and Tannen (1997), have drawn on the notion of 'framing', following Goffman's (1974) work. Similar to the framing of events by the media through alignment with different perspectives (see examples of rape reporting in Chapter 5), framing in the course of interaction involves the alignment of speakers with one another. Women and men 'frame' themselves based on societal gendered norms for appropriate behaviour. Kendall and Tannen (1997: 97) argue that the relationship between language and gender is 'sex-class' linked, i.e. spoken interaction is not necessarily identified with a woman or man but is rather associated with 'women as a class' or 'men as a class' within a society. Individuals then align themselves with a particular sex-class by talking in a particular way that is associated with that sex-class.

In a later, sole authored work, Kendall (2004) uses the framing approach to analyse how authority is framed in mixed-sex interactions at a radio station. Her analysis of interaction between Carol, a female technical director, and Ron, a male status equal, showed that Carol constructed an egalitarian 'problem-solving frame', whereas Ron created a 'hierarchical expert frame', positioning himself in a one-up position and Carol in a one-down position (ibid.: 64). When helping Harold, a male subordinate, Carol creates an 'impersonalization' frame, where she aids him but presents the information that he needs in an impersonal way, so that he is not seen as lacking in knowledge (ibid.: 71). She also creates a sense of competence for Harold by constructing a frame of expertise whereby she asks his advice on what kind of computer she should purchase. However, while Carol's managerial style is very effective, it has not necessarily aided her career. Kendall raises important points here regarding the existence of the 'glass ceiling'; this will be discussed later.

Discursive and social constructionist approaches have tended to dominate gender and language in the workplace studies in recent years. Studies by Janet Holmes and her colleagues are good examples of work following these approaches. In 1996, Holmes set up a government-funded project in Wellington, New Zealand, entitled *Language in the Workplace*. This has been a highly successful endeavour, which has helped raise the profile of language and gender workplace studies, as well as greatly expand the field by focusing on professional–professional interaction. Early publications associated with this project clearly demonstrate the influence of the transition in language and gender studies away from the dominance and difference paradigms, to the more dynamic, communities of practice, social constructionist approaches

(Holmes, 2000a; Holmes *et al.*, 2001). In an early summary of the findings relating to gender in the project thus far, Holmes (2000b) alerts us that any dichotomizing of male and female speech styles results in over-simplification and over-generalization (see Chapter 3 for similar arguments). She argues that

> It is simply not possible to make meaningful generalisations about the behaviour of 'women' vs. 'men' at work which ignore the complexities of the influence of their particular roles, professional identities and specific goals, and the social contexts in which they are operating.
>
> (Holmes, 2000b: 10)

While there is some evidence of gendered patterning in these findings, there is also clear evidence that challenges stereotypical expectations surrounding the behaviour of women and men in the workplace. To begin with, Holmes (2000a) questions the findings of earlier work that sought to highlight gender differences between women and men in the workplace. She summarizes these differences of masculine and feminine interactional styles in a useful table reproduced below (Table 6.1).

The distinctions that West (1984, 1990), Ainsworth-Vaughan (1992), Eakins and Eakins (1979), Edelsky (1981), Woods (1989) and Tannen (1994) have found, and which were highlighted above, are all represented in Holmes' summary. Holmes points out that, despite criticism of earlier studies, the findings reported in her table are still persistent. As such, they provide a very useful background for viewing how individuals are expected to behave and how they are treated based on societal gender stereotypes about spoken interaction. This is also important because, as Holmes points out, career consultants often regard some of the features on the masculine side of the table to be *the* characteristics of successful managers, and these assumptions are also at work within training programmes in organizations (see later). Therefore, if individuals perform gender identities that do not conform to societal expectations, this can lead to negative evaluation and disadvantage in the workplace. This fundamentally important issue will be discussed later in the chapter.

Table 6.1 Widely cited features of 'feminine' and 'masculine' interactional style

Masculine	Feminine
direct	indirect
aggressive	conciliatory
competitive	facilitative
autonomous	collaborative
dominates talking time	talks less than men
interrupts aggressively	has difficulty getting a turn
task-oriented	person-oriented
referentially oriented	affectively oriented

Source: Holmes (2000a: 3)

Contrary to the findings of older research, Holmes' analysis of the speech strategies of women managers in positions of power found that they were using a 'wide-verbal-repertoire style' (Holmes, 2000a: 13). This is defined, borrowing Case's (1995) term, as displaying traits stereotypically associated with both masculine and feminine speech styles. All the women managers Holmes examined were evaluated as being effective by their colleagues. Holmes attributes this success to the mixture of stereo-typical masculine and feminine discourse styles that these women managers used to achieve their goals. They dominated the talking time and issued directives without mitigation, thus displaying stereotypical masculine traits. However, they also saved face by using supportive humour, along with cooperative strategies which included ensuring that consensus was a negotiated process and that progress was summarized at regular intervals for clarity. In fact, Case's (1995) work was rather ahead of its time, as her analysis illustrated that there were more similarities in the speech patterns of certain women and men than studies had previously found. Whilst Holmes did not look at men managers in her (2000a) work, five years earlier, Case had found both women and men using the 'wide-verbal-repertoire'. She argued that this repertoire, with women displaying characteristics stereotypically associated with a masculine speech style, and vice versa, enables participants to be simultaneously assertive and supportive.

Despite this evidence, we also need to be aware of constraints surrounding the use of a wide-verbal-repertoire by women and by men. In a recent study in Germany, Thimm *et al.* (2003) examined how the role of gender stereotypes influences the atti-tudes of a variety of professionals engaged in workplace communication. They found that men were using a far wider variety of speech strategies than women, frequently including patterns stereotypically associated with female, powerless styles. Thimm *et al.* argued that women often have fewer options open to them due to social stigmas and the fact that they are evaluated very differently to men. We will explore the issue of evaluation later in this section, and the idea that women can be subject to a 'double bind' later in the chapter. After covering those parts, readers can return to Question 1.

Question 1

In what ways are women and men evaluated differently when communicating in the workplace?

How could this vary from workplace to workplace?

Let us now turn to current theorizations, which investigate language and gender in the workplace by drawing upon the notions of communities of practice and gendered dis-courses. The communities of practice approach (see Chapter 3, henceforth CofP) is particularly useful for workplace studies, as it enables comparisons to be drawn across different workplace groups (Holmes and Meyerhoff, 1999). In addition, Wenger's (1998) three dimensions of practice (mutual engagement, a joint negotiated enterprise and a shared repertoire – see Chapter 3) fit well into the workplace environment (ibid.), and can be used to identify different workplace sub-cultures (Holmes and Marra, 2002).

In her analyses of gender in managerial business interaction, Mullany (2003, 2006 and forthcoming) argues that business meetings provide an excellent arena through which communities of practice can be observed within businesses. Meetings are good examples of occasions where participants of CofPs mutually engage with one another in a joint negotiated enterprise, and they have a shared repertoire of resources to achieve this. She uses the CofP framework to examine the language managers use both to their status equals and to their subordinates in two ethnographic studies of UK corporate companies (a manufacturing and a retail company). She found evidence that the institutional status and role of individuals within specific CofPs, along with a number of other situated, contextual features, play a far more salient role than gender in governing the speech strategies managers used on numerous occasions. There was ample evidence to disprove the older views of males favouring competitive discourse styles and females favouring cooperative styles. Extract (6E) is taken from a departmental CofP in a retail company. Manager Steve is the meeting chair and direct superior of all the other meeting participants, Mike, Matt and Sue. At this point in the meeting, Steve is attempting to get his subordinates to run their own induction day, similar to what the sales department in the company (another CofP) had previously done:

Extract (6E)

Steve:	Do you feel that (-) we need to do perhaps something like (-) the sales department did?
Mike:	Set a date to sort it out
Steve:	Cos as Sue's quite rightly pointed out, all it's all been done for us and the things etc why don't we just take advantage of that? (.) Sue's offered her support with perhaps John? (-) Err you know perhaps to run that (.) why don't we just set a date now?
Matt:	Yeah
Steve:	And say right okay let's do it
Sue:	Just get everybody in
Matt:	Yeah

Mullany (2003: 136)

The extract shows that there are numerous examples of Steve using linguistic forms stereotypically associated with feminine speech styles. In contrast to the direct versus indirect dichotomy evident in Holmes's table and reported by Tannen (1994), and the aggravated versus mitigated directive dichotomy discussed by West (1990), Steve uses numerous cooperative mitigation strategies when issuing directives. His use of indirectness (e.g. 'perhaps'), hedging (e.g. 'you know', 'just') and collaborative rapport-building (e.g. 'we', 'let's') demonstrates a male manager performing his professional identity using numerous speech strategies stereotypically associated with a feminine speech style.

Extract (6F) is taken from a departmental CofP in the manufacturing company, and illustrates a woman manager talking to one of her subordinates who has asked for advice:

Extract (6F)

Phyllis is informing her manager Carrie, the female Chair, of a problem she has with the local media.

Phyllis: I'm still getting a lot of er external like students (.) press getting through
Carrie: Tell the board

(Mullany, 2003: 108)

Here, Carrie tells Phyllis what to do in the form of a direct command, without any mitigation, uttered in a forceful tone, thus providing a good illustration of a woman manager using a stereotypically masculine speech style. Both Steve and Carrie perform their professional identities in these examples by drawing on speech strategies stereotypically associated with the other gender, thus neatly proving that it is too simplistic to look for and then simply categorize gender differences in the speech of women and men. The language they choose demonstrates that expectations of gendered language can be misleading. Consequently, a more fine-grained, contextualized analysis which takes account of norms and conventions of CofPs becomes necessary.

It is, however, useful to critically examine stereotypically male/female styles and strategies in other ways, particularly in terms of the effect they have as symbolic categories drawn upon to evaluate men and women in the workplace, as was pointed out earlier in reference to Holmes' (2000a) research. Recently, there has been interesting work on the notion of *relational practice* in the workplace (Holmes and Marra, 2004; Holmes and Schnurr, 2005), that is, behaviour oriented to the 'face needs' of others and aimed at mutual empowerment, self-achievement, solidarity in teams, consensus and good working relationships. Mutual empowerment includes networking on behalf of others, or putting people in touch with others who can help them fulfil their workplace goals. Self-achievement refers to an ability to reflect upon and understand the motivations of yourself and your colleagues (see Holmes and Marra, 2004: 380). Adapting the term from Fletcher (1999), Holmes and Marra (2004: 378) define relational practice (henceforth RP) as practice that is regarded as 'dispensable, irrelevant and peripheral', but which 'serves to advance the primary objectives of the workplace'. Despite the fact that in more than half of their examples, RP was used by males, Holmes and Marra argue that RP is gendered work, perceived as stereotypically 'feminine behaviour' (see also Fletcher, 1999). Therefore, RP can be seen as a form of gendered discourse, being perceived as more feminine than masculine, regardless of who is using it.

Holmes and Marra also point out that, despite the fundamental importance of RP in terms of achieving workplace goals, it is often overlooked due to its association with the feminine. It thus becomes important to look at RP within specific CofPs, where it is used in a variety of ways. For example, in a more 'masculine' CofP (a factory), a woman manager was seen to be using humour (as one form of RP) in a stereotypically masculine, challenging manner, whereas in a more 'feminine' CofP (a white-collar firm), another female manager used humour in more supportive, traditionally feminine ways (Holmes and Stubbe, 2003; Holmes and Schnurr, 2005). However, it was also interesting that a man who worked in a more 'masculine' CofP could not use language that is seen as indexing femininity as freely as a man employed in a more 'feminine' CofP (Holmes and Schnurr, 2005). The studies above show convincingly that predictable or stereotypical ways of 'doing gender' are drawn on differently by different participants in different communities of practice.

GENDERED DISCOURSES AT WORK

As discussed in detail in Chapter 3, the notion of gendered discourses has become an influential theoretical and analytical concept in language and gender studies in general. We have seen that gendered discourses position women and men in certain ways, and at the same time, people take up particular gendered subject positions that constitute gender more widely. Broader gendered discourses (e.g. of femininity, masculinity, gender differences) and more specific ones (such as 'women as relational' or 'women as emotional') are constitutive and ideological. Such an understanding has increasingly led to a reframing of key questions (Chapter 3): What identities are created as a result of different positioning through discourses, in different contexts and situations? What opportunities and inequalities are created and maintained as a result? Workplace researchers have embraced the conception of gendered discourses and identities in their research (Baxter, 2003; Holmes and Marra, 2004; Holmes and Schnurr, 2005; Mullany, forthcoming), often in conjunction with the communities of practice approach.

We will now look at some dominant gendered discourses in the workplace: discourses of femininity; discourses of motherhood; discourses of women as emotional/irrational (pertaining to an overarching 'gender differences' discourse); and discourses of equality and discrimination.

Mullany (2003) examined gendered discourses in interviews with female and male managers at middle and senior managerial levels. One of the aims of these interviews was to discuss participants' managerial roles and the impact of gender on their everyday work lives. The range of gendered discourses that were evident in the interview data revealed that women in positions of authority can be negatively evaluated and disadvantaged in the workplace. This is due to dominant discourses of femininity, which these successful women have to negotiate. Discourses of femininity appear natural but in reality they serve to maintain the status quo and 'emphasize meanings and values which assume the superiority of males' (Coates, 1997: 292). One such discourse, seen in Mullany's interview data from the manufacturing company (2003, forthcoming), emphasizes an 'ideal' feminine image of the slim, sexually attractive woman in the workplace. This image was also evident in the descriptions of female athletes and a female doctor in Extracts (1A) and (1B) of Chapter 1. It is highlighted below in a commentary by Carrie, a director who had been on maternity leave at the time prior to this recording.

Extract (6G)

Carrie:	Coming back off maternity leave I'm a lot bigger than before and you know I think there's quite a change in attitude towards me because of that ... for people underneath yes they're definitely more switched on to me for people above or whatever are much more don't take your opinions seriously when you're fatter definitely I'm sure about that so I've been on a diet and I'm not getting any younger either.

(Mullany, 2003: 226)

Carrie believes that her opinions are not taken as seriously now by her superiors and status equals because she has put on weight. When she states that 'I'm not getting any younger either', this implies that she feels her opinion is also not as respected now as it was before when she was a slimmer, younger woman manager. Another comment which highlights the consequences of dominant discourses of femininity in relation to gendered image is provided by Jane, a middle-manager in the manufacturing company. She comments that she has noticed a difference in the manner in which some male colleagues treat her since she has gained promotion to middle-management.

Extract (6H)

Jane:	I've come across comments ermm which are completely related to your sex and the way you look ... I've often got my hair in a ponytail or up like I have today I don't wear make-up ... I distinctly get the impression from a lot of men in meetings that they look at me as if I'm a kind of twenty-one year old being given an opportunity to sit in and listen ... the meetings where those two gentlemen are in I do tend to end up putting on a bit of eye liner and wearing something slightly smarter ... you'll get kind of the male chauvinist he'll sit on the desk and kind of lean over and go 'oh well-done' when you do something and you think it's my job.

(Mullany, 2003: 235)

By putting her hair in a ponytail and not wearing make-up, Jane implies that she has disrupted the expected feminine image for a woman in the workplace. Jane is 30 years old at the time of the interview, and has considerable experience in her role. However, it is not her actual age but the age she is perceived to be, based on her appearance, that she believes is causing her to be negatively evaluated. The view perpetuated by the dominant discourse of femininity regarding feminine image appears to be that, in order to succeed and be taken seriously in this workplace, women need to be slim, attractive, and well groomed. To the extent that this is not a crucial requirement for men in the same way and in similar positions, this view may contribute to a double standard for women and men, and may further mark women as 'other' and men as the 'norm' in those communities of practice.

Alvesson and Billing (1997) comment on the problems that women can face in terms of portraying an acceptable social identity for themselves. They argue that while the 'modern career woman' has now become an acceptable social identity, it must not deviate too far from the traditional view of femininity associated with 'sexual attractiveness' and 'family orientation' (1997: 98). This view of the 'mother' as a legitimate social role for women in the workplace was observed by Wodak (1997), who reported that head teachers were successfully adopting the mother role in school meetings. Holmes and Stubbe (2003: 592) also argue that women managers in their data adopted the mother role by being both 'bossy' and supportive in a nurturing manner. The mother role neatly illustrates how women attempt to construct socially acceptable identities for themselves in order to avoid negative evaluation. However, while the mother role can be socially acceptable within the workplace, this is not to obscure the problems that working mothers face when trying to balance their careers and home lives. This important issue will be discussed in relation to the glass ceiling (see later).

Finally, the discourse of 'female emotionality', which is part of an overarching gender differences discourse (see Chapters 2 and 3) is also encountered in the workplace. As we have seen in Part I of the book, we have to be extremely cautious of biological explanations of gender, as these typically transform difference into female disadvantage. This is illustrated in the following extract (Mullany, 2003), which suggests that women are less suited to the workplace, their bodies physically preventing them from being good managers. In this extract, one of the male interviewees in a manufacturing company, Martin, replies to the question of whether he would prefer to work under the supervision of a woman or a man.

Extract (6I)

| **Martin:** | I just find men in general I mean in the workplace and in general I just find them to be more stable and straight really than women ... if you look at sort of even just on the biological clock you know you've got one week a month when women are you know not as they are the other three weeks of the month you know and and that is bound to have an effect I mean that is whatever people say about men and women are the same they're not because we- you know men don't go through that women do and it's very rare a woman who says she isn't affected for that week of the month so if you're working for someone and you get them in that week you know it's they will be emotionally they will be more |

> susceptible to emotional swings and not making decisions erm with the kind of same sort of accuracy that they normally would.
>
> (Mullany, 2003: 237)

Martin here overtly espouses the sexist, stereotypical view that for 'one week a month' women are incapable of making rational decisions due to their hormones. A distinction is implicit here between what Martin perceives as the norm, the rational efficient male, as opposed to the emotional, irrational female. The fact that Martin openly espoused this view to a female interviewer in a matter of fact, non-aggressive manner, indicates that he perceives this view to be a universal truth.

Martin's comment above is not necessarily typical of professional men's talk on topics of equality and discrimination. In interviews with professional men (architects, accountants and lawyers), Riley (2002) found that they tended to minimize the gendered nature of their workplace experiences and instead replace this with the notion of individualism. Riley makes the point that the dominant view of equality in western societies comes from the perspective that while there will always be inequalities, these have to be based on merit, not on social categorization. However, Riley argues that such ideas are androcentric, failing to challenge the values and the social structures that serve to underpin gender inequalities. Therefore, despite the implementation of equal opportunities policies, the impact and importance of such policies have been minimized. In her interview data, the males draw on discourses which assume that women and men are completely interchangable in terms of status and power. However, Riley argues that such talk is premised on a principle of individualism which results in

> absenting historical discrimination against women, absenting common experiences between members of a social category; masking the importance of gender through an emphasis on the plurality of social categories; and presenting special needs arguments as both discriminatory and against the interests of those they serve.
>
> (Riley, 2002: 456–7)

She concludes that such attitudes result in a state of 'political nothingness', where not taking any action at all is seen as the norm. Gendered differences that exist are buried by the production of an alleged symmetry between women and men which obscures gendered differences in both experiences and expectations.

Others have similarly argued that gender ideologies in institutions and organizational cultures promote a tacit androcentrism, in which men, and often women, are complicit (Lazar, 2005; Martin-Rojo and Gómez Esteban, 2005). In their work on the discourse of Spanish executives, Martin-Rojo and Callejo (1995) claim that (as we saw also in Chapters 1 and 5) sexism is inhibited in discourse. Their critical discourse analysis of male executives' responses identifies inhibited sexism as a kind of rationalization that involves the intention of avoiding non-legitimate overt sexist expressions, and so turns into a type of imperfect censorship. Social changes in women's position in general, and their access to the workplace in particular, have meant that nowadays we come across fewer explicitly sexist remarks, such as Martin's in Extract (6I). Rather, as Martin-Rojo and Callejo (1995) maintain, the men's excessive emphasis on self-exoneration in discourse shows that there is awareness of a feminist criticism which accuses men of discriminating in the workplace (see also Connell, 1995). This is also evident in the ways in which female managers oppose normalization and domination through a 'discourse of deconstruction' and a 'discourse of liberation or reconstruction' (Martin-Rojo, 1995). The former reproduces and then challenges dominant discourses, and explores new ways of understanding; an example of this is a female executive's challenging of views held about pregnancy and maternity leave:

> [imitating the voice of a businessman] 'give me a real male executive and free me from all these problems, because…', […] men complain a lot, they all do it, … they stay in bed, so I really laugh at [what they say about] pregnancies, because we don't get pregnant systematically every year.

In addition, a 'discourse of liberation' describes the female executives' attempt to resist dominant discourses, by ignoring them and by asserting their personal autonomy.

The resistance of dominant discourses is, nevertheless, a complex endeavour, and people's appropriation of discourses in general is neither predictable nor necessarily consistent. As Wetherell *et al.* (1987) illustrate through interviews with final year university students about employment opportunities for women, discourses around the endorsement of equal opportunities often co-occur and conflict with discourses around the practical considerations supposedly limiting those opportunities. Both female and male students draw on these themes, examples of which are cited here:

Extract (6J)

'Equal opportunities'
Female student: Um, yeah, I think there could be more equal opportunities, for example, when women take maternity leave they often miss out on promotion

'Practical considerations'
Male student: I suppose you can always see how an employer's mind will work, if he has a choice between two identically qualified and identically, identical personalities, and one is male and one is female, you can sympathize with him for perhaps wondering if the female is not going to get married and have children and then there's always the risk that she may not come back after, she may well do, a lot of women do, but uh I don't know he may well decide that the risk is not worth taking, play safe um and from the nature of things it looks like that is uh, the way it would stay.

(Wetherell *et al.*, 1987: 62)

Wetherell *et al.* argue that this type of accounting, which they call 'unequal egalitarianism' (ibid.: 65), neutralizes efforts for change and is effective in maintaining the status quo. This claim is similar to Riley's argument earlier about the ways in which certain discourses work to establish inaction as the norm. 'Practical considerations' discourses help to normalize double standards in the workplace (and elsewhere), thus obscuring one of the many reasons why women 'hit the glass ceiling' in many professions. These issues are considered in the next section.

Question 2
What gender ideologies are premised upon and sustained by the discourses discussed above? What inequalities or imbalances are shored up by these discourses?

IN A DOUBLE BIND, UNDER A GLASS CEILING

In the previous sections, we saw that stereotypes have a strong influence on workplace communication, and that gendered social evaluations and stigmas may contribute to limiting women's options with language. More particularly, Kendall and Tannen (1997) argue that women in positions of authority face a *double bind* in the workplace. The concept of a double bind has been put forward by a number of researchers including feminist linguists, social psychologists and organization studies researchers (Lakoff, 1990; Coates, 1995; Cameron, 1995; Crawford, 1995; Freed, 1996; Alvesson and Billing, 1997; Jones, 2000; Brewis, 2001; Martin-Rojo and Gómez Esteban, 2002). The term is used to describe the dual constraint that women face when they interact in public arenas. If women adopt a more assertive speech style typically associated with masculine speech, then they will be subject to negative evaluation, being viewed as overly aggressive and unfeminine. Alternatively, if women adopt the speech style typically associated with femininity, then they risk being negatively evaluated as ineffective and weak. When the linguistic behaviour of individuals 'does not conform to society's expectations, a set of judgements is formed about them. Their language is seen as marked and they themselves are often seen as deviant' (Freed, 1996: 70).

Graddol and Swann (1989) and Eckert and McConnell-Ginet (2003) argue that gender ideologies work to ensure that the same speech style is given a different meaning and interpretation when used by a woman rather than a man. This perspective accords with Bem's (1993) view that in society there is a lens of gender polarization which works to maintain the view that male and female behaviour is inherently different (see Chapter 2; also for a broader discussion of the problems with 'difference'). When viewed through this gender lens, if female (or male) speakers diverge from the linguistic norms that are stereotypically deemed to be appropriate behaviour for their sex, they face negative evaluation. Lakoff (1990) points out that the double bind is a paradox that professional women face when they find themselves in situations where assertive behaviour is necessary. She argues that a female has two choices: 'she can be a good woman but a bad executive or professional; or vice versa. To do both is impossible' (1990: 206). Jones (2000) details the picture for women managers in particular, arguing that if a woman speaks like a manager, then she transgresses the boundaries of femininity; if she talks like a woman, then she is no longer representing her managerial identity. That gender polarization often leads to female disadvantage and the limiting of women's access to positions of power has been emphasized in this chapter and elsewhere in the book (e.g. how ideas about women as mothers, carers, irrational, emotional and men as active, competitive, assertive are used in courts and other debates (Bing and Bergvall, 1998; Litosseliti, 2006), in order to justify employer discrimination against women or to limit women's access to traditionally 'male' domains).

The existence of the double bind in the workplace is illustrated by Case (1988) and Crawford (1988, 1995). Case (1988) reports that a female manager who combined feminine speech styles with more masculine assertive styles was widely disliked and her behaviour provoked hostile comments from her fellow employees. In matched-guise tests, Crawford (1988) discovered that women who displayed assertive behaviour were perceived as less likeable than men who adopted identical behaviour. Mullany's (2003) ethnographic business case studies also showed a negative evaluation of women who are perceived to be 'too direct' or 'domineering'. The following is an example of a commentary by Lucy, describing Amy, her manager:

Extract (6K)

Lucy: Amy is very domineering … if you'd have asked me when I was younger I'd have said yes men would domineer but now Amy's come along … Amy is very different from the rest of the females in the company she's quite honest you know where you stand with her … she's quite abrupt you know … sometimes she scares the pants off me.

(Mullany, 2003: 224)

Lucy draws a clear delineation between Amy and other females in the company, and identifies her as having domineering masculine traits. She then implies that other females in the company are not honest, by stating that Amy is 'very different from the rest of the females' in being 'quite honest'. In this way, Lucy appears to be drawing on the stereotypical assumption that women are indirect and thus hide their 'honest' opinions. The end result is that both being indirect and being direct present problems for the female managers – a 'no win' situation.

Earlier in this chapter, it was highlighted that Kendall's (2004) findings raise some important issues for the existence of the 'double bind', as well as the 'glass ceiling'. In her analysis, Kendall found evidence that Carol, the female technical director at the radio station, was very competent at her job, but despite this, soon after Kendall's recording took place, Carol was demoted. Kendall argues that the gendered speech strategies which Carol used, i.e. an egalitarian approach which minimized status differences, were seen as lacking authority; and that men in higher ranking, gatekeeping, positions considered such strategies as ineffective and inappropriate for Carol's position of power. This is a prime example of the double bind, as Carol was prevented from sustaining her senior management position, despite having broken through the glass ceiling and having achieved success.

Coates (1995) argues that male speech patterns are the norm in the public domain due to the historical male dominance of public arenas. As a consequence of this

> women are linguistically at a double disadvantage when entering the public domain: first, they are (normally) less skilful at using the adversarial, information-focused style expected in such contexts; second, the (more cooperative) discourse styles which they *are* fluent in are negatively valued in such contexts
>
> (1995: 14)

Although, as we have seen, more recent research shows that in specific contexts women draw effectively on a range of both 'masculine' and 'feminine' styles and strategies (Holmes and Schnurr, 2005; Stubbe *et al.*, 2000), the second point has even wider implications for the role of women in the public sphere. Whether women are fluent in cooperative styles or not, we know that they are assumed and expected to be, yet are evaluated negatively when they are not. Especially in (historically and currently) male-dominated workplaces – business organizations, government, politics, the church, the police, the law – where assertive behaviour is necessary, women must constantly negotiate these assumptions and expectations. So, for example, women police officers tend to 'masculinize' their behaviour and refrain from cooperative strategies in order to achieve their goals (McElhinny, 1998, 2003; Ostermann, 2003). At the same time, these women are redefining traditional notions of masculinity and femininity in positive ways – for example, by disrupting established notions of feminine appearance – and are providing new role models (McElhinny, 2003).

The appropriation of 'masculine' styles by women in such communities of practice is understandable, given the historical context of their struggle to gain access to, and recognition in, the public arena. As Litosseliti discusses (2006), women often adopt the interactional approaches that are characteristic of these environments, whereby leadership and authority have traditionally been associated with masculinity. Indeed, leadership style often equates masculine style (Hearn and Parkin, 1988), and our views of a successful entrepreneur may still include typically male characteristics: 'a charismatic individual who recognizes new opportunities, takes risks, perseveres through adversity, and eventually changes the face of the economy' (McManus, 2001: 79). Women's appropriation of 'masculine' styles, or their adoption of a combination of stereotypically 'masculine' and stereotypically 'feminine' styles, will vary from one CofP to the next, as seen above. A recent collection on the female voice in public contexts (Baxter, 2006) provides insight on how women both appropriate masculine public discourse and find new ways of combining 'doing leadership' and 'doing gender' successfully. Settings explored in this book include the academic community, parliament, education, the media, courtrooms, and the business world.

Another important question concerns the role of the double bind described here in keeping women below the *glass ceiling*, that is:

> the invisible barrier that seems to keep even some exceptionally capable women from ascending to the top in the many professions dominated by men. Its companion, the glass elevator, is the invisible leverage that propels even relatively mediocre men upward in female-dominated occupations.
>
> (McConnell-Ginet, 2000: 260)

Despite the extraordinary impact of feminism and equal opportunities legislation and implementation over the past 30 or 40 years, women are still significantly outnumbered by men – across time, locations and cultures – in the highest positions of social power (e.g. company presidents/CEOs, government ministers, judges, bishops, police chiefs, union leaders, university vice-chancellors). In addition, women continue to earn less than their male counterparts across the professions, continue to be exploited and marginalized in part-time or temporary employment, and continue to shoulder the burden of combining career and family in ways not assumed of their partners and colleagues. In fact, most women leave the workforce long before they reach the glass ceiling, in order to look after young children (as was also assumed in the students' discourse, in Extract (6J)). What all the above means, from a feminist linguistic perspective, is that females are marginalized or excluded from dominant linguistic practices and from highly valued speech genres.

In addition, the glass ceiling often operates in professions where women are not necessarily outnumbered by men. Academia is a good example. A recent report in *The Guardian* (2004), on findings by the Association of University Teachers (AUT) in British higher education, tells us that the number of female academics employed in British universities has increased by 43 per cent in the past 10 years, with women comprising almost 40 per cent of the total workforce. However, the report points out that the women's jobs tend to be more casualized and junior than those of their male colleagues. In short:

- women academics tend to be involved in teaching and learning rather than research, while more men are counted as 'research active' in the Research Assessment Exercise (a key factor in influencing promotion opportunities);
- more women than men academics are involved in pastoral care;
- more women than men are on casualized fixed-term contracts;
- women occupy the lower academic grades, while only 30 per cent of heads of department are women, and even fewer are professors;
- more women than men academics work on a part-time basis;
- women academics working full-time earn 85 per cent of the salary of their male colleagues on average.

The article cited family responsibilities as an issue for women, who may be deterred by the 'long hours culture', and the need to publish research, attend conferences and network with colleagues in their country and abroad.

McConnell-Ginet (2000) argues that a key reason for the existence of the glass ceiling is the perpetuation of dominant gender schemas, even by those committed to gender equality, which make us expect different things of women and men, and as a consequence, evaluate them differently. Drawing on the work of Valian (1998), she argues that the expectations we have of individuals based upon the sex category we have assigned to them cause distortions that result in women being disadvantaged. One example of this is that when achievement is rewarded, men get credited with hard work and determination, whereas women are seen to have just been lucky, or to have had an easy task to begin with, or to have had to work extraordinarily hard to fulfil the task.

A whole range of gendered practices, as well as discourses, contribute to the maintenance of the glass ceiling, and raising linguistic awareness is as essential as collective political action towards sustainable social change (McConnell-Ginet, 2000). One way to successfully break through the glass ceiling, according to McConnell-Ginet, is for academic researchers to work collectively to reveal hidden gender schemas, implemented during childhood, which remain covert. Collective action is also advocated by Walsh (2001), who has researched the rise of female priests in the Church of England, along with the rise of women politicians in the British political system (including Westminster and the Northern Ireland Women's Coalition). Has the increased participation of women in these workplaces changed traditional dominant masculinist discourse norms? Walsh shows that it has resulted in a questioning of masculine norms, but on some occasions, this has led to men strengthening fraternal networks. An example of this is the development of a 'new lads' network' in the British House of Commons, coined as the ability to talk about football as a way to bridge the gap between the government and the (male) citizens of Britain (Walsh, 2001: 99). In response, women have had to also develop strong networks, which are based upon alternative discourse patterns and norms. For example, the Northern Ireland's Women's Coalition aims to give priority to the interpersonal function of language instead of its referential, information-focused content. Walsh makes the crucial point that women-only groups can make a difference if they manage to assimilate the perspectives of large numbers of women (2001: 204).

From a feminist perspective, it is also worth thinking more carefully about celebrating women's entry into some of the previously male-dominated fields. Reskin and Roos (1990) claim that women typically enter fields that men no longer find desirable due to loss of pay, prestige, and autonomy. As a consequence, it may be more possible for women to break through the glass ceiling in those particular jobs, rather than, say, becoming leaders of governments or corporations. In this respect, one may consider the following article from *The Guardian*:

Extract (6L)

From *The Guardian*, 2 August 2004
Women doctors at top 'harm status'
By Sam Jones

> The female head of Britain's foremost royal medical college has warned that the medical profession could lose power and status because of the increasing number of successful women doctors.
>
> Carol Black, the president of the Royal College of Physicians, said Britain's doctors risked ending up like their Russian counterparts, who she said were ignored by their government and had lost influence as a body.
>
> 'We are feminising medicine,' Professor Black told the *Independent* newspaper. 'It has been a profession dominated by white males. What are we going to do to ensure it retains its influence? In Russia, medicine is an almost entirely female profession ... they have lost influence as a body that had competency, skills and a professional ethic. They have become just another part of the workforce. It is a case of downgrading professionalism.'
>
> Her comments come at a time when more than 60% of new doctors are female, and women make up the majority of the junior medical workforce. She said she would like to see action taken to equalise the number of male and female doctors.
>
> Women doctors were as good as, and sometimes better than, male colleagues, she said, but they often chose specialities that involved shorter working hours because of family pressures. 'They choose to go into dermatology, geriatrics and palliative care – not cardiology and gastroenterology where they would be required to work long hours.
>
> What worries me is, who is going to be the professor of cardiology in the future? Where are we going to find the leaders of British medicine in 20 years' time?'
>
> If women were not enabled to participate fully, the profession would lose its influence, she said. 'It worries me if we don't make it possible for women to do all the things we expect a doctor to do to be at the top of the profession.'
>
> © Guardian Newspapers Limited 2004.

The article above illustrates that issues of access and equal opportunities are never straightforward, and that issues of 'feminization' of a profession are necessarily complex. The article can be used effectively as material for seminar activities and a starting point for student research projects, especially alongside another article, also published in *The Guardian* (2005), entitled 'Men "winning" caring profession sex war' (see Other references). This article reports on the findings of academic research on the position of men in 'caring' professions, such as primary school teachers and nurses. It emerges that men in those professions get more respect and more challenging roles than their female counterparts. The majority of male nurses interviewed had chosen to specialize in male-dominated areas of nursing, such as mental health and accidents and emergencies, while male primary school teachers stressed their involvement in sports development, particularly of boys. The men reported that they believed their masculinity led them to be given more responsible or difficult roles than their female colleagues – such as breaking bad news to patients' relatives and dealing with suicide patients, or taking the role of disciplinarian and authority figure at school. In the words of the author of the research report: 'While the caring performed by a woman is often devalued as a "natural" part of femininity, the emotional labour performed by men is often seen as an asset.' While female nurses are seen as too 'deferential and unassertive' to be taken seriously, as well as being unable to take part in socializing with senior male doctors, male nurses are successfully raising the status of their jobs, and additionally cementing that status through 'male bonding' with senior staff.

Question 3

What gendered discourses are at work in the articles mentioned above?

How can they influence the material conditions of women and men's lives differently in different cultures?

CHANGING THE DISCOURSE IN ORGANIZATIONS

The research by Holmes and her colleagues, presented earlier in this chapter, reminds us that academic research can have implications and real practical uses outside academic contexts (see Sarangi and Roberts, 1999; also Chapter 7). In addition to academic publications, Holmes and her team have published numerous articles in business magazines, along with detailed recommendations and training programmes for improving business communication based on their research. It is not easy to see (and much less to control) which components of academic research are taken on board in organizations, and which research findings are used to shape their policies and practices. However, there *is* some cross-fertilization between academia and industry, and this is intensifying – for example, with the help of 'third stream' research programmes in universities that aim to do precisely that.

Nowadays, gender awareness and diversity issues feature highly within organizations. As observed in Chapter 1, linguistic intervention in terms of gender, in particular, can be evidenced in guidelines, codes of practice, and equal opportunities policies in industry; in awareness training seminars in organizations; in the promotion of gender-neutral terms in job advertisements, and so on (for a discussion of why these may not succeed, see Chapter 1).

> **Question 4**
>
> In what ways can change in the discourse in organizations bring about social change, as regards gender?
>
> What else is necessary for discourse change to be effective?
>
> (Readers can also refer back to Chapter 1.)

A closer look at systematic plans to integrate diversity and inclusiveness within one of the largest and most successful multinational corporations, reveals that they have as many as 40 different intervention points and programmes in place in this area. These focus on attracting, developing, retaining, and promoting diverse talent in the organization; promoting a workplace free from harassment and discrimination; and providing safe and effective ways for employees to report problems and concerns with negative behaviour (*Strategic HR Review*, 2004).

It is interesting that this organization 'pays particular attention to equal opportunities guidelines in the UK and in the US, where awareness is already high and this topic has a legislative basis' (Stewart, 2005). However, as suggested in Chapter 1, although legislation is a step in the right direction, the emphasis for feminist linguistics is on the gendered discourses circulating in the workplace (and elsewhere). Some of the diversity programmes mentioned above, within this particular organization, deal specifically with gender: gender awareness and women's career development. Perhaps not surprisingly, the gendered discourses circulating in those programmes are articulated within the dominance and difference frameworks. Videos by Pat Heim (see www.heimgroup.com for a list) and Deborah Tannen (based on her 1994 book) are used to pinpoint differences in female and male communication styles and behaviours, which are linked to differences in women's and men's socialization patterns. As a result, participants broadly explore difference through dominance (who speaks more? who interrupts more in interaction?) and through assessing a range of conversational styles associated with women and men. A random examination of some of the handouts given to participants in the courses shows lists, such as the following:

> WOMEN say 'we' more, play down achievements, downplay certainty, ask more questions, use ritual apologies and ritual compliments, soften feedback, nod to indicate listening. MEN say 'I' more, talk up achievements, minimize doubts, want answers, avoid apologies, give to-the-point feedback, use bantering, nod to indicate agreement.

We have discussed the problems with such binary understandings in various parts of the book. Nevertheless, it appears that the videos and materials used 'get a lot of positive response in [the company] culture, where women are often talked over in meetings or have difficulty getting credit for their ideas' (Stewart, 2005).

In addition to such discourses, participants in the programmes mentioned above are encouraged to use gender-neutral language to be more inclusive (e.g. when address-ing people via e-mail), and to be aware of their use of sports analogies and metaphors which can be seen to be based on male culture (ibid.). Metaphors, in particular, have been the subject of research which claims that they reveal many underlying attitudes, and can reinforce particular mental models for people. Harragan's work (1977) drew attention to the predominance of war and sports metaphors in business talk: talk about 'strategy', 'tactics' and 'team players', 'pulling rank', 'biting the bullet', 'ball-park figures', 'left fields', 'end runs', and 'scoring' – to give a few examples. These metaphors are also common in other public contexts, such as courtrooms, the media, and politics. Their effects are complex and the viability of gender-neutral metaphors is highly debatable. However, it is claimed that metaphoric language allows speakers to hide behind it, by presenting its message as beyond their control, unproblematic, common sense, and eventually naturalized, that is, stripped of its ideology (Cameron and Low, 1999; Fairclough, 1995). In her corpus analysis of business magazines, Koller argues that the widespread use of war metaphors in business media discourse 'helps to masculinize both that discourse and related social practices' and 'reinforces society's traditional gender bias' by promoting masculine patterns of behaviour and marginalizing feminine ones (2004b: 5).

Feminist linguistics can legitimately ask what options are available to those who are not part of the in-group assumed within war and sport metaphors – and, despite some changes in the high levels of corporate business, the out-group has been, and still is, women. Harragan (1977) proposes that female executives learn to use these metaphors. Koller (2004a) asserts that women managers may respond to the hege-monic masculinity indicated in war and sports metaphors by displaying an 'empha-sized femininity' (Connell, 1987: 187) revolving around notions of nurturing, caring, and selflessness. Alternatively, women may respond by adapting the metaphors to themselves in the hope of becoming part of the dominant discourse. Both approaches are problematic, however, as they involve sustaining the gender binary and co-opting the out-group. A further problem, as Koller's analysis of business media texts shows, is that these kinds of metaphors are disproportionately used to describe business-women, but there is no similar application of 'female' metaphorical concepts to men. She concludes that 'women achieving in-group membership status in a male-defined socio-economic sphere could indeed be co-opted by being labelled in male terms' (2004a: 13).

SUMMARY

■ Early research on gender and language in the workplace was heavily influenced by theories of difference and dominance. Studies on professional–lay person interaction, such as those between doctors and patients, suggested that male patients often dominated and controlled conversations with female doctors; and that male doctors used more aggressive power-asserting strategies, compared to the female doctors' co-operative and mitigated approaches (a matter of domi-nance and of difference).

- A number of studies showed that gender was more likely to be at stake than status in the workplace.

- In recent years, discursive and social constructionist approaches have shaped research in this area, alerting us to the dangers of over-simplification and over-generalization.

- Despite evidence that challenges stereotypical expectations surrounding the behaviour of women and men in the workplace, such expectations are still persistent, and can lead to the negative evaluation of those who do not conform to them.

- Women managers in positions of power were found to be effectively using a combination of speech styles, which are stereotypically associated with men and women. This enables them to be simultaneously assertive and supportive. However, their options are also constrained by the social expectations for women as a group.

- The communities of practice approach is particularly useful for workplace studies, in enabling comparisons across different groups, as well as in drawing attention to the salient role of other contextual features and norms, in addition to gender.

- It is important to critically examine stereotypically male/female styles (e.g. competitive vs. co-operative) for the effects they have as symbolic categories drawn upon to evaluate men and women in the workplace. For example, 'relational practice' is often overlooked because it is seen as 'feminine behaviour'.

- Workplace researchers have embraced the notions of gendered discourses and identities into their research, examining the positioning of women and men through different discourses, and the opportunities and inequalities created as a result.

- Some dominant gendered discourses in the workplace include discourses of femininity, discourses of motherhood, discourses of women as emotional or irrational, and discourses of equality and discrimination.

- These discourses appear natural, but in reality they serve to maintain the status quo, emphasize androcentric meanings and values, and encourage female disadvantage. Women constantly negotiate these in the workplace, in an attempt to construct socially acceptable identities for themselves and to avoid negative evaluation.

- Sexism is inhibited in workplace discourses, and can take the form of rationalizations, self-exoneration, and contradictions. The resistance of dominant discourses is both complex and unpredictable.

- Women, especially in public and authoritative positions, often face a 'double bind', where they are negatively evaluated *both* when adopting more assertive speech styles associated with masculine speech, and when adopting styles associated with feminine speech. In the first case, they risk being seen as overly aggressive and unfeminine, while in the second case, they risk being seen as ineffective and weak.

- In male-dominated workplaces (e.g. business, politics, the church, the police, etc.), women's negotiation of expectations may involve adopting the interactional approaches that are characteristic of these environments (where leadership style equates masculine style).

- Despite the impact of feminism and equal opportunities legislation, men significantly outnumber women in the highest positions of social power. While in some professions women are forced to remain under a 'glass ceiling', men enjoy the best access and opportunities even within so-called 'female' professions. In addition, women typically enter fields that men no longer find desirable.

- A range of gendered practices and discourses, that is, different expectations and evaluations of women and men, contribute to the maintenance of the glass ceiling. Raising linguistic awareness is as essential as collective political action towards sustainable social change.

- Gender awareness and diversity issues feature highly within organizations, for example, in equal opportunities policies, career development programmes, and awareness training seminars. Difference and dominance frameworks are popular for making sense of interactional styles and strategies at work.

- War and sport metaphors in business talk are examples of language use that arguably reinforces masculine discourses and social practices, while marginalizing feminine behaviour. Feminist linguistic enquiry is important for questioning the effects of in-group out-group dichotomies and a broader gender binary.

ACKNOWLEDGEMENTS

This chapter was written collaboratively with Louise Mullany, at the University of Nottingham, UK. Citation details: Mullany, L. and Litosseliti, L. (2006) Gender and language in the workplace, in Litosseliti, L. *Gender and Language: Theory and Practice*. London: Hodder Arnold, pp. 123–147.

FURTHER READING

Coates, J. (1995) Language, gender and career, in S. Mills (ed.) *Language and Gender: Interdisciplinary Perspectives*. Harlow: Longman, pp. 13–30.

Coates, J. (2004) *Women, Men and Language*, 3rd edn. Harlow: Pearson (Chapter 11, pp. 197–211).

Holmes, J. and Marra, M. (2004) Relational practice in the workplace: women's talk or gendered discourse? *Language in Society*, 33: 377–98.

Holmes, J. and Stubbe, M. (2003) 'Feminine' workplaces: stereotype and reality, in J. Holmes and M. Meyerhoff (eds) *The Handbook of Language and Gender*. Oxford: Blackwell, pp. 573–99.

Kendall, S. and Tannen, D. (1997) Gender and language in the workplace, in R. Wodak (ed.) *Gender and Discourse*. New York: Longman, pp. 81–105.

Tannen, D. (1995) *Talking from 9 to 5*. London: Virago.

Tannen, D. (1999) The display of (gendered) identities in talk at work, in M. Bucholtz, A.C. Liang and L. Sutton (eds) *Reinventing Identities: The Gendered Self in Discourse*. Oxford: Oxford University Press.

Walsh, C. (2001) *Gender and Discourse: Language and Power in Politics, the Church and Organizations*. London: Longman.

Wodak, R. (1997) 'I know, we won't revolutionize the world with it, but …': styles of female leadership in institutions, in H. Kotthoff and R. Wodak (eds) *Communicating Gender in Context*. Amsterdam: John Benjamins.

Other references

P. Heim videos: www.heimgroup.com

Sam Jones, Women doctors at top 'harm status', *The Guardian*, 2 August 2004.

Strategic HR Review, 3(6), September/October 2004.

Rebecca Smithers, More women move into academia despite the glass ceiling, *The Guardian*, 1 October 2004.

Lucy Ward, Men 'winning' caring profession sex war, *The Guardian*, 26 July 2005.

RESEARCHING GENDER AND LANGUAGE

This part introduces some key elements and principles involved in conducting research on gender and language. It aims to be a starting point for researchers in the area and a resource for those who are teaching and studying gender and language. In the first section of Chapter 7, the relevant ideas are introduced, rather than developed in detail (which is not within the scope of this book), and framed through reference to readings where in-depth discussions can be found. The other sections in the chapter list samples of activities, study questions, and sources for carrying out gender and language research.

7 Starting points for researchers, teachers and students

PRINCIPLES OF FEMINIST LINGUISTIC RESEARCH

Feminist research shares many of the principles underlying different methodological frameworks, such as post-structuralism, post-modernism, and Marxism. These include a questioning of, most notably, the validity of 'universal truths' or 'objectivity' (notions which make the researcher invisible), of Western forms of knowledge, and of the androcentrism of science.

The central tenet of feminism, 'the personal is political', means that personal experience is fundamental to the feminist research process, something which manifests itself in a number of ways:

1 Feminist research is characterized by a self-reflection, self-reflexivity, or conscious partiality

Feminist researchers refute the idea that facts can be divorced from values or that impartiality is possible, and aim to engage with their own value positions. More specifically from a feminist linguistic perspective, impartiality is not possible: if language choices are sociologically and ideologically determined, then analysts are also inextricably involved in understanding, interpreting and shaping the processes, functions and meanings of social interaction (Sunderland and Litosseliti, 2002). Self-reflexivity in academic enquiry means an effort on the part of the analysts to declare their interest in the research; to be explicit about their own decisions regarding what becomes a topic for study, which questions are asked or not, which methods of analysis are followed and why, how conclusions are reached; and to continuously reassess their own presuppositions. The need to be reflexive is also important because sometimes feminists may perpetuate rather than subvert the inequalities they try to address (Lazar, 2005).

Readings
Cameron *et al.* (1992)
Bergvall *et al.* (1996)

2 Feminist researchers locate themselves within, rather than outside the research topic and the participants. This entails being alert to the existence of power relationships between the researcher and those researched

The aim here is for scholarship 'which does not transform those it studies into objects but preserves in its analytic procedures the presence of the subject as actor and experiencer' (Smith, 1981: 1). This is especially important for feminist research, as it is often centred around marginal or oppressed individuals and groups. The participants' perspectives during the research process, as well as them setting the agenda and identifying what is important for them in their own terms, take precedence over those of an 'expert' researcher – a notion that is questioned as well. However, feminist researchers often find themselves in a difficult situation, when it comes to insider/outsider perspectives: 'We may empathize with a woman's perspective, but we cannot presume to be fully inside that situation *or* to have a better vantage point from which to evaluate that situation' (DeFrancisco, 1997: 48).

Readings
Cameron *et al.* (1992)   DeFrancisco (1997)

The necessity for this complex negotiation between the researcher and those researched has been the subject of much debate (see Cameron *et al.,* 1992; Sarangi and Roberts, 1999). It relates to the singular most fundamental aspect of feminist research, which distinguishes it from other research:

3 Feminist research is informed by feminist politics

Feminist research grounds its critique in emancipatory action, and the transformation or empowerment of participants (see DeFransisco, 1997, for a good discussion of issues regarding such action). Along these lines, feminist linguistics (see Part I) is grounded in identifying, demystifying, and resisting the various ways in which language reflects, creates and helps sustain gender inequalities. Seeing linguistic change as a crucial part of social change, it explicitly aims to draw connections between gender-related linguistic phenomena and gender inequality or discrimination. For example, it acknowledges that it is problematic to speak of 'woman' as a universal category where characteristics and experiences are assumed to be shared by all women, as this effectively means excluding 'other' (black, working-class, lesbians, etc.) less privileged women (Christie, 2000). In this sense, all research is political, located within a particular standpoint, in the same way that any knowledge is 'interested', that is, held by particular interest groups, and maintaining power relations that need to be made visible (see Chapter 3).

Reading
Baxter (2003)

As we saw in Part I, the study of gender and language has been developing, towards recognizing that the meanings generated by language use are not self-evident or derivable from linguistic 'content' (Christie, 2000); that linguistic features cannot straightforwardly be mapped on to individual characteristics such as a person's sex; and that there are different gender ideologies that frame everyday interactions and practices, and render them sensible within social contexts. These new concerns and lines of enquiry involve new methodological possibilities and constraints. Swann (2002) explores whether the current models of gender and language, which see meaning as ambiguous and context-dependent, allow an analyst to make any general statements about gendered language use. She asks a number of questions that I list here, because they are pertinent for anyone researching gender and language in the current climate.

> [W]hat implications does [a fluid conception of language and meaning] have for the authority with which analysts interpret texts? How do analysts establish the meaning of an utterance? Is one interpretation as good as any other? ... for the analyst, what should count as *relevant* context, and what sort of warrants do analysts need to make inferences about this? ... How does the analyst assess whether a speaker is doing gender, or another aspect of identity? How does this relate to any one of a number of other things speakers and listeners may be doing in an interaction?
>
> (Swann, 2002: 47–8)

To address these questions, Swann usefully identifies and discusses a set of warrants used by researchers, both historically and currently, to justify interpretations of data as gendered in some way. These warrants for language and gender research are as follows (2002: 49):

- quantitative and/or general patterns (derived from correlational studies of language use, large (computerized) corpora or other systematic comparison between the language of different social groups);
- indirect reliance on quantitative/general patterns;
- participants' orientations as evident in the text;
- speakers'/participants' solicited interpretations;
- analysts' theoretical positions;
- analysts' intuitions;
- speakers/participants are female, male (or whatever).

Reading
Swann (2002)

Swann's paper is very useful in drawing attention to how difficult it is for researchers not to use gender 'as an *a priori* explanatory category'; and in suggesting 'a wider range of warrants and associated research methods drawn on as and when to target specific questions and issues' (ibid.: 60). For example, quantitative approaches may be used to complement qualitative, contextualized analyses. At present, feminist linguistic research draws overwhelmingly on qualitative methodologies that examine the *why* and the *how* of language use, and much less on quantitative methods, which have tended to identify the frequency of instances of particular language use. One reason for this, as seen in much of feminist critique, is the tendency for past quantitative sociolinguistic research to measure women's language with instruments designed for men (Coates and Cameron, 1988). Qualitative methods – such as interviews, participant observation, ethnography, and so on – are seen as suitable for illuminating the complexity of meanings, processes, and contexts, and for exploring a range of interpretations (Cohen and Manion, 1994; Silverman, 1993). They put emphasis on meanings situated in context and as they emerge from the participants themselves and what they actually do, rather than being pre-determined by the researcher or measured by variables. The research described in Chapter 3 is based on the premise that the researcher can get close to the interaction, and to participants' situated use of language and discourses in instantiating a practice. The shift towards qualitative procedures, across the social sciences, is part of an ongoing debate about moving away from *positivistic* paradigms of research (e.g. positivism) towards more *interpretative* (e.g. phenomenology, ethno-methodology, sociolinguistics, ethnography) and more *critical* paradigms (e.g. Marxism, feminism) – see Sarantakos (1998) for a comprehensive discussion.

Antaki *et al.* (2003) observe that qualitative analysis in general, and discourse analysis in particular, can be misunderstood by those trained in quantitative methods as analysis where 'anything goes'. With the aim to emphasize the analytic basis of discourse analysis (of any type – see Chapter 3), they outline some basic requirements for the analysis of discourse and a number of things that give the appearance of conducting such analysis, but which they call 'non-analyses'. We are alerted to the following six non-analyses, which are useful reminders for those of us involved in discourse analytic work in the social sciences, as well as for students being introduced to such work:

1. under-analysis through summarizing themes in an interaction;
2. under-analysis through taking sides;
3. under-analysis through over-quotation or through isolated quotation;
4. the circular identification of discourses and mental constructs;
5. under-analysis through treating findings as surveys;
6. under-analysis through simply spotting features.

In her response to Antaki *et al.*, Burman problematizes the idea that avoiding taking sides in analysis is possible, but stresses the importance of being reflexive about 'how the tools of our own discursive practice inevitably speak of their own assumptions'

(2003: 2). She further alerts researchers to three additional failures to do discourse analysis fruitfully:

7. under-analysis through uncontested readings;
8. under-analysis through decontextualization (i.e. not situating a text in the historical, social and political context which gave rise to it);
9. under-analysis through not having a question (i.e. *why* this analysis is being done).

In particular, the idea of situating texts in context has been both assumed and advocated by those types of discourse analysis that describe themselves broadly as 'critical' (see Chapter 3). Such situatedness involves providing a rationale about our choices of texts as data, where they come from, why they are important, and why they are useful for providing answers to specific research questions.

Readings

Antaki *et al.* (2003)
Burman (2003)

The ideas presented briefly in this section serve as starting points for approaching one's involvement with feminist research in general and gender and language research in particular. They can be followed through the indicated readings, and these readings can also be used to prepare students for working on hands-on activities, such as the ones that follow.

SAMPLES OF ACTIVITIES

In addition to activities given in previous chapters, the activities below can be used (as such or adapted) during seminar work with students, to encourage them to reflect on some of the issues introduced in this book:

---

1. Transcript of an extract from a focus group discussion on the topic of marriage (Litosseliti, 1999). For transcript conventions see p. 36.

[*Discussion turns to the topic of women taking their husband's surname after marriage*]

[…]

Phil: [there are] very practical reasons =
Simon: = no I think it's more than that actually
/ I think this taking the same name is sometimes a symbolic thing / certainly in my first marriage I wanted my name to (…) / but my relationship now is very different from my first relationship . it's very much two individuals / I think I'd be quite happy if Mary kept her own name /

Irene:	I think a side of you feels as if you're giving in / I feel as if I was giving up something =
Phil:	= it's pretty bad when you feel that this is your husband's name
Irene:	yes
Phil:	that strikes me as very much a putdown /
Irene:	I still don't think that it's MY name / my name is X / it's how I was born and it will always be / I like X but it's not my name /
Anna:	so it's the name you go by ! /
Irene:	yes that's right / *[Laughs]*
Simon:	I can sympathise with that / I think if the situation reversed I would be very unhappy losing my name /
Irene:	I was . perhaps I was 36 I think when I got married / and so yeah I had my own name for a long time / it was me /
George:	*[referring to him and his wife having different surnames]* whenever . you know like the car needs to be serviced and they ring up and they say is it Mr X . and they use her name . and I suddenly become HER /
Lia:	what is that like? /
George:	well I say I'm NOT Mr X but =
Irene:	= and it's not important / it's unnecessary
George:	but yes you get a glimpse into what it feels like to actually not having . being who you want to be /

Questions

1. What questions of interest for gender and language might arise from this text?
2. To pursue these questions in a research project, what would you need to find out about the text?
3. What theoretical and methodological approaches would be useful/appropriate?

2. Extract from a brochure for seminars for working women (CareerTrack International)

High-Impact Communication Skills for Women

A one-day CareerTrack seminar

26 skills and insights to help you communicate powerfully

Speaking up and getting heard
Timing is everything: when you're most likely to be heard and when it's better to hold your tongue.

Crucial differences in how men and women communicate – and how to use this awareness to get more respect.

The simple secret of creating immediate rapport.

How taking yourself seriously affects the way others see you … and specific ways to demonstrate your own self-respect.

Gently redefining relationships with your co-workers so they know where you stand, and how you want to be treated.

Making requests in a way that encourages people to cooperate with you.

How to bring 'hidden resistance' out in the open.

Moving from self-consciousness to self-confidence

How to mentally prepare for a difficult confrontation … an all-important presentation … or a high-powered meeting.

Courage-builders to help you face high-stakes situations and difficult people.

Specific techniques that enable you to keep your composure when you feel yourself losing control.

Listening (and responding) to what people mean, not what they say.

Setting limits without making enemies

What to do when you're ignored or interrupted (so you don't get flustered and do get results).

When you have to criticize others: how to do it in a way that minimizes resentment and defensiveness.

When you're being criticized: how to stay open to the message without overreacting or being 'hurt'.

What to do when someone tries to intimidate or bully you.

Empathy: your secret weapon for defusing a hothead.

How to say no in a way people respect.

What to do when people don't respect your limits.

Specific techniques for dealing with lying, guilt trips and unreasonable requests.

How to avoid inconsistent behaviors that make it harder for you to set limits the next time.

Gaining visibility and getting ahead

5 steps that help you manage the stress of speaking in groups.

How to be an 'active player' and contribute during meetings.

Selling your point of view: how to make your idea their idea – so it's supported enthusiastically.

How to react when you're challenged so you come across even stronger.

A quick and simple way to get over your fear of speaking up.

How to use conflicts to build stronger relationships.

Questions

1. What gendered discourses can you identify in the text? How are women positioned through them?
2. What do we need to know about gender in organizations in order to make sense of the different layers of the text?
3. What gender ideologies and possible inequalities are shored up by the discourses above?

3. Editorial in *Good Housekeeping* (February 1999)

Most of us try not to think too much about fitness and diet right now, as we haven't shifted those few extra pounds from Christmas. But Rosemary Conley will get you into that leotard before you can say chocolate! Her philosophy is that we can all look better and feel fitter (…and look what it did for her!). But it has to be done at your own pace, which is why we've devised a healthy diet and exercise routine that anyone can follow. If you think that you've tried them all, try ours. The Hay Diet, the F-plan – you name it, we've done it too – so we're well placed to create a weight-loss and well-being plan that will work for you.

Questions

1. What linguistic resources are used in the editorial that are typical of media discourse in general, and magazines in particular?
2. Who is the ideal reader of this text?
3. In what ways are women positioned here? What kind of femininities are constructed through the text, and for what purpose?
4. What are some possible ways in which readers can respond to the positionings in the text?

4. Extracts from 'head-to-head' debate on the question 'What are the moral duties of business?' (*The Guardian*, November 1996)

(1a) **Anita Roddick:** […]You have said that what makes you happy is seeing the company's prosperity trickle down to employees. I have a broader vision: our employees want to participate in social change to give their work more meaning. That's what makes me happy – when I see employees involved, when the connection between life and work appears seamless. Is your apparently money-based view of business really so narrow?

(1b) **Stanley Kalms:** On the other hand my tribe goes back several thousand years and we have accumulated quite a lot of carefully documented wisdom. So I start from a sound ethical base – age-old values and proven rules of social obligation. No need to make them up on the hoof – instant ethics can be tiresome. [...] At Dixons we do it differently. Our writ runs to paying our staff on a Friday afternoon. 'Life and work seamless' – that is truly nonsense. Our role is to create the means, not impose the ends.

Anita, our differences may not be so sharp but I can't tell from your scattered thoughts. I believe in a focused, rational approach in which man has it within himself to improve. But it needs a reasoned acceptance of the real world. Might I suggest to you that Margaret Thatcher would be a better role model than Don Quixote.

(2a) **Anita Roddick:** Now I know where you're coming from. I'm the irrational female imposing my world view on employees, ignorant of how markets work. But you seem to know the price of everything and the value of nothing [...] By the way, unlike Mrs Thatcher, I believe there is an alternative, so we don't tilt at windmills, we invest in them!

(2b) **Stanley Kalms:** Your attempt to monopolize the 'caring' market fails. I also care but in an ordered and studied manner, not merely based on public relations geared to selling my products [...] Your cliché-ridden response is disappointing, albeit predictable. Let me pose you a quiet question – can't you accept that your frenetic, self-righteous approach may not always be the best way to draw attention to issues that actually concern us all? [...*continues*]

© Dame Anita Roddick, founder of the Body Shop, www.AnitaRoddick.com

Questions

1. In what ways does gender become relevant in this debate?
2. What gendered discourses can you identify in the text? How are women positioned through them? In what ways do participants respond to such discourses?

STUDY QUESTIONS (PARTS I AND II)

The following questions appear within each chapter in Parts I and II, and are explored mainly in the particular chapter. They have been partly modified here in order to stand independently. These questions can be adapted to develop group seminar questions, essay questions, or questions for small-scale research projects.

Chapter 1

1. In what ways can language shape how we see ourselves and the world?
2. What are some examples of biological explanations of gender differences? What are their possible effects and implications?
3. Consider the following topics being debated in some European countries at the time of writing:

- the preaching, by some Christian groups, of sexual abstinence to teenagers;
- boys' academic under-achievement;
- the ban on wearing Islamic head-scarves in French schools;
- single-sex schools;
- the pay gap for women and men in paid employment;
- the availability of contraception to girls and boys under 16;
- the provision of maternity and paternity leave for employees.

First, would it be possible in each case to talk about the sexes (men, women, boys, girls) without saying something about gender?

Second, would it be possible to talk about gender without saying something about race, ethnicity, religion, class, sexuality, education levels, and the geographical/historical/political/social context pertinent to each of these issues?

Chapter 2

1. What assumptions is Lakoff making in the quote below?

    > Women's speech seems in general to contain more instances of 'well', 'you know', 'kind' and so forth: words that convey the sense that the speaker is uncertain about what he (or she) is saying, or cannot vouch for the accuracy of the statement ... [These words] appear ... as an apology for making an assertion at all.
    >
    > (Lakoff, 1975: 53–4)

2. Consider each of the features of 'women's language', as described by Lakoff. Think of as many *functions* of the same feature as possible, and of different *situations* where the same feature is used in different ways.
3. In what ways can language be used to dominate and control interaction?
4. What are some of the ways in which adults talk to boys and girls differently, and some of the ways in which adults respond to them differently? What are the possible effects of such talk?
5. Read Extract (2B) in Chapter 2. Can you see evidence of the linguistic choices and interaction styles that are associated with women's and men's language, according to difference theorists?
6. If we conceptualize the interactions of gender, class and race as intersecting circles (West and Fenstermaker, 1995), what are some examples where different members of groups share some, but not all of these characteristics?
7. What are some concrete examples where gender polarization effectively justifies the limiting of options – in terms of educational, vocational, public office or political opportunities – for women? And for men?

Chapter 3

1. Identify some 'sexist' discourses that draw on sexist wordings, and some that do not.

2. Read Extracts (1A) and (1B) in Chapter 1. What gendered discourses do you think are evident in the texts? How are women and men positioned through them? What identities is Heather Clark producing in Extract (1B)? What identities are attributed to her by the interviewer?

Chapter 4

1. In what ways can classroom interaction be gendered? What gender stereotypes are likely to be produced and reproduced at school?
2. Discuss classroom research findings that can be explained through theories of dominance.
3. Discuss classroom research findings that can be explained through theories of difference.
4. In what ways can analyses of the quantity and of the quality of interaction produce different findings, as regards gender in the classroom?
5. What are possible responses to perceived sexism in language learning materials, on the part of teachers and education policy-makers?

Chapter 5

1. Read Extract (1A) in Chapter 1. How are women and men represented in the texts (e.g. as passive or active, and in specific roles and domains)? What femininities and masculinities, and what gender relations, are constructed for women and men in the texts? Who is the ideal reader and what subject positions are available in the texts? What power relations, particularly unequal power relations, are created through certain inclusions/exclusions?
2. Consider any of the extracts in Chapter 5. Alternatively, choose a text from a women's magazine, e.g. an article on health or beauty, an interview, an advice column, etc. You may also use the Corby Trouser Press advertisements in Chapter 5.

   ■ Who is the ideal reader of the texts?
   ■ In what ways are women/men positioned in the texts? What femininities and masculinities are constructed? Why?
   ■ What kind of power relations are assumed/created?
   ■ What are some possible ways in which readers can respond to the various positionings in the texts?
   ■ How do the cultural practices in the texts compare with those in other cultures?

Chapter 6

1. In what ways are women and men evaluated differently when communicating in the workplace? How could this vary from workplace to workplace?
2. What gender ideologies are premised upon and sustained by the discourses discussed in Chapter 6? What inequalities or imbalances are shored up by these discourses?

3. What gendered discourses are at work in *The Guardian* articles seen in Chapter 6? How can they influence the material conditions of women's and men's lives differently in different cultures?

4. In what ways can change in the discourse in organizations bring about social change, as regards gender? What else is necessary for discourse change to be effective?

RESOURCES FOR TEACHERS

General texts

Cohen, L. and Manion, L. (1985) *Research Methods in Education*, 2nd edn. London: Croom Helm.

Johnstone, B. (2000) *Qualitative Methods in Sociolinguistics*. New York: Oxford University Press.

Silverman, D. (1993) *Interpreting Qualitative Data*. London: Sage.

Wray, A., Trott, K. and Bloomer, A. (1998) *Projects in Linguistics: A Practical Guide to Researching Language*. London: Hodder Arnold.

Gender-related texts

See texts listed in Chapter 3, Further reading.

Cameron, D. (1993) *Feminism and Linguistic Theory*, 2nd edn. London: Longman.

Eckert, P. and McConnell-Ginet, S. (2003) *Language and Gender*. Cambridge: Cambridge University Press.

Talbot, M. (1998) *Language and Gender: An Introduction*. Cambridge: Polity.

Websites

Mary Bucholtz's Language and Gender Page,
   www.linguistics.ucsb.edu/faculty/bucholtz/lng

Andrew Moore's teaching resource site,
   www.universalteacher.org.uk/lang/gender.htm

The Council on the Status of Women in Linguistics (COSWL),
   www-personal.umich.edu/~jlawler/gender.html

Syllabi on the Web for Women- and Gender-Related Courses
   www.umbc.edu/cwit/syl_ling.html

Gender and Genre Bibliography, www.ling.lancs.ac.uk/groups/gal/ggb/genre.htm

International Gender and Language Association (IGALA),
   www.stanford.edu/group/igala/

Gender and Language journal, www.equinoxpub.com/journals

FURTHER READING

Bergvall, V., Bing, J. and Freed, A. (eds) (1996) *Rethinking Language and Gender Research: Theory and Practice*. London: Longman.

Cameron, D., Frazer, E., Harvey, P., Rampton, B. and Richardson, K. (1992) *Researching Language: Issues of Power and Method.* London: Routledge.

Crawford, M. and Kimmel, E. (1999) Promoting methodological diversity in feminist research, *Psychology of Women Quarterly*, 23: 1–6.

Gergen, M. (1988) Toward a feminist metatheory and methodology in the social sciences, in M. Gergen (ed.) *Feminist Thought and the Structure of Knowledge.* New York: New York University Press, pp. 87–104.

Hall, K. and Bucholtz, M. (1995) *Gender Articulated: Language and the Socially Constructed Self.* London: Routledge.

Krolokke, C. and Scott Sorensen, A. (2005) *Gender Communication Theories and Analyses: From Silence to Performance.* London: Sage.

Nielsen, J. (ed.) (1990) *Feminist Research Methods: Exemplary Readings in the Social Sciences.* Boulder, CO: Westview Press.

Roberts, H. (ed.) (1981) *Doing Feminist Research.* London: Routledge.

Russo, N. (1999) Feminist research: questions and methods, *Psychology of Women Quarterly*, 23: i–iv.

Weedon, C. ([1987] 1997) *Feminist Practice and Poststructuralist Theory.* Oxford: Blackwell.

References

INTRODUCTION

Butler, J. (1990) *Gender Trouble: Feminism and the Subversion of Identity*. London: Routledge.

Cameron, D. (1998) Gender, language and discourse: a review essay, *Signs*, 1: 945–73.

Eckert, P. and McConnell-Ginet, S. (1994) Think practically and look locally: language and gender as a community-based practice, in C. Roman, S. Juhasz and C. Miller (eds) *The Woman and Language Debate*. New Brunswick, NJ: Rutgers University Press.

Fairclough, N. (1992) *Discourse and Social Change*. Cambridge: Polity Press.

Johnson, S. and Meinhoff, U. (eds) (1997) *Language and Masculinity*. Oxford: Blackwell.

Talbot, M. (1997) *Language and Gender: An Introduction*. Cambridge: Polity Press.

Wodak, R. (ed.) (1997) *Gender and Discourse*. London: Sage.

I PUTTING GENDER AND LANGUAGE ON THE MAP

Antaki, C. (ed.) (1988) *Analysing Everyday Explanation: A Casebook of Methods*. London: Sage.

Antaki, C. (1994) *Explaining and Arguing: The Social Organisation of Accounts*. London: Sage.

August, E. (1995) Real men don't: anti-male bias in English, in W. Roberts and G. Turgen (eds) *About Language: A Reader for Writers*. Boston: Houghton, pp. 267–77.

Baxter, J. (2003) *Positioning Gender in Discourse: A Feminist Methodology*. Basingstoke: Palgrave Macmillan.

Beard, A. (2004) *Language Change*. London: Routledge.

Bem, S.L. (1993) *The Lenses of Gender: Transforming the Debate on Sexual Inequality*. New Haven, CT: Yale University Press.

Bing, J. and Bergvall, V. (1996) The question of questions: beyond binary thinking, in V. Bergvall, J. Bing and A. Freed (eds) *Rethinking Language and Gender Research: Theory and Practice*. London: Longman, pp. 1–30.

Blaubergs, M. (1980) An analysis of classic arguments against changing sexist language. *Women's Studies International Quarterly*, 3: 135–47.

Bourke, J. (1999) *An Intimate History of Killing: Face-to-Face Killing in 20th Century Warfare*. New York: Basic Books.

Bourke, J. (2001) *The Second World War: A People's History*. Oxford: Oxford University Press.

Bucholtz, M. (1999) Bad examples: transgression and progress in language and gender studies, in M. Bucholtz, A.C. Liang and L. Sutton (eds) *Reinventing Identities: The Gendered Self in Discourse*. New York: Oxford University Press, pp. 3–24.

Butler, J. (1990) *Gender Trouble: Feminism and the Subversion of Identity*. London: Routledge.

Cameron, D. (ed.) (1990) *The Feminist Critique of Language: A Reader*. New York: Routledge.

Cameron, D. (1992) *Feminism and Linguistic Theory*. Basingstoke: Macmillan.

Cameron, D. (1995) *Verbal Hygiene*. London: Routledge.

Cameron, D. (1997) Theoretical debates in feminist linguistics: questions of sex and gender, in R. Wodak (ed.) *Discourse and Gender*. Thousand Oaks, CA: Sage, pp. 21–36.

Cameron, D. (ed.) (1998) *The Feminist Critique of Language*, 2nd edn. London: Routledge.

Cheshire, J. (1978) Present tense verbs in reading English, in P. Trudgill (ed.) *Sociolinguistic Patterns in British English*. London: Edward Arnold, pp. 52–68.

Christie, C. (2000) *Gender and Language: Towards a Feminist Pragmatics*. Edinburgh: Edinburgh University Press.

Coates, J. (1998) 'Thank God I'm a woman': the construction of differing femininities, in D. Cameron (ed.) *The Feminist Critique of Language*. London: Routledge, pp. 295–320.

Cowie, C. and Lees, S. (1987) Slags or drags?, in *Feminist Review* (ed.) *Sexuality: A Reader*. London: Virago.

Dion, K. (1987) What's in a title? The *Ms.* stereotype and images of women's titles of address, *Psychology of Women Quarterly*, 11: 21–36.

Eckert, P. (1989) The whole woman: sex and gender differences in variation, *Language Variation and Change*, 1: 254–67.

Ehrlich, S. (2004) Gendered ideologies and the structuring of 'experiences' of coerced sex, paper presented at IGALA 3 conference, Cornell University, NY, 7 June.

Epstein, J. (1990) Either/or–neither/both: sexual ambiguity and the ideology of gender, *Genders*, 7: 99–142.

Fairclough, N. (1992) *Discourse and Social Change*. Cambridge: Polity Press.

Giddens, A. (1989) *Sociology*. Cambridge: Polity Press.

Graddol, D. and Swann, J. (1989) *Gender Voices*. Oxford: Blackwell.

Hall, K. and O'Donovan, V. (1996) Shifting gender positions among Hindi-speaking hijras, in V. Bergvall, J. Bing and A. Freed (eds) *Rethinking Language and Gender Research: Theory and Practice*. London: Longman, pp. 228–66.

Hekman, S. (1990) *Gender and Knowledge: Elements of a Postmodern Feminism*. Cambridge: Polity Press.

Hellinger, M. and Hadumod, B. (eds) (2001) *Gender across Languages: The Linguistic Representation of Women and Men*, vol. I. *IMPACT: Studies in Language and Society* 9.

Jacobs, S. and Cromwell, J. (1992) Visions and revisions of reality: reflections on sex, sexuality, gender, and gender variance, *Journal of Homosexuality*, 23: 43–69.

Labov, W. (1990) The intersection of sex and social class in the course of linguistic change. *Language Variation and Change*, 2(2): 205–54.

Lees, S. (1996) *Carnal Knowledge: Rape on Trial*. London: Hamish Hamilton.

Lorber, J. and Farrell, S.A. (eds) (1991) *The Social Construction of Gender*. Newbury Park, CA: Sage.

Miller, C. and Swift, K. (1981) *The Handbook of Non-Sexist Writing for Writers, Editors and Speakers*. London: The Women's Press.

Mills, S. (2002) Third wave feminist linguistics and the analysis of sexism, plenary talk at IGALA 2 conference, 12–14 April, Lancaster. Also in *Discourse Analysis Online*, www.shu.ac.uk/daol/

Pauwels, A. (1998) *Women Changing Language*. New York: Longman.

Poynton, C. (1989) *Language and Gender: Making the Difference*. Oxford: Oxford University Press.

Rattansi, A. (1995) Just framing; ethnicities and racisms in a 'postmodern' framework, in L. Nicholson and S. Seidman (eds) *Social Postmodernism: Beyond Identity Politics*. New York: Cambridge University Press, pp. 250–86.

Schulz, M. (1975) The semantic derogation of woman, in B. Thorne and N. Henley (eds) *Language and Sex: Difference and Dominance*. Rowley, MA: Newbury House, pp. 64–73.

Spender, D. (1990) *Man-Made Language*, 2nd edn. London: Pandora.

Stanley, J. (1977) Gender marking in American English, in A.P. Milsen *et al. Sexism and Language*. Urbana, IL: NCTE, pp. 44–76.

Sunderland, J. (2004) Contradictions in gendered discourses, paper presented at IGALA 3 conference, Cornell University, NY, 7 June.

Sunderland, J. and Litosseliti, L. (2002) Gender identity and discourse analysis: theoretical and empirical considerations, in L. Litosseliti and J. Sunderland (eds) *Gender Identity and Discourse Analysis*. Amsterdam: John Benjamins, pp. 1–39.

Talbot, M. (1998) *Language and Gender: An Introduction*. Cambridge: Polity Press.

Trudgill, P. (1974) *Sociolinguistics: An Introduction*. Harmondsworth: Penguin.

van Dijk, T. (2005) *Racism and Discourse in Spain and Latin America*. Amsterdam: John Benjamins.

Wodak, R. (ed.) (1997) *Gender and Discourse*. London: Sage.

Wood, L.A. and Rennie, H. (1994) Formulating rape: the discursive construction of victims and villains, *Discourse and Society*, 5: 125–48.

2 THE 'LANGUAGE OF WOMEN': LACKING, POWERLESS, DIFFERENT

Barnett, R. and Rivers, C. (2004) Men are from earth, and so are women. It's faulty research that sets them apart, *The Chronicle Review*, 51(2): B11.

Bem, S.L. (1993) *The Lenses of Gender: Transforming the Debate on Sexual Inequality*. New Haven, CT: Yale University Press.

Bergvall, V., Bing, J. and Freed, A. (eds) (1996) *Rethinking Language and Gender Research: Theory and Practice*. London: Longman.

Bilous, F. and Krauss, R. (1988) Dominance and accommodation in the conversational behaviors of same- and mixed-gender dyads, *Language and Communication*, 8(3/4): 183–95.

Bing, J. (1999) Brain sex: how the media reports and distorts brain research, *Women and Language*, XXII: 2, 4–12.

Bing, J. and Bergvall, V. (1998) The question of questions: beyond binary thinking, in J. Coates (ed.) *Language and Gender: A Reader*. Oxford: Blackwell, pp. 496–510.

Borker, R. and Maltz, D. (1989) Anthropological perspectives on gender and language, in *Gender and Anthropology: Critical Reviews for Research and Teaching*. Washington, DC: AAA.

Bucholtz, M. (ed.) (2004) *Language and Woman's Place: Text and Commentaries*, rev. and expanded edn, original text by R. Lakoff, ed. M. Bucholtz. New York: Oxford University Press.

Cameron, D. (1990) Why is language a feminist issue?, in D. Cameron (ed.) *The Feminist Critique of Language: A Reader*. New York: Routledge, pp. 1–32.

Cameron, D. (1992) Review of Tannen, *Feminism and Psychology*, 2: 475–8.

Cameron, D. (1995) *Verbal Hygiene*. London: Routledge.

Cameron, D. (1996) The language-gender interface: resisting co-optation, in V. Bergvall, J. Bing and A. Freed (eds) *Rethinking Language and Gender Research*. London: Longman, pp. 31–53.

Cameron, D. and Coates, J. (1989) Some problems in the sociolinguistic explanation of sex differences, in J. Coates and D. Cameron (eds) *Women in their Speech Communities*. New York: Longman, pp. 13–26.

Cameron, D., McAlinden, F. and O'Leary, K. (1988) Lakoff in context: the social and linguistic function of tag questions, in J. Coates and D. Cameron (ed.) *Women in their Speech Communities: New Perspectives on Language and Sex*. New York: Longman, pp. 74–93.

Christie, C. (2000) *Gender and Language: Towards a Feminist Pragmatics*. Edinburgh: Edinburgh University Press.

Coates, J. (1988) Gossip revisited: language in all-female groups, in J. Coates and D. Cameron (eds) *Women in their Speech Communities: New Perspectives on Language and Sex*. New York: Longman, pp. 94–122.

Coates, J. (1993) *Women, Men, and Language: A Sociolinguistic Account of Sex*. New York: Longman.

Coates, J. (1996a) *Women Talk: Conversation between Women Friends*. Oxford: Blackwell.

Coates, J. (1996b) 'You know so I mean I probably ...': hedges and hedging, in *Women Talk: Conversation between Women Friends*. Oxford: Blackwell, pp. 152–73.

Coates, J. (1997) One-at-a-time: the organization of men's talk, in S. Johnson and U. Meinhoff (eds) *Language and Masculinity*. Oxford: Blackwell.

Coates, J. and Cameron, D. (eds) (1988) *Women in their Speech Communities*. London: Longman.

Cohn, C. and Ruddick, S. (2004) A feminist ethical perspective on weapons of mass destruction, in S. Hashmi and S. Lee (eds) *Ethics and Weapons of Mass Destruction: Religious and Secular Perspectives*. New York: Cambridge University Press, pp. 405–35.

Crawford, M. (1995) *Talking Difference: On Gender and Language*. London: Sage.

Eckert, P. (1990) Cooperative competition in adolescent girl talk, *Discourse Processes*, 13: 92–122.

Fishman, P. (1983) Interaction: the work women do, in B. Thorne, C. Kramarae and N. Henley (eds) *Language, Gender, and Society*. Rowley, MA: Newbury House, pp. 89–102.

Fishman, P. (1990) Conversational insecurity, in D. Cameron (ed.) *The Feminist Critique of Language: A Reader*. New York: Routledge, pp. 234–50.

Gaudio, R. (2004) They way we wish we were: sexuality and class in language and woman's place, in *Language and Woman's Place: Text and Commentaries*, rev. and expanded edn, original text by R. Lakoff, ed. M. Bucholtz. New York: Oxford University Press.

Goffman, E. (1976) Gender advertisements, *Studies in the Anthropology of Visual Communication*, 3: 69–154.

Goodwin, M.H. (1980) Directive-response speech sequences in girls' and boys' task activities, in S. McConnell-Ginet, R. Borker and N. Furman (eds) *Women and Language in Literature and Society*. New York: Praeger, pp. 157–73.

Goodwin, M.H. (1998) Cooperation and competition across girls' play activities, in J. Coates (ed.) *Language and Gender: A Reader*. Oxford: Blackwell, pp. 121–46.

Gray, J. (1992) *Men Are from Mars, Women Are from Venus*. New York: HarperCollins.

Gumperz, J. (1982) *Discourse Strategies*. Cambridge: Cambridge University Press.

Hall, K. and Bucholtz, M. (eds) (1995) *Gender Articulated: Language and the Socially Constructed Self*. New York: Routledge.

Holland, P. (1987) When a woman reads the news, in H. Bachr and G. Dyer (eds) *Boxed In: Women and Television*. London: Pandora Press, pp. 133–50.

Holmes, J. (1986) Functions of 'you know' in women's and men's speech, *Language in Society*, 15(1): 1–22.

Holmes, J. (1990) Hedges and boosters in women's and men's speech, *Language and Communication*, 10(3): 185–206.

Holmes, J. (1995) *Women, Men and Politeness*. London: Longman.

Ide, S. (2004) Exploring woman's language in Japan, in *Language and Woman's Place: Text and Commentaries*, rev. and expanded edn, original text by R. Lakoff, ed. M. Bucholtz. New York: Oxford University Press.

James, D. and Clarke, S. (1993) Women, men and interruptions: a critical review, in D. Tannen (ed.) *Gender and Conversational Interaction*. Oxford: Oxford University Press, pp. 231–80.

Jespersen, O. (1990) The woman, in D. Cameron (ed.) *The Feminist Critique of Language: A Reader*. New York: Routledge, pp. 201–20.

Jones, D. (1990) Gossip: notes on women's oral culture, in D. Cameron (ed.) *The Feminist Critique of Language: A Reader*. New York: Routledge, pp. 242–50.

Lakoff, R. (1975) *Language and Women's Place*. New York: Harper and Row.

Leap, W. (2004) Language and woman's place: blueprint studies of gay men's English, in *Language and Woman's Place: Text and Commentaries*, rev. and expanded edn, original text by R. Lakoff, ed. M. Bucholtz. New York: Oxford University Press.

Litosseliti, L. (1999) *Moral Repertoires and Gender Voices in Argumentation*. PhD thesis, Department of Linguistics, Lancaster University, UK.

Litosseliti, L. (2002) The discursive construction of morality and gender: investigating public and private arguments, in S. Benor, M. Rose, D. Sharma, J. Sweetland and Q. Zhang (eds) *Gendered Practices in Language*. Stanford: Center for the Study of Language and Information, Stanford University, pp. 45–63.

Litosseliti, L. (2006) Constructing gender in public arguments: the female voice as emotional voice, in J. Baxter (ed.) *Speaking Out: The Female Voice in Public Contexts*. London: Palgrave Macmillan.

Livia, A. (2004) Language and woman's place: picking up the gauntlet, in *Language and Woman's Place: Text and Commentaries*, rev. and expanded edn, original text by R. Lakoff, ed. M. Bucholtz. New York: Oxford University Press.

Maltz, D. and Borker, R. (1998) A cultural approach to male–female miscommunication, in J. Coates (ed.) *Language and Gender: A Reader*. Oxford: Blackwell, pp. 417–34.

McElhinny, B. (2004) 'Radical feminist' as label, libel, and laudatory chant: the politics of theoretical taxonomies in feminist linguistics, in *Language and Woman's Place: Text and Commentaries*, rev. and expanded edn, original text by R. Lakoff, ed. M. Bucholtz. New York: Oxford University Press.

McMillan, S.R *et al.* (1973) Women's language: uncertainty or interpersonal sensitivity and emotionality?, *Sex Roles*, 3(6): 545–59.

Morgan, M. (2004) 'I'm every woman': black women's (dis)placement in women's language study, in *Language and Woman's Place: Text and Commentaries*, rev. and expanded edn, original text by R. Lakoff, ed. M. Bucholtz. New York: Oxford University Press.

Mullany, L. (2003) Identity and role construction: a sociolinguistic study of gender and discourse in management, unpublished PhD thesis, Nottingham: Nottingham Trent University, UK.

Nichols, P. (1983) Linguistic options and choices for black women in the rural South, in B. Thorne, C. Kramarae and N. Henley (eds) *Language, Gender and Society*. Rowley, MA: Newbury House, pp. 54–68.

O'Barr, W. and Atkins, B. (1998) 'Women's language' or 'powerless language'?, in J. Coates (ed.) *Language and Gender: A Reader*. Oxford: Blackwell, pp. 377–87.

Pilkington, J. (1998) 'Don't try and make out that I'm nice!' The different strategies women and men use when gossiping, in J. Coates (ed.) *Language and Gender: A Reader*. Oxford: Blackwell, pp. 254–69.

Sheldon, A. (1997) Talking power: girls, gender enculturation and discourse, in R. Wodak (ed.) *Gender and Discourse*. London: Sage, pp. 225–44.

Sheldon, A. and Johnson, D. (1998) Preschool negotiators: linguistic differences in how girls and boys regulate the expression of dissent in same-sex groups, in J. Cheshire and P. Trudgill (eds) *The Sociolinguistics Reader*, vol. 2: *Gender and Discourse*. London: Arnold, pp. 76–98.

Shields, S.A. (2000) Thinking about gender, thinking about theory: gender and emotional experience, in A. Fischer (ed.) *Gender and Emotion: Social Psychological Perspectives*. Cambridge: Cambridge University Press.

Simpson, A. (1997) 'It's a game!': the construction of gendered subjectivity, in R. Wodak (ed.) *Gender and Discourse*. London: Sage, pp. 197–224.

Spender, D. (1980) *Man Made Language*. London: Pandora.

Swann, J. (2002) 'Yes, but is it gender?', in L. Litosseliti and J. Sunderland (eds) *Gender Identity and Discourse Analysis*. Amsterdam: John Benjamins, pp. 43–67.

Tanaka, L. (2004) *Gender, Language and Culture: A Study of Japanese Television Interview Discourse*. Amsterdam: John Benjamins.

Tannen, D. (1990) *You Just Don't Understand: Women and Men in Conversation*. New York: William Morrow.

Tannen, D. (1993) The relativity of linguistic strategies: rethinking power and solidarity in gender dominance, in D. Tannen (ed.) *Gender in Conversational Language*. New York: Oxford University Press, pp. 165–88.

Thorne, B. and Henley, N. (eds) (1975) *Language and Sex: Difference and Dominance*. Rowley, MA: Newbury House.

Trudgill, P. (1974) *Sociolinguistics: An Introduction*. Harmondsworth: Penguin.

Uchida, A. (1992) When 'difference' is 'dominance': a critique of the 'anti-power-based' cultural approach to sex differences, *Language in Society* 21(4): 547–68.

West, C. and Fenstermaker, S. (1995) Doing difference, *Gender and Society*, 9(1): 8–37.

West, C. and Zimmerman, D. (1983) Small insults: a study of interruptions in cross-sex conversations between unacquainted persons, in B. Thorne, C. Kramarae and N. Henley (eds) *Language, Gender and Society*. Rowley, MA: Newbury House, pp. 103–17.

Wooffitt, R. (2005) *Conversation Analysis and Discourse Analysis: A Comparative and Critical Introduction*. London: Sage.

Zimmerman, D. and West, C. (1975) Sex roles, interruptions and silences in conversation, in B. Thorne and N. Henley (eds) *Language and Sex: Difference and Dominance*. Rowley, MA: Newbury House.

3 THE SHIFT TO DISCOURSE: THE DISCURSIVE CONSTRUCTION OF GENDERED IDENTITIES

Antaki, C. (1994) *Explaining and Arguing: The Social Organisation of Accounts.* London: Sage.

Antaki, C., Billig, M., Edwards, D. and Potter, J. (2002) Discourse analysis means doing analysis: a critique of six analytic shortcomings, *Discourse Analysis Online*, www.shu.ac.uk/daol/articles/v1/n1/a1/antaki2002002.html

Ashcraft, K.L. and Mumby, D. (2004) Organizing a critical communicology of gender and work, *International Journal of the Sociology of Language*, 166: 19–43.

Barrett, R. (1999) Indexing polyphonous identity in the speech of African American drag queens, in M. Bucholtz, A.C. Liang and L.A. Sutton (eds) *Reinventing Identities: The Gendered Self in Discourse*. New York: Oxford University Press, pp. 313–31.

Baxter, J. (2003) *Positioning Gender in Discourse: A Feminist Methodology.* Basingstoke: Palgrave.

Bergvall, V., (1996) Constructing and enacting gender through discourse: negotiating multiple roles as female engineering students, in V. Bergvall, J. Bing and A. Freed (eds) *Rethinking Language and Gender Research: Theory and Practice*. New York: Longman, pp. 173–201.

Bergvall, V., Bing, J. and Freed, A. (eds) (1996) *Rethinking Language and Gender Research: Theory and Practice*. London: Longman.

Billig, M. (1999a) Whose terms? Whose ordinariness? Rhetoric and ideology in conversation analysis, *Discourse and Society*, 10(4): 543–58.

Billig, M. (1999b) Conversation analysis and the claims of naivety, *Discourse and Society*, 10(4): 572–6.

Billig, M. (2000) Guest editorial: towards a critique of the critical, *Discourse and Society*, 11(3): 291–2.

Blommaert, J. (2005) *Discourse: A Critical Introduction.* Cambridge: Cambridge University Press.

Bourdieu, P. (1977) *Outline of a Theory of Practice.* Cambridge: Cambridge University Press.

Bourdieu, P. (1984) *Distinction.* London: RKP.

Bucholtz, M. and Hall, K. (2004) Theorizing identity in language and sexuality research, *Language in Society*, 33: 469–515.

Burman, E. (2002) Discourse analysis means analysing discourse: some comments on Antaki, Billig, Edwards and Potter 'Discourse analysis means doing analysis: a critique of six analytic shortcomings', *Discourse Analysis Online*, www.shu.ac.uk/daol/articles/v1/n1/a1/antaki2002002.html

Butler, J. (1990) *Gender Trouble: Feminism and the Subversion of Identity.* New York: Routledge.

Cameron, D. (1997a) Performing gender identity: young men's talk and the construction of heterosexual masculinity, in S. Johnson and U. Meinhoff (eds) *Language and Masculinity*. Oxford: Blackwell, pp. 86–107.

Cameron, D. (1997b) Theoretical debates in feminist linguistics: questions of sex and gender, in R. Wodak (ed.) *Gender and Discourse*. London: Sage, pp. 21–35.

Cameron, D. (1998a) Performing gender identity: young men's talk and the construction of heterosexual masculinity, in J. Coates (ed.) *Language and Gender: A Reader*. Oxford: Blackwell, pp. 270–84.

Cameron, D. (ed.) (1998b) *The Feminist Critique of Language*, 2nd edn. London: Routledge.

Cameron, D. (2000) Styling the worker: gender and the commodification of language in the globalized service economy, *Journal of Sociolinguistics*, 4(3): 323–47.

Cameron, D. (2001) *Working with Spoken Discourse*. London: Sage.

Cameron, D. and Kulick, D. (2003) *Language and Sexuality*. Cambridge: Cambridge University Press.

Cameron, D. and Kulick, D. (2005) Identity crisis?, *Language and Communication*, 25(2): 107–25.

Chouliaraki, L. and Fairclough, N. (1999) *Discourse in Later Modernity*. Edinburgh: Edinburgh University Press.

Christie, C. (2000) *Gender and Language: Towards a Feminist Pragmatics*. Edinburgh: Edinburgh University Press.

Coates, J. (1996) *Women Talk*. Oxford: Blackwell.

Coates, J. (1997) Competing discourses of femininity, in H. Kotthoff and R. Wodak (eds) *Communicating Gender in Context*. Amsterdam: John Benjamins, pp. 285–313.

Coates, J. (1999) Changing femininities: the talk of teenage girls, in M. Bucholtz, A. Liang and L.A. Sutton (eds) *Reinventing Identities: The Gendered Self in Discourse*. Oxford: Oxford University Press, pp. 123–44.

Coupland, J. and Williams, A. (2002) Conflicting discourses, shifting ideologies: pharmaceutical, 'alternative' and feminist emancipatory texts on the menopause, *Discourse and Society*, 13: 419–45.

Crawford, M. (1995) *Talking Difference: On Gender and Language*. London: Sage.

Eckert, P. (2000) *Linguistic Variation as Social Practice*. Oxford: Blackwell.

Eckert, P. and McConnell-Ginet, S. (1992a) Communities of practice: where language, gender and power all live, in K. Hall, M. Bucholtz and B. Moonwomon (eds) *Locating Power: Proceedings of the Second Berkeley Women and Language Conference*. Berkeley, CA: Berkeley Women and Language Group, pp. 89–99.

Eckert, P. and McConnell-Ginet, S. (1992b) Think practically and look locally: language and gender as community-based practice, *Annual Review of Anthropology*, 21: 461–90.

Eckert, P. and McConnell-Ginet, S. (1994) Think practically and look locally: language and gender as a community based practice, in C. Roman, S. Juhasz and C. Miller (eds) *The Woman and Language Debate*. New Brunswick, NJ: Rutgers University Press.

Erlich, S. (1999) Communities of practice, gender and the representation of sexual assault, *Language in Society*, 28(2): 239–57.

Fairclough, N. (1989) *Language and Power*. London: Longman.

Fairclough, N. (1992) *Discourse and Social Change*. Cambridge: Polity Press.

Fairclough, N. (1995) *Critical Discourse Analysis*. London: Longman.

Foucault, M. (1972) *The Archaeology of Knowledge*. London: Routledge.

Gal, S. (1995) Language, gender and power: an anthropological review, in K. Hall and M. Bucholtz (eds) *Gender Articulated: Language and the Socially Constructed Self*. London: Routledge, pp. 169–82.

Galazinski, D. (2004) *Men and the Language of Emotions*. Basingstoke: Palgrave.

Gee, J. (2005) *An Introduction to Discourse Analysis: Theory and Method*, 2nd edn. London: Routledge.

Gee, J.P. (1989) Literacy, discourse and linguistics: introduction, *Journal of Education*, 171(1): 5–17.

Gee, J.P. (1990) *Social Linguistics and Literacies*. London: Falmer.

Gill, R. (1995) Relativism, reflexivity, and politics: interrogating discourse analysis from a feminist perspective, in S. Wilkinson and C. Kitzinger (eds) *Feminism and Discourse: Psychological Perspectives*. London: Sage, pp. 165–86.

Griffin, C. (1991) Experiencing power: dimensions of gender, 'race' and class, proceedings of POWS/WIPS Women and Psychology conference, Lancaster University, July, *BPS Psychology of Women Section newsletter*, 8(Winter): 43–58.

Hall, K. (1995) Lip service on the fantasy lines, in K. Hall and M. Bucholtz (eds) *Gender Articulated: Language and the Socially Constructed Self*. New York: Routledge, pp. 183–216.

Hall, K. and Bucholtz, M. (eds) (1995) *Gender Articulated: Language and the Socially Constructed Self*. New York: Routledge.

Hollway, W. (1984) Gender differences and the production of the subject, in J. Henriques *et al.* (eds) *Changing the Subject: Psychology, Social Regulation and Subjectivity*. London: Methuen.

Holmes, J. and Meyerhoff, M. (1999) The community of practice: theories and methodologies in language and gender research, *Language in Society*, 28(2): 173–83.

Holmes, J. and Schnurr, S. (2004) Doing femininity at work: more than just relational practice, paper presented at IGALA 3 conference, 5–7 June, Cornell University, NY.

Jaworski, A. and Coupland, N. (eds) (1999) *The Discourse Reader*. London: Routledge.

Johnson, S. (1997) Theorising language and masculinity: a feminist perspective, in Johnson, S. and Meinhof, U. (eds) *Language and Masculinity*. Oxford: Blackwell, pp. 8–26.

Joseph, J. (2004) *Language and Identity: National, Ethnic, Religious*. Basingstoke: Palgrave Macmillan.

Kiesling, S. (2004) What does a focus on 'men's language' tell us about language and woman's place?, in *Language and Woman's Place: Text and Commentaries*, rev. and expanded edn, original text by R. Lakoff, ed. M. Bucholtz. New York: Oxford University Press.

Kitzinger, C. (2002) Doing feminist conversation analysis, in P. McIlvenny (ed.) *Talking Gender and Sexuality*. Amsterdam: John Benjamins, pp. 49–77.

Kotthof, H. and Wodak, R. (eds) (1997) *Communicating Gender in Context*. Amsterdam: John Benjamins.

Kress, G. (1985) *Linguistic Processes in Sociocultural Practice*. Victoria: Deakin University Press.

Kress, G. (1989) *Linguistic Processes in Sociocultural Practice*, 2nd edn. Oxford: Oxford University Press.

Kristeva, A. (1986) Word, dialogue and novel, in T. Moi (ed.) *The Kristeva Reader*. Oxford: Columbia University Press, pp. 34–61.

Lave, J. and Wenger, E. (1991) *Situated Learning: Legitimate Peripheral Participation*. Cambridge: Cambridge University Press.

Lazar, M. (1993) Equalising gender relations: a case of double talk, *Discourse and Society*, 4(4): 443–65.

Lazar, M. (2000) Gender, discourse and semiotics: the politics of parenthood representations, *Discourse and Society*, 11(3): 373–400.

Lazar, M. (ed.) (2005) *Feminist Critical Discourse Analysis*. London: Palgrave.

Leap, W. (ed.) (1995) *Beyond the Lavender Lexicon*. Newark: Gordon and Breech Press.

Litosseliti, L. (2002) 'Head to Head': gendered repertoires in newspaper arguments, in L. Litosseliti and J. Sunderland (eds) *Gender Identity and Discourse Analysis*. Amsterdam: John Benjamins, pp. 129–148.

Litosseliti, L. (2006) Constructing gender in public arguments: the female voice as emotional voice, in J. Baxter (ed.) *Speaking Out: The Female Voice in Public Contexts*. London: Palgrave Macmillan.

Litosseliti, L. and Sunderland, J. (eds) (2002) *Gender Identity and Discourse Analysis*. Amsterdam: John Benjamins.

Livia, A. and Hall, K. (eds) (1997) *Queerly Phrased*: *Language, Gender and Sexual Politics*. London: Cassell.

Lorber, J. and Farrell, S.A. (eds) (1991) *The Social Construction of Gender*. London: Sage.

McConnell-Ginet, S., Borker, R. and Furman, N. (eds) (1980) *Women and Language in Literature and Society*. New York: Praeger.

McIntosh, P. (1989) White privilege: unpacking the invisible knapsack, *Peace and Freedom*, July–August: pp. 10–12.

Mills, S. (1997) *Discourse*. London: Routledge.

Mills, S. (2002) Third wave feminist linguistics and the analysis of sexism, plenary talk at IGALA 2 conference, 12–14 April, Lancaster. Also in *Discourse Analysis Online*, www.shu.ac.uk/daol/

Mills, S. (2003) Caught between sexism, anti-sexism and 'political correctness': feminist women's negotiations with naming practices, *Discourse and Society*, 14(1) 87–110.

Ostermann, A.C. (2003) Communities of practice at work: gender, facework and the power of habitus at an all-female police station and a feminist crisis intervention center in Brazil, *Discourse and Society*, 14(4): 473–505.

Pavlenko, A., Blackledge, A., Piller, I. and Teutsch-Dwyer, M. (eds) (2001) *Multilingualism, Second Language Learning, and Gender*. Berlin: Mouton de Gruyter.

Pichler, P. (2002) Sex talk and (gender) identity in three groups of adolescent girls, paper presented at Interdisciplinary Seminar on Language, Love and Sexuality, Kingston University, UK, 8–9 April.

Potter, J., Wetherell, M., Gill, R. and Edwards, D. (1990) Discourse – noun, verb or social practice?, *Philosophical Psychology*, 3: 201–17.

Pujolar i Cos, J. (1997) Masculinities in a multilingual setting, in S. Johnson and U. Meinhof (eds) *Language and Masculinity*. Oxford: Blackwell, pp. 86–106.

Renkema, I. (2004) *Introduction to Discourse Studies*. Amsterdam: John Benjamins.

Rich, A. (1980) Compulsory heterosexuality and lesbian existence, *Signs* 5(4): 631–60.

Schegloff, E.A. (1997) Whose text? Whose context?, *Discourse and Society*, 8(2): 165–87.

Schegloff, E.A. (1998) Reply to Wetherell, *Discourse and Society*, 9(3): 413–16.

Schegloff, E.A. (1999a) 'Schegloff's text as Billig's data': a critical reply, *Discourse and Society*, 10(4): 558–72.

Schegloff, E.A. (1999b) Naivete vs sophistication or discipline vs. self-indulgence: a rejoinder to Billig, *Discourse and Society*, 10(4): 577–82.

Simpson, A. (1997) 'It's a game!': the construction of gendered subjectivity, in R. Wodak (ed.) *Gender and Discourse*. London: Sage, pp. 197–224.

Stubbs, M. (1996) Whorf's children: critical comments on critical discourse analysis (CDA), in A. Ryan and A. Wray (eds) *Evolving Models of Language*. Clevedon: Multiligual Matters.

Sunderland, J. (2000) State of the art review article: gender, language and language education. *Language Teaching*, 33(4): 203–23.

Sunderland, J. (2002) Baby entertainer, bumbling assistant and line manager: discourses of paternal identity in parentcraft texts, in L. Litosseliti and J. Sunderland (eds) *Gender Identity and Discourse Analysis*. Amsterdam: John Benjamins, pp. 293–324.

Sunderland, J. (2004) *Gendered Discourses*. Basingstoke: Palgrave.

Sunderland, J. and Litosseliti, L. (2002) Gender identity and discourse analysis: theoretical and empirical considerations, in L. Litosseliti and J. Sunderland (eds) *Gender Identity and Discourse Analysis*. Amsterdam: John Benjamins, pp. 1–39.

van Dijk, T. (1990) Social cognition and discourse, in H. Giles and W.P. Robinson (eds) *Handbook of Social Psychology and Language*. Chichester: Wiley, pp. 163–83.

van Dijk, T. (1993) Principles of Critical Discourse Analysis, *Discourse and Society*, 4(2): 249–83.

van Dijk, T. (1998) *Ideology. A Multidisciplinary Approach*. London: Sage.

Weatherall, A. (2002a) *Gender, Language and Discourse*. London: Routledge.

Weatherall, A. (2002b) Towards understanding gender and talk-in-interaction, *Discourse and Society*, 13(6): 767–81.

Weedon, C. (1987) *Feminist Practice and Poststructuralist Theory*. Oxford: Blackwell.

Wenger, E. (1998) *Communities of Practice*. Cambridge: Cambridge University Press.

West, C. and Fenstermaker, S. (1995) Doing difference, *Gender and Society*, 9(1): 8–37.

Wetherell, M. (1998) Positioning and interpretative repertoires: conversation analysis and post-structuralism in dialogue, *Discourse and Society*, 9(3): 387–412.

Wetherell, M., Stiven, H. and Potter, J. (1987) Unequal egalitarianism: a preliminary study of discourses concerning gender and employment opportunities, *British Journal of Social Psychology*, 26: 59–71.

Wetherell, M., Taylor, S. and Yates, S.J. (eds) (2001) *Discourse as Data: A Guide for Analysis*. London: Sage/Open University.

Widdowson, H.G. (1995) Discourse analysis: a critical view, *Language and Literature*, 4(3): 157–72.

Wilkinson, S. and Kitzinger, C. (eds) (1995) *Feminism and Discourse: Psychological Perspectives*. London: Sage.

Wodak, R. (ed.) (1989) *Language, Power and Ideology: Studies in Political Discourse*. Amsterdam: John Benjamins.

Wodak, R. (ed.) (1997) *Gender and Discourse*. London: Sage.

Wooffitt, R. (2005) *Conversation Analysis and Discourse Analysis: A Comparative and Critical Introduction*. London: Sage.

4 GENDER AND LANGUAGE IN EDUCATION

Alcón, E. (1994) The role of participation and gender in non-native speakers' classroom interaction, *Working Papers on Language, Gender and Sexism*, 4(1): 51–68.

Arnot, M., Gray, J., James, M., Ruddock, J. and Duveen, G. (1998) *Recent Research on Gender and Educational Performance*. London: HMSO/Ofsted.

Bacon, S. and Finnemann, M. (1992) Sex differences in self-reported beliefs about foreign-language learning and authentic oral and written input, *Language Learning*, 42(4): 471–95.

Batters, J. (1987) Pupil and teacher perceptions of foreign language learning, PhD thesis, University of Bath.

Baxter, J. (2002) A juggling act: a feminist post-structuralist analysis of girls' and boys' talk in the secondary classroom, *Gender and Education*, 14(1): 5–19.

Bayyurt, Y. (in progress) The analysis of the interactional strategies of female and male university students in an EFL setting, research report, supported by the

Commission of Bogazici University Scientific Research Projects (Project Number: 99HD601) and Turkish Academy of Sciences Post-Doctoral Research Award.

Brophy, J. and Good, T. (1974) *Teacher–Student Relationships: Causes and Consequences*. New York: Holt, Rinehart and Winston.

Carrell, P.L. and Wise, T.E. (1998) The relationship between prior knowledge and topic interest in second language reading, *Studies in Second Language Acquisition*, 20(3): 285–309.

Cheshire, J. and Jenkins, N. (1991) Gender issues in the GCSE oral English examination: part 2, *Language and Education*, 5(1): 19–40.

Cincotta, M.S. (1978) Textbooks and their influence on sex-role stereotype formation, *BABEL: Journal of the Australian Federation of MLTS Associations*, 14(3): 24–9.

Clark, A. and Trafford, J. (1995) Boys into modern languages: an investigation in attitudes and performance between boys and girls in modern languages, *Gender and Education*, 7(3): 315–25.

Clarricoates, K. (1978) Dinosaurs in the classroom: a re-examination of some aspects of the 'hidden curriculum' in primary schools, *Women's Studies International Quarterly*, 1: 353–64.

Clarricoates, K. (1983) Classroom interaction, in J. Whyld (ed.) *Sexism in the Secondary Curriculum*. New York: Harper and Row.

Coates, J. (1996) *Women Talk: Conversations Between Women Friends*. Oxford: Blackwell.

Corson, D. (1997) Gender, discourse and senior education: ligatures for girls, options for boys, in R. Wodak (ed.) *Gender and Discourse*. London: Sage, pp. 140–64.

Crawford, M. (1995) *Talking Difference: On Gender and Language*. London: Sage.

Davies, J. (2003) Expressions of gender: an analysis of pupils' gendered discourse styles in small group discussions, *Discourse and Society*, 14(2): 115–32.

Delamont, S. (1990) *Sex Roles and the School*, rev. edn. London: Methuen.

Dennison, C. and Coleman, J. (2000) *Young People and Gender: A Review of Research*. London: Women's Unit, Cabinet Office.

Diamond, A. (1987) Gender-typed subjects: their influence on some secondary students' occupational choice variable, *Curriculum Perspectives*, 7: 23–29.

Edelsky, C. (1981) Who's got the floor?, *Language in Society*, 10: 383–421.

Ehrlich, S. (1997) Gender as social practice: implications for second language acquisition, *Studies in Second Language Acquisition* 19(4): 421–46.

Ekstrand, L. (1980) Sex differences in second language learning?: empirical studies and a discussion of related findings, *International Review of Applied Psychology*, 29: 205–59.

Elwood, J. and Gipps, C. (1998) *Report: Review of Recent Research on the Achievement of Girls in Single-Sex Schools*. London: AMGS.

Ferguson, B. (1994) Overcoming gender bias in oral testing: the effect of introducing candidates, *System*, 22(3): 341–8.

Francis, B. (2000) The gendered subject: students' subject preferences and discussions of gender and subject ability, *Oxford Review of Education*, 26: 35–48.

Freeman, R. and McElhinny, B. (1996) Language and gender, in S.L. McKay and N.H. Hornberger (eds) *Sociolinguistics and Language Teaching*. Cambridge: Cambridge University Press, pp. 218–80.

French, J. and French, P. (1984) Gender imbalance in the primary classroom: an interactional account, *Educational Research*, 26(2): 127–36.

Gass, S. and Varonis, E. (1986) Sex differences in nonnative speaker–nonnative speaker interactions, in R. Day (ed.) *Talking to Learn: Conversation in Second Language Acquisition*. New York: Newbury House.

Goh, C. and Foong, K.P. (1997) Chinese ESL students' learning strategies: a look at frequency, proficiency and gender, *Hong Kong Journal of Applied Linguistics*, 2(1): 39–53.

Goodwin, M.H. (1980a) Directive-response speech sequences in girls' and boys' task activities, in S. McConnell-Ginet, R. Borker and N. Furman (eds) *Women and Language in Literature and Society*. New York: Praeger, pp. 157–73.

Goodwin, M.H. (1980b) He-said-she-said: formal cultural procedures for the construction of a gossip dispute activity, *American Ethnologist*, 7(4): 674–95.

Goodwin, M.H. (1998) Cooperation and competition across girls' play activities, in J. Coates (ed.) *Language and Gender: A Reader*. Oxford: Blackwell, pp. 121–46.

Gupta, A. and Lee, A.S.Y. (1990) Gender representation in English language textbooks used in the Singapore primary classroom: an interactional account, *Language and Education*, 4(1): 29–50.

Harris, V. (1998) Making boys make progress, *Language Learning Journal*, 18: 56–62.

Hartman, P. and Judd, E.L. (1978) Sexism and TESOL materials, *TESOL Quarterly*, 14: 383–93.

Hellekant, J. (1994) Are multiple choice tests unfair for girls?, *System*, 22(3): 349–52.

Hellinger, M. (1980) 'For men must work and women must weep': sexism in English language textbooks used in German schools, *Women's Studies International Quarterly*, 3: 267–75.

Hirst, G. (1982) An evaluation of evidence for innate sex differences in linguistic ability, *Journal of Psycholinguistic Research*, 11(2): 95–113.

Holmes, J. (1989) Is sex relevant in the ESL classroom?, *Language Issues* 3(1): 14–18.

Holmes, J. (1994) Improving the lot of female language learners, in J. Sunderland (ed.) *Exploring Gender: Questions and Implications for English Language Education*. Hemel Hempstead: Prentice Hall.

Holmes, J. (1995) *Women, Men and Politeness*. London: Longman.

Holmes, J. and Meyerhoff, M. (eds) (2003) *The Handbook of Language and Gender*. Oxford: Blackwell.

Jimenez Catalan, R. and Ojeda Alba, J. (2000) Gender and sex in the illustrations of an ESL dictionary, in *Estudios de la Mujer en ámbito de los países de habla inglesa*, IV. Madrid: Editorial Universidad Complutense.

Jones, M., Kitetu, C. and Sunderland, J. (1997) Discourse roles, gender and language textbook dialogues: who learns what from John and Sally?, *Gender and Education*, 9(4): 469–90.

Kelly, A. (1988) Gender differences in teacher–pupil interactions: a meta analytic review, *Research in Education*, 39: 1–24.

Kelly, A., Baldry, A., Bolton, E., Edwards, S., Emery, J., Levin, C., Smith, S. and Wills, M. (1985) Traditionalists and trendies: teachers' attitudes to educational issues, *British Educational Resesarch Journal*, 11: 91–104.

Ludwig, J. (1983) Attitudes and expectations: a profile of female and male students of college French, German and Spanish. *Modern Language Journal*, 67(3): 216–27.

Maccoby, E. and Jacklin, C. (1974) *The Psychology of Sex Differences*. Stanford, CA: Stanford University Press.

Mahony, P. (1983) How Alice's chin really came to be pressed against her foot: sexist processes of interaction in mixed-sex classrooms, *Women's Studies International Forum*, 6(1): 107–15.

Mercer, N., Wegerif, R. and Dawes, L. (1999) Children's talk and the development of reasoning in the classroom. *British Educational Research Journal*, 35: 95–111.

Merrett, F. and Wheldall, K. (1992) Teachers' use of praise and reprimands to boys and girls, *Education Review*, 44(1): 73–9.

Morris, L.A. (1998) Differences in men's and women's ESL writing at the junior college level: consequences for research on feedback, *The Canadian Modern Language Review/La Revue canadienne des langues vivantes*, 55(2): 219–38.

Mulac, A. Bradac, J.J. and Gibbons, P. (2001) Empirical support for the gender-as-culture hypothesis: and intercultural analysis of male/female language differences, *Human Communication Research*, 27(1): 121–152.

Murphy, P. and Elwood, J. (1998) Gendered learning outside and inside school: influences on assessment, in D. Epstein, J. Elwood, V. Hey and J. Maw (eds) *Failing Boys? Issues in Gender and Achievement*. Buckingham: Open University Press, pp. 162–81.

Norton, B. and Pavlenko, A. (2004) Addressing gender in the ESL/EFL classroom, *TESOL Quarterly*, 38(3): 504–14.

Norton, B. and Toohey, K. (eds) (2004) *Critical Pedagogies and Language Learning*. Cambridge: Cambridge University Press.

Ogbay, S. (1999) Gendered perceptions, silences and resistance in two Eritrean secondary schools: reasons for girls' lower performance than boys, PhD thesis, Lancaster University.

Oxford, R. (1994) 'La différence continue …': gender differences in second/foreign language learning styles and strategies, in J. Sunderland (ed.) *Exploring Gender: Questions and Implications for English Language Education*. Hemel Hempstead: Prentice Hall.

Pavlenko, A., Blackledge, A., Piller, I. and Teutsch-Dwyer, M. (2001) *Multilingualism, Second Language Learning, and Gender*. Berlin: Mouton de Gruyter.

Pavlidou, T.-S. (2001) Politeness in the classroom? Evidence from a Greek high school, in A. Bayraktaroglu and M. Sifianou (eds) *Linguistic Politeness across the Boundaries: The Case of Greek and Turkish*. Amsterdam: John Benjamins, pp. 105–36.

Porreca, K.L. (1984) Sexism in current ESL textbooks, *TESOL Quarterly*, 18(4): 704–24.

Porter, D. (1991) Affective factors in language testing, in J.C. Alderson and B. North (eds) *Language Testing in the Nineties*. London: Macmillan/British Council, pp. 32–40.

Poulou, S. (1997) Sexism in the discourse roles of textbook dialogues, *Language Learning Journal*, 15: 68–73.

Provo, J. (1991) Sex differences in nonnative speaker interaction. *The Language Teacher*, 15(7): 25–8.

Pugsley, J. (1992) Sexist language and stereotyping in ELT materials, *Working Papers on Language, Gender and Sexism*, 2(2): 5–13.

Sadker, M. and Sadker, D. (1985) Sexism in the schoolroom of the '80s, *Psychology Today*, March: 54–7.

Sarah, E. (1988) Teachers and students in the classroom: an examination of classroom interaction, in D. Spender and E. Sarah (eds) *Learning to Lose*, rev. edn. London: The Women's Press, pp. 155–64.

Sargeant, J. (1993) Gender and power: the meta-ethics of teaching argument in schools. *Curriculum*, 14(1): 6–13.

Skelton, C. (1996) Learning to be 'tough': the fostering of maleness in one primary school, *Gender and Education* 8(2): 185–97.

Spender, D. (1982) *Invisible Women: The Schooling Scandal*. London: The Women's Press.

Spender, D. (1988) Talking in class, in D. Spender and E. Sarah (eds) *Learning to Lose: Sexism and Education*. London: The Women's Press, pp. 149–54.

Spender, D. and Sarah, E. (eds) (1988) *Learning to Lose: Sexism and Education*, rev. edn. London: The Women's Press.

Stern, R. (1976) Review article: sexism in foreign language textbooks, *Foreign Language Annals*, 9: 294–9.

Sunderland, J. (ed.) (1994) *Exploring Gender: Questions and Implications for English Language Education*. Hemel Hempstead: Prentice Hall.

Sunderland, J. (1996) Gendered discourse in the foreign language classroom: teacher–student and student–teacher talk, and the social construction of children's femininities and masculinities, PhD thesis, Lancaster University, UK.

Sunderland, J. (2000a) New understandings of gender and language classroom research: texts, teacher talk and student talk, *Language Teaching Research*, 4(2): 149–73.

Sunderland, J. (2000b) State of the art review article: gender, language and language education, *Language Teaching*, 33(4): 203–23.

Sunderland, J., Cowley, M., Abdul Rahim, F., Leontzakou, C. and Shattuck, J. (2002)

From representation towards discursive practices: gender in the foreign language textbook revisited, in L. Litosseliti and J. Sunderland (eds) *Gender Identity and Discourse Analysis*. Amsterdam: John Benjamins, pp. 223–56.

Swann, J. (1992) *Girls, Boys, and Language*. Oxford: Blackwell, chapters 2, 3 and 4.

Swann, J. (2003) Schooled language: language and gender in educational settings, in J. Holmes and M. Meyerhoff (eds) *The Handbook of Language and Gender*. Oxford: Blackwell, pp. 624–44.

Swann, J. and Graddol, D. (1988) Gender inequalities in classroom talk, *English in Education*, 22(1): 48–65.

Swann, J. and Graddol, D. (1995) Feminising classroom talk?, in S. Mills (ed.) *Language and Gender*. London: Longman.

Wedman, I. and Stage, C. (1983) The significance of contents for sex differences in test results, *Scandinavian Journal of Educational Research*, 27(1): 49–71.

Wernersson, I. (1982) Sex differentiation and teacher–pupil interaction in Swedish-compulsory schools, in Council of Europe (eds) *Sex Stereotyping in Schools*. Lisse: Swets and Zeitlinger.

Wodak, R. (ed.) (1997) *Gender and Discourse*. London: Sage.

Wood, R. (1978) Sex differences in answers to English language comprehension items, *Educational Studies*, 4(2): 157–65.

Younger, M., Warrington, M. and Williams, J. (1999) The gender gap and classroom interactions: reality and rhetoric? *British Journal of Sociology of Education*, 20(3): 325–341.

5 GENDER AND LANGUAGE IN THE MEDIA

Aitchison, J. and Lewis, D. (eds) (2003) *New Media Language*. London: Routledge.

Ballaster, R. *et al.* (1996) A critical analysis of women's magazines, in H. Baehr and A. Gray (eds) *Turning it On: A Reader in Women and Media*. London: Arnold.

Ballaster, R., Beetham, M., Frazer, E. and Hebron, S. (1991) *Women's Worlds: Ideology, Femininity and the Woman's Magazine*. London: Macmillan.

Benwell, B. (2002) Is there anything 'new' about these lads? The textual and visual construction of masculinity in men's magazines, in L. Litosseliti and J. Sunderland (eds) *Gender Identity and Discourse Analysis*. Amsterdam: John Benjamins, pp. 149–74.

Benwell, B. (ed.) (2003) *Masculinity and Men's Lifestyle Magazines*. Oxford: Blackwell.

Benwell, B. (2005) 'Lucky this is anonymous' Ethnographies of reception in men's magazines: a 'textual culture' approach, *Discourse and Society*, 16(2): 147–72.

Bing, J. and Lombardo, L. (1997) Talking past each other about sexual harassment: an exploration of frames for understanding, *Discourse and Society* 8(3): 293–311.

Brown, G. and Yule, G. (1983) *Discourse Analysis*. Cambridge: Cambridge University Press.

Burn, A. and Parker, D. (2003) *Analysing Media Texts*. London: Continuum.

Caldas-Couthard, C.R. (1996) 'Women who pay for sex. And enjoy it': transgression versus morality in women's magazines, in C.R. Caldas-Coulthard and M. Coulthard (eds) *Texts and Practices*. London: Routledge.

Cameron, D. (2004) Language, gender and media: past, present, future, plenary paper presented at IGALA 3 conference, 5–7 June 2004, Cornell University, NY.

Christie, C. (2000) *Gender and Language: Towards a Feminist Pragmatics*. Edinburgh: Edinburgh University Press.

Connell, R.W. (1995) *Masculinities*. Oxford: Polity.

Cosslett, T. (1996) Fairytales: revising the tradition, in T. Cosslett, A. Easton and P. Summerfield (eds) *Women, Power and Resistance*. Buckingham: Open University Press, pp. 81–90.

Crewe, B. (2003) *Representing Men: Cultural Production and Producers in the Men's Magazine Market*. Oxford: Berg.

Edwards, T. (1997) *Men in the Mirror: Men's Fashion, Masculinity and Consumer Fashion*. London: Cassell.

Eggins, S. and Iedema, R. (1997) Difference without diversity: semantic orientation and ideology in competing women's magazines, in R. Wodak (ed.) *Gender and Discourse*. London: Sage.

Fairclough, N. (1989) *Language and Power*. London: Longman.

Fairclough, N. (1995) *Media Discourse*. London: Arnold.

Ferguson, M. (1983) *Forever Feminine: Women's Magazines and the Cult of Femininity*. London: Heinemann.

Gilbert, P. and Taylor, S. (1991) *Fashioning the Feminine: Girls, Popular Culture and Schooling*. Sydney: Allen and Unwin.

Goffman, E. (1974) *Frame Analysis: An Essay on the Organization of Experience*. New York: Harper and Row.

Goffman, E. (1976) *Gender Advertisements*. London: Macmillan.

Goffman, E. (1981) *Forms of Talk*. Philadelphia: University of Pennsylvania Press.

Greenslade, R. (2004) Prejudice, distortion and the cult of celebrity: are the press going to hell in a handcart?, *City Insights* lecture, 22 January, City University, London, UK.

Hall, S., Crichter, C., Jefferson, T., Clake, J. and Roberts, B. (1978) *Policing the Crisis: Mugging, the State and Law and Order*. London: Macmillan.

Hermes, J. (1995) *Reading Women's Magazines*. Cambridge: Polity.

Hodge, R. and Kress, G. (1988) *Social Semiotics*. Cambridge: Polity Press.

Hollway, W. (1984) Gender differences and the production of the subject, in J. Henriques *et al.* (eds) *Changing the Subject: Psychology, Social Regulation and Subjectivity*. London: Methuen.

Jackson, P., Stevenson, N. and Brooks, K. (2001) *Making Sense of Men's Magazines*. Cambridge: Polity Press.

Janoschka, A. (2004) *Web Advertising: New Forms of Communication on the Internet*. Amsterdam: John Benjamins.

Kress, G. and van Leeuwen, T. (2001) *Multi-Modal Discourse: The Modes and Media of Contemporary Communication*. London: Arnold.

Lazar, M. (2002) Consuming personal relationships: the achievement of feminine self-identity through other-centeredness, in L. Litosseliti and J. Sunderland (eds) *Gender Identity and Discourse Analysis*. Amsterdam: John Benjamins, pp. 11–28.

Lazar, M. (ed.) (2005) *Feminist Critical Discourse Analysis*. London: Palgrave.

Litosseliti, L. (2002) The discursive construction of morality and gender: investigating public and private arguments, in S. Benor, M. Rose, D. Sharma, J. Sweetland and Q. Zhang (eds) *Gendered Practices in Language*. Stanford, CA: Center for the Study of Language and Information, Stanford University, pp. 45–63.

Macdonald, M. (1995) *Representing Women: Myths of Femininity in the Popular Media*. London: Arnold.

Machin, D. and Thornborrow, J. (2003) Branding and discourse: the case of *Cosmopolitan, Discourse and Society*, 14(4): 453–71.

McCracken, E. (1993) *Decoding Women's Magazines: from Mademoiselle to Ms.* Macmillan Press.

McLoughlin, L. (2000) *The Language of Magazines*. London: Routledge.

McRobbie, A. (1978) *Jackie*: an ideology of adolescent femininity, occasional paper, Centre for Contemporary Studies, University of Birmingham.

McRobbie, A. (1999) MORE! New sexualities in girls' and women's magazines, in A. McRobbie *In the Culture Society: Art, Fashion and Popular Music*. London: Routledge.

Mills, S. (ed.) (1994) *Gendering the Reader*. Hemel Hempstead: Harvester Wheatsheaf.

Mills, S. (1995) *Feminist Stylistics*. London: Routledge.

Mills, S. (1998) Introduction to special issue ('Feminist Text Analysis and the Media') of *Language and Literature*, 7(3): 235–53.

Mills, S. (2002) Third wave feminist linguistics and the analysis of sexism, plenary talk at IGALA 2 conference, 12–14 April, Lancaster. Also in *Discourse Analysis Online*, www.shu.ac.uk/daol/

Myers, G. (1994) *Words in Ads*. London: Arnold.

Myers, G. (1998) *Ad Worlds: Brands, Media, Audiences*. London: Arnold.

Nixon, S. (1996) *Hard Looks*: *Masculinities, Spectatorship and Contemporary Consumption*. London: UCL Press.

Nixon, S. (2001) Resignifying masculinity: from 'new man' to 'new lad', in D. Morley and K. Robins (eds) *British Cultural Studies*, Oxford: Oxford University Press.

Rich, A. (1980) Compulsory heterosexuality and lesbian existence, *Signs*, 5(4): 631–60.

Schaff, A. (1984) The pragmatic function of stereotypes, *International Journal of the Sociology of Language*, 45: 89–100.

Scollon, R. (2004) Intertextuality across communities of practice: academics, journalism and advertising, in C. Moder and A. Martinovic-Zic (eds) *Discourse across Languages and Cultures*. Amsterdam: John Benjamins.

Seidler, V. (ed.) (1992) *Men, Sex and Relationships: Writings from Achilles Heel.* London: Routledge.

Slovic, P., Fischoff, B. and Lichtenstein, S. (1980) Risky assumptions, *Psychology Today* (June): 44–8.

Southwell, T. (ed.) (2000) *Loaded* magazine, April.

Stevenson, N., Jackson, P. and Brooks, K. (2000) The politics of 'new' men's lifestyle magazines, *European Journal of Cultural Studies*, 3(3): 366–85.

Stubbs, M. (1996) Whorf's children: critical comments on critical discourse analysis (CDA), in A. Ryan and A. Wray (eds) *Evolving Models of Language.* Clevedon: Multiligual Matters.

Sunderland, J. and Litosseliti, L. (2002) Gender identity and discourse analysis: theoretical and empirical considerations, in L. Litosseliti and J. Sunderland (eds) *Gender Identity and Discourse Analysis.* Amsterdam: John Benjamins, pp. 1–39.

Talbot, M. (1992) The construction of gender in a teenage magazine, in N. Fairclough (ed.) *Language Awareness: Critical Perspectives.* London: Longman.

Talbot, M. (1995) A synthetic sisterhood: false friends in a teenage magazine, in K. Hall and M. Bucholtz (eds) *Gender Articulated: Language and the Socially Constructed Self.* New York: Routledge.

Talbot, M. (1997) *Randy Fish Boss* Branded a stinker: coherence and the construction of masculinities in a British tabloid newspaper, in S. Johnson and U. Meinhof (eds) *Language and Masculinity.* Oxford: Blackwell.

Talbot, M. (1998) Multiple voices in magazines, in *Language and Gender: An Introduction.* Cambridge: Polity Press, pp. 176–84.

Tannen, D. (ed.) (1993) *Framing in Discourse.* New York: Oxford University Press.

Tannen, D. (1998) *The Argument Culture.* New York: Virago.

Tester, K. (1994) *Media, Culture and Morality.* London: Routledge.

Tetlow, H. (1991) The reinvented man: constructions of masculinity in one issue of *Arena*, MA dissertation, Lancaster University.

Thompson, K. (1998) *Moral Panics.* London: Routledge.

Thornborrow, J. (1998) Playing hard to get: metaphor and representation in the discourse of car advertisements, *Language and Literature*, 7(3): 254–72.

van Zoonen, L. (1994) *Feminist Media Studies.* London: Sage.

Watney, S. (1987) *Policing Desire.* London: Methuen.

Weedon, C. (1987) *Feminist Practice and Poststructuralist Theory.* Cambridge: Blackwell.

Widdowson, H.G. (1995) Discourse analysis: a critical view, *Language and Literature*, 4(3): 157–72.

Winship, J. (1987) *Inside Women's Magazines.* London: Pandora.

6 GENDER AND LANGUAGE IN THE WORKPLACE

Ainsworth-Vaughan, N. (1992) Topic transitions in physician–patient interviews: power, gender and discourse change. *Language in Society*, 21: 409–26.

Alvesson, M. and Billing, Y.D. (1997) *Gender, Work and Organization.* London: Sage.

Baxter, J. (2003) *Positioning Gender in Discourse: A Feminist Methodology.* Basingstoke: Palgrave.

Baxter, J. (ed.) (2006) *Speaking Out: The Female Voice in Public Contexts.* London: Palgrave Macmillan.

Bem, S. (1993) *The Lenses of Gender.* New Haven, CT: Yale University Press.

Bing, J. and Bergvall, V. (1998) The question of questions: beyond binary thinking, in J. Coates (ed.) *Language and Gender: A Reader.* Oxford: Blackwell, pp. 496–510.

Brewis, J. (2001) Telling it like it is? Gender, language and organizational theory, in R. Westwood and S. Linstead (eds) *The Language of Organization.* London: Sage, pp. 283–309.

Cameron, D. (1995) *Verbal Hygiene.* London: Routledge.

Cameron, L. and Low, G. (eds) (1999) *Researching and Applying Metaphor.* Cambridge: Cambridge University Press.

Case, S.S. (1988) Cultural differences not deficiencies: an analysis of managerial 'women's language', in L. Larwood and S. Rose (eds) *Women's Careers: Pathways and Pitfalls.* New York: Praeger, pp. 41–63.

Case, S.S. (1995) Gender, language and the professions: recognition of wide-verbal-repertoire speech, *Studies in the Linguistic Sciences,* 25(2): 149–92.

Coates, J. (1995) Language, gender and career, in S. Mills (ed.) *Language and Gender: Interdisciplinary Perspectives.* London: Longman, pp. 13–30.

Coates, J. (1997) Competing discourses of femininity, in H. Kotthoff and R. Wodak (eds) *Communicating Gender in Context.* Amsterdam: John Benjamins, pp. 285–313.

Connell, R. (1987) *Gender and Power: Society, the Person and Sexual Politics.* Stanford, CA: Stanford University Press.

Connell, R. (1995) *Masculinities.* Cambridge: Polity.

Crawford, M. (1988) Gender, age and the social evaluation of assertion, *Behavior Modification* 12: 549–64.

Crawford, M. (1995) *Talking Difference: On Gender and Language.* London: Sage.

Eakins, B. and Eakins, G. (1979) Verbal turn-taking and exchanges in faculty dialogue, in B.-L. Dubois and I. Crouch (eds) *The Sociology of the Languages of American Women.* San Antonio, TX: Trinity University Press, pp. 53–62.

Eckert, P. and McConnell-Ginet, S. (2003) *Language and Gender.* Cambridge: Cambridge University Press.

Edelsky, C. (1981) Who's got the floor? *Language in Society* 10: 383–421.

Fairclough, N. (1995) *Media Discourse.* London: Edward Arnold.

Fisher, S. (1993) Gender, power and resistance: is care the remedy?, in S. Fisher and K. Davis (eds) *Negotiating at the Margins: The Gendered Discourse of Power and Resistance.* New Brunswick, NJ: Rutgers University Press.

Fletcher, J. (1999) *Disappearing Acts: Gender, Power and Relational Practice at Work.* Cambridge, MA: MIT Press.

Freed, A. (1996) Language and gender in an experimental setting, in V. Bergvall, J. Bing and A. Freed (eds) *Rethinking Language and Gender Research: Theory and Practice.* New York: Longman, pp. 54–76.

Goffman, E. (1974) *Frame Analysis*. New York: Harper and Row.

Goodwin, M.H. (1980) Directive-response speech sequences in girls' and boys' task activities, in S. McConnell-Ginet, R. Borker and N. Furman (eds) *Women and Language and Literature in Society*. New York: Praeger, pp. 157–73.

Graddol, D. and Swann, J. (1989) *Gender Voices*. Oxford: Blackwell.

Harragan, B. (1977) *Games Mother Never Taught You: Corporate Gamesmanship for Women*. New York: Warner Books.

Hearn, J. and Parkin, W. (1988) Women, men, and leadership: a critical review of assumptions, practices, and change in the industrialized nations, in N. Adler and D. Izraeli (eds) *Women in Management Worldwide*. London: M.E. Sharpe, pp. 17–40.

Holmes, J. (2000a) Women at work: analysing women's talk in New Zealand. *Australian Review of Applied Linguistics*, 22(2): 1–17.

Holmes, J. (2000b) Victoria University of Wellington's Language in the Workplace Project: an overview, *Language in the Workplace Occasional Papers* 1: 1–18.

Holmes, J. and Marra, M. (2002) Having a laugh at work: how humour contributes to workplace culture. *Journal of Pragmatics* 34: 1683–710.

Holmes, J. and Marra, M. (2004) Relational practice in the workplace: women's talk or gendered discourse? *Language in Society*, 33: 377–98.

Holmes, J., Marra, M. and Burns, L. (2001) Women's humour in the workplace: a quantitative analysis. *Australian Journal of Communication*, 28(1): 83–108.

Holmes, J. and Meyerhoff, M. (1999) The community of practice: theories and methodologies in language and gender research. *Language in Society*, 28(2): 173–83.

Holmes, J. and Schnurr, S. (2005) Politeness, humour and gender in the workplace: negotiating norms and identifying contestation, *Journal of Politeness Research: Language, Behaviour, Culture*, 1(1): 121–49.

Holmes, J. and Stubbe, M. (2003) 'Feminine' workplaces: stereotype and reality, in J. Holmes and M. Meyerhoff (eds) *The Handbook of Language and Gender*. Oxford: Blackwell, pp. 573–99.

Jones, D. (2000) Gender trouble in the workplace: 'language and gender' meets 'feminist organisational communication', in J. Holmes (ed.) *Gendered Speech in Social Context: Perspectives from Gown to Town*. Wellington: Victoria University Press, pp. 192–210.

Kendall, S. (2004) Framing authority: gender, face and mitigation at a radio network, *Discourse and Society*, 15(1): 55–79.

Kendall, S. and Tannen, D. (1997) Gender and language in the workplace, in R. Wodak (ed.) *Gender and Discourse*. New York: Longman, pp. 81–105.

Koller, V. (2004a) Businesswomen and war metaphors: 'Possessive, jealous and pugnacious'?, *Journal of Sociolinguistics*, 8(1): 3–22.

Koller, V. (2004b) *Metaphor and Gender in Business Media Discourse: A Critical Cognitive Study*. Basingstoke: Palgrave.

Lakoff, R. (1990) *Talking Power: The Politics of Language*. San Francisco: Basic Books.

Lazar, M. (ed.) (2005) *Feminist Critical Discourse Analysis*. London: Palgrave.

Litosseliti, L. (2006) Constructing gender in public arguments: the female voice as emotional voice, in J. Baxter (ed.) *Speaking Out: The Female Voice in Public Contexts*. London: Palgrave Macmillan.

Martin-Rojo, L. (1995) Strategies of resistance to normative discourse: the emergence of a new female identity, in B. Dendrinos, *Language, Social Life and Critical Thought*, proceedings of the 4th International Symposium on Critical Discourse Analysis.

Martin-Rojo, L. and Callejo, J. (1995) Argumentation and inhibition: sexism in the discourse of Spanish executives, *Pragmatics*, 5(4): 455–84.

Martin-Rojo, L. and Gómez Esteban, C. (2002) Discourse at work: when women take on the role of manager, in G. Weiss and R. Wodak (eds) *Critical Discourse Analysis: Theory and Interdisciplinarity*. London: Palgrave Macmillan.

Martin-Rojo, L. and Gómez Esteban, C. (2005) The gender of power: the female style in labour organizations, in M. Lazar (ed.) *Feminist Critical Discourse Analysis: Gender, Power and Ideology in Discourse*. London: Palgrave Macmillan.

McConnell-Ginet, S. (2000) Breaking through the glass ceiling: can linguistic awareness help?, in J. Holmes (ed.) *Gendered Speech in Social Context: Perspectives from Gown to Town*. Wellington: Victoria University Press, pp. 259–82.

McElhinny, B. (1998) 'I don't smile much anymore', in J. Coates (ed.) *Language and Gender: A Reader*. Oxford: Blackwell, pp. 309–27.

McElhinny, B. (2003) Theorizing gender in sociolinguistics and linguistic anthropology, in J. Holmes and M. Meyerhoff (eds) *The Handbook of Language and Gender*. Oxford: Blackwell, pp. 21–42.

McManus, P. (2001) Women's participation in self-employment in Western industrialized nations, *International Journal of Sociology*, 31(2): 70–97.

McRae, S. (2004) Language, gender and status in the workplace: the discourse of disagreement in meetings, unpublished PhD thesis, Open University, Milton Keynes.

Mullany, L. (2003) Identity and role construction: a sociolinguistic study of gender and discourse in management, unpublished PhD thesis, Nottingham Trent University, UK.

Mullany, L. (2004a) Gender, politeness and institutional power roles: humour as a tactic to gain compliance in workplace business meetings, *Multilingua*, 23: 13–37.

Mullany, L. (2004b) An examination of the discourse strategies of female and male chairs in managerial business meetings, in C. Gouveia and C. Silvestre (eds) *Discourse, Communication and the Enterprise*. Lisbon: University of Lisbon Press.

Mullany, L. (2006) 'Girls on tour': politeness, small talk and gender identity in managerial business meetings, *Journal of Politeness Research: Language, Behaviour, Culture*, 2(1): 55–77.

Mullany, L. (forthcoming) *Gendered Discourse in Professional Communication*. Basingstoke: Palgrave.

Ostermann, A.C. (2003) Communities of practice at work: gender, facework and the power of habitus at an all-female police station and a feminist crisis intervention center in Brazil, *Discourse and Society*, 14(4): 473–505.

Pizzini, F. (1991) Communication hierarchies in humour: gender differences in the obstetrical/gynaecological setting, *Discourse and Society*, 2: 477–88.

Reskin, B. and Roos, P. (1990) *Job Queues, Gender Queues*. Philadelphia: Temple University Press.

Riley, S. (2002) Constructions of equality and discrimination in professional men's talk, *British Journal of Social Psychology*, 41: 443–61.

Sarangi, S. and Roberts, C. (1999) The dynamics of interactional and institutional orders in work-related settings, in S. Sarangi and C. Roberts (eds) *Talk, Work and Institutional Order: Discourse in Medical, Mediation and Management Settings*. Berlin: Mouton de Gruyter, pp. 1–57.

Stewart, L. (2005) Senior Consultant, Shell Learning, Shell International plc, The Hague, Netherlands (personal communication on issues of diversity and inclusiveness).

Stubbe, M., Holmes, J., Vine, B. and Marra, M. (2000) Forget Mars and Venus: let's get back to earth!: challenging gender stereotypes in the workplace, in J. Holmes (ed.) *Gendered Speech in Social Context: Perspectives from Gown to Town*. Wellington: Victoria University Press, pp. 231–58.

Tannen, D. (1994) *Talking from 9 to 5: Women and Men in the Workplace: Language, Sex and Power*. New York: Avon.

Thimm, C., Koch, S. and Schey, S. (2003) Communicating gendered professional identity: competence, cooperation, and conflict in the workplace, in J. Holmes and M. Meyerhoff (eds) *The Handbook of Language and Gender*. Oxford: Blackwell, pp. 528–49.

Valian, V. (1998) *Why So Slow? The Advancement of Women*. Cambridge, MA: MIT Press.

Walsh, C. (2001) *Gender and Discourse: Language and Power in Politics, the Church and Organisations*. London: Longman.

Wenger, E. (1998) *Communities of Practice*. Cambridge: Cambridge University Press.

West, C. (1984) When the doctor is a lady, *Symbolic Interaction*, 7: 87–106.

West, C. (1990) Not just 'doctor's orders': directive response sequences in patients' visits to women and men physicians, *Discourse and Society*, 1(1): 85–112.

Wetherell, M., Stiven, H. and Potter, J. (1987) Unequal egalitarianism: a preliminary study of discourses concerning gender and employment opportunities, *British Journal of Social Psychology*, 26: 59–71.

Wodak, R. (1997) 'I know we won't revolutionize the world with it, but …': styles of female leadership in institutions, in H. Kotthoff and R. Wodak (eds) *Communicating Gender in Context*. Amsterdam: John Benjamins, pp. 335–70.

Woods, N. (1989) Talking shop: sex and status as determinants of floor apportionment in a work setting, in J. Coates and D. Cameron (eds) *Women in their Speech Communities: New Perspectives on Language and Sex*. London: Longman, pp. 141–57.

7 STARTING POINTS FOR RESEARCHERS, TEACHERS AND STUDENTS

Antaki, C., Billig, M., Edwards, D. and Potter, J. (2003) Discourse analysis means doing analysis: a critique of six analytic shortcomings, *Discourse Analysis Online*, 1(1), www.shu.ac.uk/daol/previous/v1/n1/index.htm

Baxter, J. (2003) *Positioning Gender in Discourse: A Feminist Methodology*. Basingstoke: Palgrave.

Burman, E. (2003) Discourse analysis means analysing discourse: some comments on Antaki, Billig, Edwards and Potter 'Discourse analysis means doing analysis: a critique of six analytic shortcomings', *Discourse Analysis Online*, 1(1), www.shu.ac.uk/daol/previous/v1/n1/index.htm

Cameron, D., Frazer, E., Harvey, P., Rampton, B. and Richardson, K. (1992) *Researching Language: Issues of Power and Method*. London: Routledge.

Christie, C. (2000) *Gender and Language: Towards a Feminist Pragmatics*. Edinburgh: Edinburgh University Press.

Coates, J. and Cameron, D. (eds) (1988) *Women in their Speech Communities: New Perspectives on Language and Sex*. New York: Longman.

Cohen, L. and Manion, L. (1994) *Research Methods in Education*, 4th edn. London: Routledge.

DeFrancisco, V. (1997) Gender, power and practice: or, putting your money (and your research) where your mouth is, in R. Wodak (ed.) *Gender and Discourse*. London: Sage, pp. 37–56.

Lakoff, R. (1975) *Language and Women's Place*. New York: Harper and Row.

Lazar, M. (ed.) (2005) *Feminist Critical Discourse Analysis*. London: Palgrave.

Litosseliti, L. (1999) Moral repertoires and gender voices in argumentation, PhD thesis, Department of Linguistics, Lancaster University, UK.

Sarangi, S. and Roberts, C. (1999) The dynamics of interactional and institutional orders in work-related settings, in S. Sarangi and C. Roberts (eds) *Talk, Work and Institutional Order: Discourse in Medical, Mediation and Management Settings*. Berlin: Mouton de Gruyter, pp. 1–57.

Sarantakos, S. (1998) *Social Research*, 2nd edn. Macmillan Education, Australia, South Melbourne.

Silverman, D. (1993) *Interpreting Qualitative Data: Methods for Analysing Talk, Text, and Interaction*. London: Sage.

Smith, D. (1981) *The Experienced World as Problematic: A Feminist Method*. (Sorokin Lecture No. 12). Saskatoon: University of Saskatchewan.

Sunderland, J. and Litosseliti, L. (2002) Gender identity and discourse analysis: theoretical and empirical considerations, in L. Litosseliti and J. Sunderland (eds) *Gender Identity and Discourse Analysis*. Amsterdam: John Benjamins, pp. 1–39.

Swann, J. (2002) 'Yes, but is it gender?', in L. Litosseliti and J. Sunderland (eds) *Gender Identity and Discourse Analysis*. Amsterdam: John Benjamins, pp. 43–67.

West, C. and Fenstermaker, S. (1995) Doing Difference, *Gender and Society*, 9(1): 8–37.